FALSE PROPHETS

Also by James Hoopes:

Community Denied

Consciousness in New England

Van Wyck Brooks

Oral History

FALSE PROPHETS

*The Gurus Who Created Modern
Management and Why Their Ideas
Are Bad for Business Today*

JAMES HOOPES

PERSEUS
PUBLISHING
A Member of the Perseus Books Group

For Carol, Johanna, and Ben

Quote from Lawrence Richley's letter to Lillian Gilbreth:
Lawrence Richley to Lillian Gilbreth, March 15, 1929, "Gilbreth, Dr. Lillian M., 1929–1933," Presidential Secretary's File, Hoover Papers, Hoover Library.

Library of Congress Control Number: 2003101363
ISBN 0-7382-0798-5

Perseus Publishing is a member of the Perseus Books Group.
Find us on the World Wide Web at http://www.perseuspublishing.com.
Perseus Publishing books are available at special discounts for bulk purchases in the U.S. by corporations, institutions, and other organizations. For more information, please contact the Special Markets Department at the Perseus Books Group, 11 Cambridge Center, Cambridge, MA 02142, or call (800) 255-1514 or (617) 252-5298, or e-mail j.mccrary@perseusbooks.com.

Text design by Brent Wilcox
Set in 11-point Berkeley by the Perseus Books Group

First printing, March 2003

1 2 3 4 5 6 7 8 9 10—06 05 04 03

CONTENTS

PART 3
Social Philosophy: Management as
Everybody's Business ◦ 193

LIST OF ILLUSTRATIONS

Figures

ACKNOWLEDGMENTS

DURING THE FIVE YEARS THAT I WORKED ON THIS BOOK AND for many years before, Carol Hoopes supported me in more ways than I can ever adequately acknowledge. So did Johanna and Benjamin Hoopes, while also growing into fine young adults. I thank them and love them.

I owe a large debt to friends and colleagues at Babson College, who over a course of more than twenty years have taught me much of what I know about the potential of management to do both good and ill. I have been lucky during the last five years to work for two exemplary managers of high standards and character—Michael Fetters, vice president of Academic Affairs, and Stephen Collins, chairman of the Division of History and Society. Without their support, this book might not have been written or, for certain, would have been much longer in the writing. They were also faithful friends.

Two other good friends gave indispensable emotional and intellectual support. Ross Wolin discussed this book with me for more evenings and gave me more good advice than he probably cares to remember. George Cotkin read parts of a wayward first draft, gently nudged me toward a course correction, and since then has supplied limitless encouragement.

Three Babson College colleagues read parts of the manuscript, saving me from errors and giving me the benefit of their insights—Allan Cohen, Ismael Dambolena, and Jack Stamm. Stephen Collins read it all, adding to the large personal and intellectual debt I have come to owe him. Many other faculty, administrators, and staff at Babson have supported this project in small ways and large while contributing to my understanding of management. I thank them all and especially Mary Driscoll and Pat MacAlpine.

The world knows what a generous man Peter Drucker is, but I thank him anyway for a three-hour lunch conversation that profoundly affected the viewpoint of this book. He also read the chapter on himself and two other chapters as well, correcting me on several factual matters, chiding me for my praise of him, and refusing to take issue with my criticisms.

I am grateful to The W. Edwards Deming Institute for permission to read the papers of W. Edwards Deming at the Library of Congress. Diana Deming Cahill, Albie Davis, Brad Jackson, and Bruce Kuklick all read drafts of one or more chapters, for which they have my thanks. My late friend Kenneth Lynn read a chapter and, many years ago, taught me most of what I know about scholarship and intellectual standards.

I found gracious and generous hospitality during a research trip to Japan. Professor Kenji Okuda, an eminent management scholar, introduced me to Professor Izumi Nonaka, an expert on quality control. Professor Nonaka arranged for me to do research in the Japanese Union of Scientists and Engineers (JUSE) library with the assistance of an excellent translator, Suphawan Srisupha. Professors Okuda and Nonaka also arranged interviews with managers who had been influenced by W. Edwards Deming or who had known him during his early visits to Japan— Mister Kennkichi Yamaji, Mister Junichi Ishiwata, Mister Tadasu Fujita, and Mister Eizou Watanabe. I thank them all for their time and assistance. I am also grateful for the opportunity to discuss Deming's influence in Japan with Professor Hiroshi Kume.

In England, Pauline Graham generously shared her notes and insights on Mary Parker Follett. I must also particularly thank Gail Thomas and Jane Goldsmith for their help with the Mary Parker Follett Papers at Henley Management College, Henley-on-Thames.

Librarians and archivists are the unsung heroes of historical scholarship. I am obligated to many dozens of them on four continents and especially to Kate Buckley, Barbara Kendrick, and the rest of the staff at the Horn Library, Babson College, for research assistance and patience far beyond the call of duty.

Linda Rosenthal provided expert assistance with photographs. Jerry Burgess and John Piccolo of TrizecHahn Office Properties gave me a tour of the old GM headquarters in Detroit while it was being converted into a Michigan state office building. Soraya Rodriguez of Bell-Atlantic New Jersey (now Verizon) kindly arranged for me to visit the former headquarters of the New Jersey Bell Telephone Company in Newark, to read the Chester Barnard files there, and to see his office.

I am grateful to the Alfred P. Sloan Foundation and to Gail Pesyna, director of the Sloan Foundation's program on business organizations, for a timely grant that provided released time from teaching.

Several funding agencies at Babson College provided assistance and time for writing—the Board of Research, the Faculty Research Facility, and the William F. Glavin Center for Global Entrepreneurial Leadership. Lee Higdon, during his presidency of Babson College, provided support without which I could not have researched this book.

My thanks, finally, to Barbara Rifkind, a wonderful agent, and to Nick Philipson and Arlinda Shtuni of Perseus Publishing for their patient and excellent editorial guidance.

INTRODUCTION

THIS IS A STORY OF MISFITS AND PHONIES, RUTHLESS BOSSES and generous philosophers, shrewd executives and honest engineers. They were the management gurus who led the way in reconciling Americans to corporate life, sometimes by improving our understanding of human organization, sometimes by intellectual chicanery aimed at making us feel freer than we are. They were an ersatz set of founding fathers (and mothers), jury-rigging an informal constitution for our other, unofficial government, not the political institutions that keep us free but the managerial corporations that make us rich. Most of them are forgotten, but their ideas still shape our lives. This book aims to help us as managers, employees, and citizens get what is best from the gurus' ideas and protect us from the worst.

The gurus have had a big job on their hands, getting freedom-loving Americans to accept management power. America is the premier market for management gurus not just because it pioneered big business but also because working in such organizations contradicts some of our deepest, democratic values. We have a love-hate relationship with corporations, an ambivalence that complicates the challenges we face both in managing and being managed.

To make corporate life palatable to Americans, some of the gurus have unrealistically minimized the amount of power it takes to manage, whereas others have claimed management power can be made morally legitimate. Either way, they have contradicted, often with the best of intentions, the traditional democratic attitude toward power, which is to reluctantly admit its necessity, suspect it of bad intentions, and try to fence it in.

Management power is an American paradox, a vital necessity of our economic well-being and an obvious contradiction of our democratic values. In practice, the United States and many other modern democracies have dealt with that paradox in an extraordinarily fortunate way. We have developed a mix of corporate and governmental institutions that let us enjoy the economic benefit of top-down power at work and, in the rest of society, allow us to have civil rights and political freedom.

But Americans do not like to admit their inconsistencies any more than other people do. Free people want to feel as free at work as they do elsewhere in society. As much as we can, we ignore the fact that we check many of our freedoms at the workplace door and that ordinary citizens get their closest exposure to undemocratic government when they go to work for a corporation.

For example, corporations can legally curtail employees' civil rights to a degree the government cannot. A highly visible case occurred in the spring of 2000, when the commissioner of baseball suspended Atlanta Braves pitcher John Rocker for racist and homophobic remarks. It took a constitutional lawyer to observe that only the commissioner's status as "chief executive of a private corporation" made it legal for him to violate "the spirit of free speech" in the First Amendment to the Constitution of the United States.

Few sympathized with Rocker, not just because his remarks were disgusting but also because he was well paid, which is the nutshell principle of corporate life, the exchange of some freedom and independence for a lot of productivity and wealth. Although it turned out to have cost Rocker some of his freedom of speech when he became a professional player, major league baseball clearly treated him well in return.

But corporations do not always uphold their end of the bargain with employees as well as major league baseball did with Rocker. Anyone who has worked for a while in a large managerial organization has seen employees be verbally abused, unfairly evaluated, passed over for a well-deserved raise or promotion, be underpaid, overworked, fired despite good performance, and so on.

And employees treated wrongly often have no recourse except to keep quiet or find another job. The ancient principle in common law that "no man shall be judge in his own cause" has no corporate counterpart. In corporate life there is no independent judiciary. As long as managers have the support of their companies and have broken no laws, they decide for themselves whether they have done the right thing.

Working under such arbitrary management power leaves more than a few employees, as everyone knows, feeling like fearful inhabitants of dark planets. And because free speech often stops when work begins, those shrunken souls suffer, in addition to tyrannous wrong, the guilty anguish of complicit silence.

A management job is no safeguard. Managers are managed themselves and run the same risk as other employees, maybe more, of top-down blindsiding. Even those who love their jobs remember, if they're smart, that everything can change in an instant, that a new boss, or even the old boss, can turn work into hell.

Does it have to be that way? Do even the best companies have to be potential tyrannies? Of course they do if we want speed, flexibility, and above all profit in a competitive world. Our ability to create wealth depends at least partly on managerial authority. Top-down power and its potential abuse are here to stay in corporate America. It is foolish to think otherwise.

What a contrast with American ideals! We celebrate freedom and the rule of law. We work for corporations whose managers, like Boss Hague in Jersey City, *are* the law.

America's greatest prophet of democracy, Thomas Jefferson, had a different vision—a nation of farmers living freely on their own land, answering to no one but themselves. Believing that working for others was the first step in a walk away from freedom, Jefferson hoped never to find his "fellow citizens at a work-bench." He would have hated to see us in our cubicles.

We pound keyboards in our cubbies because it pays better than tilling the land. Jefferson's agrarian ideal was outmatched economically by industrialism and its promise of prosperity, provided that nineteenth-century Americans organized themselves for mass production. The corporation therefore prospered, and we with it. The surest way for gurus, managers, employees, or anyone else to misinterpret the corporation is to forget the historical fact that money has been Americans' primary motive for living corporate lives.

Intangibles have been a nice bonus. Corporations have opened for ordinary citizens a chance at creativity, honor, and power once reserved for aristocrats. From coordinating human resources to building information technology networks, corporations offer stimulating work that, done with others, provides many people with a dignity and community they find nowhere else. Not least among a managerial society's rewards is the pleasure of power, which managers in democratic societies often try to exercise in a benign spirit of self-restraint, which has its own satisfactions.

But the rich personal identity the corporation offers to the ordinary citizen of peasant ancestry—wealth plus the chance to be a savant, a mentor, a patron, or even a philosopher king—can collapse into cruel spiritual death with an arrogant flick of the whip, a moment of courtly intrigue, or just a careless top-down mistake.

The upshot is our love-hate relation with corporations. They give us money and meaning by putting us to work under the arbitrary power of a boss, affronting our Jeffersonian thirst for freedom by exposing us to the risk of top-down tyranny. Even when corporate life is richly rewarding, as it often is, its beneficiaries may feel in their hearts that it is a deal with the devil.

For a century now, one of the gurus' main tactics for dealing with our ambivalence about management power has been to try to make corporate life seem freer than it is. In *What Management Is*, a recent book summarizing the state of the art, Joan Magretta and Nan Stone reflect the conventional wisdom in saying that "the real insight about managing people is that, ultimately, you don't."

That, ultimately, you *do* manage people is the argument of this book. Yes, "[t]he best performers are people who know enough and care enough to manage themselves." And true enough, managing such high performers is not a simple matter of control but of getting them to cooperate with each other in order to accomplish together more than they could alone. But a big part of what motivates them to work together is their superiors' top-down power to bestow rewards—money most important of all.

The ideas I question in *What Management Is* originated not with its authors but with the gurus I write about in the following chapters. The moral questions of freedom and power occupy only a small part of Magretta and Stone's book, which is an excellent overview of strategy, value creation, and other aspects of management.

However, *What Management Is* shows that certain of the gurus' ideas are alive and well in the present, particularly the claim that corporate life is freer and better than it can possibly be. Friendly fuzzies like managing by "culture" and "values" get lots of attention, whereas it is only briefly conceded that "[h]istorically, organizations have relied more heavily on work rules and financial incentives, and these will never go away entirely." For sure, they won't.

—◦—

Although this is not a how-to book but rather a history of management ideas, I have written with today's managers and their problems in mind. This book does not offer a prescription for managing well, but it may help immunize readers against the underemphasis on power and money as well as the unconscious moral arrogance in some of today's management ideas.

I am not a management teacher, let alone a guru, but I bring to this book more than twenty years of practical experience in working with management ideas. As a professor of history and, for half a dozen years, an administrator in a business school run with more than a little self-conscious attention to the latest management fads and fashions, I have had practical experience with most of the buzzwords and flavors of the month in living memory. I have witnessed—not as a guru, consultant, or other hired gun but close up and from the inside of an organization undergoing change—the surprising power of management ideas both to energize and disappoint.

My experience disproved the saying that familiarity breeds contempt. To the contrary, the more I came to know of management teachers and their ideas, the more interesting and attractive they seemed, especially their development of practical techniques for improving communication and human cooperation in small groups. Although I believe that some management teachers' most cherished big ideas are profoundly wrong, I do not doubt that much of their ordinary, day-to-day work in developing employees' interpersonal skills and facilitating small-group relations does great good, not just within companies but for democratic society at large. I am proud to call many management teachers friends.

Yet even as I came to admire management teachers, I recognized that some of them made a dangerous leap of faith. They often assumed that the knowledge they had won in developing individuals and promoting better intragroup relations could be applied to the oldest and weightiest of moral and political questions such as power and justice. In other words, they turned their small-group techniques of generous recognition, open communication, and so forth into a general theory of government or at least a general theory of management and applied it to large organizations as well as small groups. They seemed not to realize how flimsy a bridge they had thrown across how immense an abyss. Here, I thought, might lie at least part of the explanation for the unrealistic quality of some management ideas, especially the underestimation of the need for power and the overestimation of the moral possibilities in corporate life.

And there was the ironic fact, wryly admitted by many management professors, that those who can, do; those who can't, teach. It is not a universal truth, but in some cases the more steeped a management teacher is in management theory, the less able a manager he or she turns out to be in practice. Management ideas can be as useful for rationalizing mistakes and wrongdoing as they are for preventing them. Many business schools harbor legends of management professors who have fallen on their faces when given responsibility not for teaching management but for practicing it as academic administrators. Were these inept administrators just feckless professors, or was there also an element of "he who teaches bad ideas, can't?"

And the problem was not just academic. Some friends and acquaintances became CEOs. I heard them vow at the start that they were not going to be top-down bosses but would unleash energy from the bottom up. And I knew many young, naive managers, newly elevated, who sang the same song in an even higher key. Whether a human-relations, "soft" style of management was ever a radical idea, it had obviously become a commonplace of American culture.

All these new leaders magnanimously told employees to take charge of their departments, their offices, their janitorial closets, and make of them what they willed. And they soon grew disturbed at the result, or lack thereof. The lucky were those who did not lash out in anger and destroy what moral authority they had. One such friend, one of the most decent people I know, said, "I would start in a different way if I could do it again," as he tried to tighten the reins he had initially loosened and learned what every good teacher knows—it is easier to let the class get out of hand than to regain control.

To some extent these troubled managers had been misled by the gurus, but there also seemed to be a deeper problem, a conflict between management and democratic values to which both the gurus and managers were inadequately responding. Some of the gurus saw the conflict but, finding no way around it, minimized and even denied it. Managers, eager not to be so un-American a thing as a top-down boss, bought the gurus' message that corporate life can be freer or at least better than it really can.

This book aims to use history to help today's managers gain a more realistic perspective on a morally ambiguous world where there has always been power and injustice. Rather than denying or minimizing the conflict between management and democracy as so many gurus have done, it may be better to accept the conflict as inevitable. That approach might help managers accept their power more openly and use it a bit more effectively as well as morally. Bosses have little reason to tread lightly among the lowly if they mistake their superior power for the moral authority that so many of today's gurus suppose is the basis of effective management. Only if managerial power is understood as an undemocratic but necessary evil in an imperfect world does moral caution have a fighting chance to engage the manager's conscience.

In other words, the best response to the paradox of managerial power in a democratic society may be another paradox. Managers, faced with all the temptations that have corrupted the powerful throughout history, need all the spiritual humility they can get from remembering that their power is inherently undemocratic and that they are unworthy of being trusted with it even though they must be.

To accept that there is no resolution of the conflict between management and democracy, between power and justice, may be far from comforting to managers and still less so to employees and citizens. But there is also a potential reward. Understanding the strategies our predecessors have bequeathed us for covering up some of their conflicts and discomforts may offer us a chance to be a little more realistic and maybe manage a little better.

--o--

To reveal the origins of the lack of realism in management ideas, especially the minimizing and covering up of the conflict between management and democracy, this book tells the story of the most important gurus in American history. It follows them into the factory, the office, the classroom, the clinic, the lab, or wherever they worked in order to show how their practical experiences shaped their ideas. But precisely because management ideas involve democratic values from the larger culture outside the corporation, it is not possible to understand the gurus just in terms of their business and practical experience. The gurus also created their ideas under the sway of political events, cultural trends, and personal life. Therefore, this book tells as much as space permits about the gurus' whole lives. I hope I have communicated a little of the fun and personal profit I found in learning about these varied characters who run the gamut from sages in somber hues to corporate jesters in full motley.

The story has three parts, and so does this book. First came scientific management, meaning rationalized, top-down factory operations; second, human relations, with its emphasis on bottom-up participation; and third, social philosophy, which attempted to apply management techniques not just to business but to the rest of society as well, especially governmental and nonprofit organizations.

Scientific Management

The story of the conflict between democracy and top-down management—like so many others in American history—begins with slavery. The concerns of slaveholders may seem a world away from those of today's managers. But some Southern planters, as Chapter 1 shows, had shrewd psychological insights unfortunately relevant to the practice of management today. More important, those today who think the moral challenges of management can be met by moralistic injunctions to do the right thing may be disturbed to see how easily slave owners convinced themselves that they were on the side of the angels. Blacks were natural tyrants, the argument went, and white masters protected the weak among them from the strong.

Early American managers of free white workers spent less time than slave owners rationalizing the contradiction between their power and a democratic society. The contradiction was of course less glaring than in the case of slavery, but there was also the annoying fact that free Americans were hard to manage because of their high-flown commitment to democratic values. Only with difficulty was managerial control exerted over free-spirited women workers in textile factories and male workers in armories, on railroads, and in steel mills. But by the late nineteenth century, it was clear that the majority of Americans were destined to work not independently in the agrarian republic Jefferson had envisioned but under the control of managers, a fact that created a market for management gurus.

Frederick W. Taylor, the creator of scientific management, led the way in imposing top-down control over late nineteenth- and early twentieth-century factory workers. For a few years widely regarded as a progressive reformer, he tried to justify his concentration of power in managers' hands by claiming to be a friend and benefactor of workers. Labor leaders used congressional hearings to expose him as a tyrant, a charge that still rightly tarnishes his reputation. Yet Taylor delivered on his promise to raise productivity and create wealth through rationalized factory operations. However brutal his methods, his imposition of top-down control over the American system of production reflected a realistic understanding that not just a free market but organizational coherence created economic prosperity.

Taylor won some notable disciples who became gurus themselves and, to his chagrin, improved on his system by allowing workers more participation in management. Most publicly prominent of his followers were a husband and wife team, Frank and Lillian Gilbreth, who tried to manage workers' every motion, often with the help of workers themselves. Frank Gilbreth was Taylorism's most effective proselytizer, not only in the United States but also in Europe. After his death, Lillian became an ally of her fellow engineer Herbert Hoover, in his failed campaign for voluntary spending by the American people to lift the country out of the Great Depression, which suggested the limitation of participatory management techniques in politics.

Henry Gantt, a close friend of the Gilbreths, was Taylor's other prominent disciple. Realizing that workers' minds and hearts, not just their muscle, were necessary ingredients of efficiency, Gantt won their willing cooperation with monetary rewards, adding a carrot to the stick of scientific management by creating the system of bonus pay later used to manage millions of twentieth-century industrial workers. Yet he was also a believer in top-down power, frighteningly so in his political organization, the New Machine, which aimed at undemocratic political power for engineers in the run-up to World War I. Disappointed that the war did not bring production managers supremacy over capitalist financiers, he became, afterward, a sympathizer with the new Soviet Union. His career amounted to an ominous warning of the potential of managerial high-mindedness to promote political authoritarianism, but he was also the first important critic of the disjunction between financial accounting and operations management that is no less important in our time than his.

Human Relations

By the 1920s, Taylor's successors such as the Gilbreths and Gantt had modified scientific management and moved it toward a bit of fairness and worker participation, making it practically useful and winning wide acceptance in industry. But Taylor's reputation for tyrannical brutality stuck to the movement, costing his followers' more humane versions of scientific management any chance at broad public acceptance outside industry or among those in business who cared for public opinion. The way was opened for the human relations movement, which better appealed to the American conscience by underestimating both management power and its moral dangers.

Mary Parker Follett could have been a useful transitional figure to human relations from scientific management, where she found an audience, though far from as large as she deserved. Too little heeded in her own time and then forgotten, she has recently been rediscovered and her reputation is rapidly and rightly ascending. Her optimism was an honest aspect of the courage with which she overcame personal and gender barriers that would have laid many low. Although she hoped for more good from management power than it is ever likely to deliver, she at least never denied its reality. The first guru to come from outside the business world, Follett imposed some of her preconceptions as a philosophical idealist and political scientist on management, unrealistically hoping the corporation might contribute new social techniques not just to business but to democracy. Yet she also offered insights into the nature of leadership, conflict resolution, and the spiritual possibilities of corporate life that have never been surpassed and from which today's managers can still learn. Unfortunately, leadership of the human relations movement fell into cruder hands than hers.

Elton Mayo, a psychotherapist and an immigrant from Australia, led the Harvard Business School to prominence in the 1930s by introducing there a therapeutic style of human relations as a practical alternative to scientific management, a style that is today the staple of organizational behavior as it is taught in business schools. Charming, generous, and well-meaning, Mayo was also a charlatan. A greater-than-average deficit in intellectual integrity made his sparkling intelligence too facile and enabled him to ignore evidence that ran counter to his ideas. A lifelong skeptic of democracy, he believed it had destroyed social harmony. Mayo nevertheless created the idea of the bottom-up organization, an idea that appealed widely in America because of its at least superficial consistency with democratic values. In a creative but dubious interpretation of the famous "Hawthorne experiment" at a Chicago telephone factory of that name, Mayo argued that therapeutic supervision turned the experiment's employees into a communal group that labored with a will because workers' well-being came first, a still-influential illusion among some management theorists.

Chester Barnard, a brilliant AT&T executive who exerted great influence at the Harvard Business School in the 1930s and 1940s, extended Mayo's ideas on gentle shop-floor supervision into a theory of corporate leadership. Many of today's managers who have never heard of Barnard subscribe to his idea that the executive has little power and therefore has to lead bottom-up organizations by moral authority. His rise out of a hard childhood may have accounted for Barnard's undemocratic belief in the leader's moral superiority. Conversely, his underestimation of managers' power meshes well with democratic values and still makes his ideas appealing to the broad managerial public, his unwitting intellectual heirs. He also pioneered today's use of business management methods in nonprofit organizations and government.

Social Philosophy

The United States emerged from World War II as the world's preeminent industrial power with a seemingly insurmountable lead in managerial know-how, a lead dissipated with remarkable speed in the quarter century that followed. European and Asian economies recovered fairly rapidly from the war, and Japan in particular seemed to offer a new model of "quality" management. By the 1980s, American management was furiously reinventing itself and has been doing so ever since. During the half century of dramatic change following World War II, two enormously influential personalities were the predominant gurus. They offered different approaches to management that took note of broad social issues while sometimes including and sometimes departing from elements of both scientific management and human relations.

W. Edwards Deming, a son of the turn-of-the-century Wyoming frontier, is widely credited with inspiring the quality movement in post–World War II Japan, and there is a great deal of truth in the story as it is conventionally told. Although the Japanese were committed to quality well before Deming's famous 1950 visit, he played an important role in teaching quality as not just a manufacturing technique but as a social philosophy. But he underestimated the role of top-down power and higher wages in the Japanese postwar social model, which was heavily influenced by scientific management. Many Americans similarly underestimated the importance of management power in the 1980s when they built the quality movement in the United States, making Deming something of a popular hero in the process. Although Deming's contributions to manufacturing rival Taylor's in importance, he was ill equipped for his new role as a social philosopher of management. His frontier habit of denying conflict contributed significantly to the near utopian faith in the possibility of cooperative social systems and bottom-up power that is still a vital and often unrealistic influence in American management.

By contrast, Peter Drucker never denied the necessity of management power but spent his career trying to make it morally legitimate. His realistic recognition of power and lifelong moral concern make him, with Mary Parker Follett, the most admirable of the gurus. A native of Vienna who worked as a young man in Germany and left when Hitler came to power, Drucker attributed the Nazis' popular appeal to their creation of noneconomic status hierarchies that restored the dignity workers had lost under managerial capitalism. During his early career in the United States, Drucker aimed, with little success, to use some of the Nazis' techniques for moral ends, trying to use noneconomic status systems to turn corporations into legitimate self-governing communities. Although he had little luck achieving such democratic objectives in corporations, he succeeded brilliantly as a consultant and writer on management methods. Drucker has remained less clear on the goals of management, arguing that management power can only be made legitimate through its being used for the good of employees without reconciling that objective with profit. Now he places his hope—questionably, from the perspective of this book—in the rise of an "organizational society" where nonprofits rather than corporations will create a morally legitimate system of management.

◄○►

In the Conclusion, I try to interpret the meaning of the history of management ideas for today's managers and citizens alike. Readers will of course also find their own meanings, but they may find it useful to know at the start that the contemporary organizational issues for which I believe this story has significance include the nature of *work*, *culture*, *leadership*, and *ethics*. And given the increasing prominence of management ideas outside the business world, these issues are important to all of us—whether corporate denizens or not—who are concerned with maintaining a democratic society.

Work

Today's ideas about flat organizations, self-directed teams, values-driven companies, and so forth have a lot of underlying assumptions, but one of the main ones is that there has been a quantum change in the nature of work. "Back when work was mostly a matter of brawn," the thinking goes, "work itself could be managed." But now "there is a sizeable knowledge or service component in most jobs. The most powerful sources of value are locked in people's heads, and in their hearts."

This book offers some glimpses into the workplaces of a century ago that make it doubtful that, during the history of modern management, brawn was ever the most important aspect of work. As Chapter 2 shows, Taylor believed that the workers of his time had too much knowledge and therefore too much power. Getting that knowledge out of workers' heads and into managers' was his overriding concern. The Gilbreths and Gantt more moderately tried to get workers to participate with their hearts and minds. But in all cases, the creators of scientific management concerned themselves to a significant degree with managing knowledge.

There are real differences, of course, between knowledge in today's leading industries and those of a century ago. But do we overestimate the magnitude of those differences? Do we see them as stark and absolute when they are a matter of degree? If the nature of work has not changed as much as we like to believe, could the same be true of management? Might the insistence of Taylor and his followers on the necessity of hierarchical, top-down authority have more relevance today than we like to admit?

Culture

The idea that corporations have cultures is one of the most influential management concepts of the past quarter century. Although the idea is too recent to have affected most of the gurus in this book, it may be that the story told here also applies to the notion of corporate culture. Some of the appeal of the idea of corporate culture lies in its promise of control without the use of undemocratic power. Who has not met the new manager out to "change the culture"? If staff members will just imbibe a new set of cultural values, never mind how, they will soon be doing what the manager wants without even knowing that they are being managed.

In other words, "culture" may be only one more device for fending off any tragic understanding of management as a necessary evil in an imperfect world. If people can be managed with culture so that internalized values drive them to act in the way management wants, there is no need for a win-lose choice between corporate prosperity and individual freedom. Managed by culture change, people freely choose to do what managers want. Employee morale rises, and managers get their way without any unpleasant need to use their power. It's a neat idea, but can it really work?

Some long-established companies with loyal workforces probably do have something like a culture in the anthropological sense of the word—a system of values that exerts some control over employee behavior. But in many other companies, culture is no more than an inch deep. Given the rapidity with which many managers claim to "change the culture," how can the culture involve deeply held values? Is culture often just a polite fiction with the social function of enabling employees to pretend that they are not subject to power, not subject to a prescribed way of acting that comes down from the top? Does the pretense promote hypocrisy, with hidden costs to morale from propping up phony cultures? Or is the idea of culture a workable and profitable deception, useful in enabling employees as well as managers to deny the unpleasant fact of top-down power?

Leadership

The lineage of many of today's most influential management ideas on leadership can be traced back to the Harvard human relations group of the 1930s. But in Chapters 5 and 6, I argue that Elton Mayo's and Chester Barnard's mix of assertions—bottom-up power and top-down morality— were unrealistic and unnecessary to what was genuinely useful in their calls for a softer style of management. As Mayo admitted, most of his practical recommendations to supervisors were commonsensical enough and hardly needed confirmation by the Hawthorne experiment. Even within scientific management, Taylor's successors—Gantt and the Gilbreths—moved in the direction of softer use of power. Still, the human relations movement became the main corrective of Taylorist brutality and no doubt continues to offer an important message in a business environment that has grown harsher in recent decades.

But today we have little emphasis on top-down power among management gurus to counterbalance the teeming descendants of Barnard and Mayo. Today's multitudinous teachers of leadership place ever greater emphasis on the generous character and personality of the manager and precious little on the use of authority and power. The alert new manager picks up almost by breathing the tempting idea that the way to take hold is to let go. The *Harvard Business Review* recently devoted an entire issue to leadership, and it scarcely contained the word "power."

Has the near total eclipse—in theory if not in practice—of scientific management and its emphasis on top-down control been an unalloyed plus for the understanding and teaching of business leadership? Does the idea of moral leadership in the absence of power run the risk of becoming a recipe for managers to take their eyes off the ball, to focus on human relations issues at the expense of business goals? This book's historical approach suggests that democratic values in American culture rather than the intellectual merit of the human relations school account for that camp's victory over scientific management. If that's right, then today's managers need more help than today's leadership gurus provide in finding the best balance between bottom-up participation and top-down authority.

Ethics

As I write, a rash of accounting scandals at such companies as Enron, WorldCom, and a dozen others have revealed that CEOs and other top managers rigged the books to enrich themselves in the short term while doing long-term damage to their companies and wreaking havoc in the lives of investors and employees. The reaction to these events by leading gurus, business schools, and popular pundits is discouraging if one thinks back to the late 1980s when another series of scandals rocked Wall Street. Now, as then, there is a popular hue and cry for teaching business ethics in order to make managers more moral. No one seems to consider the possibility that for these last fifteen years, we have had too much, not too little, talk about the need for high morals in our business leaders. Some of the CEOs who may soon be sporting orange jumpsuits and mopping prison floors were only a little while ago pontificating about company values and opening business meetings with ostentatious prayers.

From the perspective of this book, there is a different sort of moral deficiency in management ideas and education than is usually diagnosed. There is an unwitting moral arrogance in much of the contemporary thinking about managing by culture and leading by moral authority. Many gurus, many teachers of business ethics, and many of the rest of us, too, think managers need to become more moral to deal with the ethical challenges of their jobs. That's a bad idea if it has the premise, as it often does, that it is possible for managers to become morally adequate for their responsibilities.

Managers and teachers of business ethics would do better to remember the most basic of democratic insights—no human being is good enough to be trusted with power. Because managers inevitably do have power, they need to remember even more than elected officials the democratic admonition that all who hold power live in a moral quagmire where no matter how good they become, they will never be good enough. In the wake of an era of celebrity CEOs who inevitably failed to live up to the foolish claims made for their virtue, the main need of managers today is for humility, not the humility that will stop them from using power but the humility that will help minimize self-righteous use of power or, worse, false denials of power's existence. We need awareness of the complexity of our moral challenges, not simplistic injunctions to do the right thing, as if character and willpower are all it takes.

At a time when American management is awash in a sea of moralistic criticism, I hope this book will help managers avoid defensive hypocrisy and misguided moral aspirations. Most managers are already fairly moral people, or at least no worse than most of the rest of us. It is less important that managers try to become better people, good though that would be, than that they recognize their inevitable shortcomings for the moral challenges they face. Such recognition might—no more than might—promote some moral caution that will help them use their power as honestly as they can to make money for their companies, which is why they have power in the first place.

—<o>—

The nature of corporate work, culture, leadership, and ethics matters not only to managers and employees but to citizens in general. Management ideas have assumed an ever more central place in American culture in the past twenty years. Formerly, the gurus, influenced by democratic values in the rest of American culture, tried to make corporate life freer or at least better than it can be. Now, the flow of ideas is often reversed. Now, management ideas increasingly leave the company and get used by government, charities, churches, hospitals, and schools to run the rest of our lives.

Should we draw a line, and if so, where? Management techniques can surely improve lots of nonbusiness organizations, and it would be a shame to miss the benefit because of a misplaced sentimentalism that wants democracy where it does not work. Yet as this book shows, there is also a mistaken sentimentalism in management ideas that denies the contradiction between management and democracy. That raises the danger that management will get used in the democratic political arena, where it can only work against, not for, the fundamental principles of a free society.

Throughout society, from college classrooms to the Oval Office, more and more Americans think in terms of management ideas. In George W. Bush we have our first MBA president, and he is unlikely to be the last, with our universities minting 100,000 MBA degrees a year. Many citizens who do not have MBAs are well acquainted with management ideas, thanks to company training programs, the how-to books sold at airport newsstands, and social contact with fellow corporate employees. Business is now the most popular subject with college undergraduates, many more of whom major in management disciplines than American history. The principles of organizational behavior, not constitutional democracy, most likely inform their social and political views.

No wonder we are told that management is "everyone's business" because it is a "universal discipline" useful everywhere. But there is a hint, maybe not recognized by those who say such things, that using management everywhere means curtailing democracy not just in managerial organizations but in our political lives as well. What does it imply about the traditional democratic right of dissent to say that we should not "ask management to pursue conflicting missions" in health and education when that is exactly what a free people will inevitably do? If "we, as citizens" must "accept our responsibility to use [management] wisely," how can we afford to "let management do its work of finding measures—even imperfect ones—of progress and performance?" Accepting responsibility while letting others set standards is a good way to dodge the essential question of democracy: Who has the power to decide?

Not just management ideas but criticism of them is everyone's business. As the gurus' ideas increasingly come home from the office and affect all our lives, we cannot accept them on faith. Regardless of whether

truth or deception, realism or the lack of it, works best in managing employees, a free society should not accept a false reconciliation of management with democracy. It is better to contain top-down administrative
power within the less-free realm of the corporation and other managed
organizations, where it has proven effective and valuable, by openly admitting that we lead two lives. At work we create wealth under top-down
management power that contradicts the freedoms and rights we cherish
in the rest of society. Some of the gurus' denials of management power
may once have helped create our fortunate balance between prosperity
and freedom by getting Americans to accept corporate life. Now we need
to prevent the extension of corporate values into our democratic institutions by honestly recognizing the reality of management power.

PART 1

---◦---

SCIENTIFIC MANAGEMENT

How Top-Down Power Increased American Productivity

THE FACT THAT MOST OF US WORK FOR MANAGERS IS AN
unintended consequence of American efforts to democratize the corporation in the 1830s. For hundreds of years only those wealthy and
powerful enough to get a monarch or a legislature to grant a charter had
been able to incorporate. But democratic Americans loathed such economic privilege. During Andrew Jackson's presidency, state legislatures
delegated to state agencies their sovereign power to issue corporate char-
ters. Ordinary Americans could fill out a form, pay a small fee, and ob-
tain the legal and economic advantages of incorporation that had formerly been available only to the favored few. The nineteenth century,
which began with only a handful of corporations in the United States,
would end with many thousands of them.

Some corporations prospered more than others, accumulating capital
that in the onrushing era of heavy industry created a new kind of special
privilege, the privilege of owning, as Karl Marx said, the means of production. The result was that the best economic choice for many Americans was not to own their own little company but to work for a big corporation owned by others, forcing many to submit to a new kind of
undemocratic power over part of their lives—management power.

1

Although nineteenth-century corporations tremendously expanded the use of management power, professional management already existed on American slave plantations, as Chapter 1 shows. For eighteenth- and nineteenth-century Americans, a significant part of the meaning of "freedom" was negative. Freedom meant *not* being a slave whose life was managed by someone else. The rhetoric of the American Revolution and its demands for liberty were intimately related to slavery as the colonists' everyday example of tyranny. Therefore, when nineteenth-century employees of mills, factories, and railroads resisted management power, they often borrowed rhetoric from the revolutionary era in order to imply that their corporate employers were tyrannical enslavers.

Management power, in short, was not easily applied to free Americans. Until the end of the nineteenth century, some employees enjoyed an amount of control over their work lives that make feeble by comparison the calls of some of today's gurus for employee empowerment. And what those workers did with their power might give pause to those who think worker empowerment fosters productivity. Many other nineteenth-century workers were of course governed tyrannically, though less by managers than by foremen who often had a large amount of autonomy from management and ran factories with less concern for profit than for their own perks.

Frederick Winslow Taylor, the "demon" of Chapter 2, invented scientific management in the late nineteenth and early twentieth centuries to achieve top-down control of factories. Believing that workers and foremen had power because they alone knew how to do their jobs, Taylor aimed to give managers knowledge of even the smallest operations. He broke jobs down into their simplest parts, made it management's responsibility to teach workers the most efficient way to do each task, set performance standards with the stopwatch, and invented new forms of incentive pay to motivate employees and hold them accountable for their performance.

Scientific management worked well, at least from the point of view of productivity, even though workers often loathed it. Yet efficient as Taylor's system was, it turned out to be improvable by his followers H. L. Gantt and Frank and Lillian Gilbreth, who saw that power was one thing and knowledge another.

Frank Gilbreth was a guru with a common touch who got workers to join him in searching for "motion savings" techniques that further sped them up. His success in enlisting workers' hearts and minds showed that management did not need the psychoanalytic methods of the 1930s "human relations" school to understand the usefulness of a gentle management style. Gilbreth helped give scientific management a more benign appearance, which made him an effective proselytizer for it, not only in the Untied States but in Europe in the years just before and after World War I.

H. L. Gantt, Gilbreth's close friend, still more systematically used workers' hearts, minds, and knowledge while hanging onto the top-down power that Taylor had seized for management. Gantt's approach offers an instructive contrast with today's management gurus, many of whom believe that because knowledge is bottom-up, power cannot be top-down. The rhetorical heat of World War I, a "war to make the world safe for democracy," stirred Gantt deeply. He confusedly believed that his desire for top-down political power in order to maximize war production made him a democrat. Yet he did somewhat humanize top-down management and improve the conditions of many industrial workers.

Gantt and Frank Gilbreth both died relatively young, leaving Lillian Gilbreth to carry on their idea of involving workers' minds in their work, an idea that by the 1920s had an enthusiastic following in the scientific management movement. The risk by then was that gurus would lose sight of the balance between top-down power and bottom-up know-how that Gantt had advocated. That was why Lillian Gilbreth failed in her largest attempt to use bottom-up methods in the 1930s, when President Herbert Hoover enlisted her to help fight the Great Depression. She energetically but unsuccessfully appealed to Americans to spend their way to bottom-up prosperity while their government tightened its purse strings. Scientific management, which began by imposing top-down power on American workers, ended with exclusive reliance on bottom-up solutions in politics and economics.

1

Handling People in Early America

Why Management Is Un-American

To call management "un-American" seems a contradiction in terms. Modern business management is an American invention. Yet the simple existence of top-down management power contradicts the democratic political values at the heart of American culture. This book argues that remembering that contradiction rather than covering it up, as many gurus have done, is the best way to manage well. Calling management un-American is a good way to remember its contradiction of democracy.

Power has a bad name in America. That's good, but it sometimes makes us aim unrealistically at running things from the bottom up. For 2,000 years, serious thinkers from Plato to Machiavelli agreed that power has to be exercised mainly from the top. The only real question was whether top-down power was capable of creating a just society.

Many American managers would like to think of themselves as exercising power in the just spirit of Plato. Warning lovers of liberty "to beware lest by an excessive and ill-timed thirst for freedom they fall into . . . anarchy," Plato believed that a just society could be created from the top down. Justice simply took a philosopher-king wise enough to know that self-restraint was in his own interest, for "despotic power benefits neither rulers nor subjects." It speaks well for managers today that many of them aspire to temper their power, as Plato advised, with sapient self-restraint.

But as many practicing managers also know, Machiavelli's implicit critique of Plato was on the mark. In his personal life, Machiavelli was a reasonably moral man, but as a political commentator he believed it "better to concentrate on what really happens rather than on theories." What really happens is that many people behave immorally. Therefore, the prince and the manager must sometimes act immorally, at least if they want to hang on to their jobs: "[H]ow men live is so different from how they should live that a ruler who . . . persists in doing what ought to be done, will undermine his power rather than maintain it." It is useful to appear like a just philosopher-king, but in reality the prince is "often forced to act treacherously, ruthlessly or inhumanely, and to disregard the precepts of religion. Hence, he must be . . . capable of entering upon the path of wrongdoing when this becomes necessary."

Fortunately, managers do not have enough power to achieve the degree of ruthlessness that Machiavelli idealized as a way of staving off the decline of Florence. Managers cannot subject employees—as the Medicis subjected Machiavelli—to prison and torture. But more than a few managers have felt forced sometime or other into making the best of a bad situation by cutting a corner in a way that does not sit easily on the conscience. In an imperfect world, all forms of power, including managerial power, involve moral compromises. To argue otherwise is to oppose the spirit of democracy, the genius of which is the recognition that power has no claim on our trust.

To suppose that power corrupts in politics but not in business is puerile. Corporate executives' self-righteous assertion of moral leadership has been one of the worst aspects of business life in recent times, far more threatening to our culture than financial corruption. Many managers' simplistic claims to be moral leaders reflect earnest consciences. But mere conscience, especially when combined with ethical and philosophical naïveté, is a poor safeguard against the temptations of power.

American managers get defensive about power because it contradicts their democratic heritage. Two centuries ago, Thomas Jefferson and many others rejected the old idea—from Plato to Machiavelli—that social order requires top-down power. The rise of democracy held out the hope of a bottom-up alternative to Plato's unlikely notion of the philosopher-king as a way of creating a just society.

The Jeffersonians believed that they lived in an unusually stable country that could preserve order without top-down power. A plentiful supply of land in America, their reasoning went, guaranteed relative equality of opportunity, at least for free white males. Long gone, of course, is Jefferson's dream of a nation of farmers living in relative equality. Many of his ideas seem hopelessly irrelevant to today's corporate society.

Yet Jefferson's fear of tyranny enabled him to analyze the moral danger that power poses to human character, including the character of managers today. Power, said Jefferson, believes "that it has a great soul and vast views, beyond the comprehension of the weak; and that it is doing God's service while it is violating all his laws."

Jeffersonian skepticism of power's claim to moral superiority became a central part of American culture and is the main reason that management is un-American. The claim in our time that managers earn their positions by moral leadership is an example of the self-deceiving rationalization Jefferson diagnosed in the powerful. His analysis of power's tendency to produce deceptive self-righteousness in its possessor explains why every time a CEO speaks on business ethics and company values, he or she runs the risk of slipping into self-righteousness. When managers need to discuss values, they may find a little caution and safety for their own souls by remembering Jefferson's humbling admonition that power is powerless to understand its own wrongdoing.

Corporations violate the Jeffersonian idea of freedom and justice because employees depend on their jobs. Independence was the basis of freedom for eighteenth-century Americans. One of Jefferson's contemporaries defined dependence as "an obligation to conform to the will . . . of that superior person . . . upon which the inferior depends." "Freedom and dependency" were "opposite and irreconcilable terms."

Jefferson's dislike of manufacturing—his hope never to see "our fellow citizens laboring at a work-bench"—resulted from his belief that only the independent could be free and virtuous. Those who made their living by producing goods for the market depended "on the casualties and caprice of customers. Dependance begets subservience and venality, suffocates the germ of virtue, and prepares fit tools for the designs of [political] ambition."

Conversely, agriculture promoted freedom because farmers could aim at self-sufficiency and economic independence. "Those who labour in the earth," said Jefferson, "are the chosen people of God." By clinging to the independent life of the farmer, Americans could preserve their free republic.

Jefferson was antimanagement. He hoped to prevent the rise of a professional class of government administrators, whom he feared would destroy freedom by making people dependent on the government. He disagreed with the idea proclaimed by today's gurus that employees should receive intellectual stimulation and personal satisfaction from work. The government should offer only "drudgery . . . to those entrusted with its administration." Bored government workers, according to Jefferson, would not stay long, providing "a wise and necessary precaution against the degeneracy of the public servants."

Jefferson's great opponent, Alexander Hamilton, took a more realistic view. As America's first secretary of the treasury, Hamilton ran a large bureaucracy, at least by the standards of the day, from the top down. "Decision, activity, secrecy, and dispatch," he said, "will generally characterize the proceedings of one man in a much more eminent degree than the proceedings of any greater number."

But Hamilton saw that top-down management had practical limits and delegated authority in order to avoid "a vast mass of details" certain to lead to "sloth of execution." The manager should consult subordinates because even the "greatest genius, hurried along by the rapidity of its own conceptions, will occasionally overlook obstacles which ordinary and more phlegmatic men will discover."

As secretary of the treasury, Hamilton convinced Congress to enact protective tariffs and incorporate a national bank—a controversial program aimed among other things at encouraging the manufacturing that Jefferson feared as a threat to freedom. Hamilton's program touched off a fierce ideological debate within the country at large and within the Washington administration. Jefferson advised President Washington that Hamilton's career was "a tissue of machinations against the liberty of the country." Hamilton, a superb infighter, won the battles in Washington's cabinet, and Jefferson eventually resigned as secretary of state.

But Jefferson won the war in culture and politics. Elected president in 1800, he dismantled much of Hamilton's economic program that had aimed to promote manufacturing. And by doubling the country's size in the Louisiana Purchase, he encouraged the westward spread of agriculture so that every man could work independently of others on his own land, prospering according to merit and suffering no arbitrary injustice from political or economic superiors. Jefferson's admirable suspicion of top-down power, not Hamilton's realistic insistence on its inevitability, became the primary value of American political culture.

Jefferson's America, however, had a nearly fatal flaw—the self-contradictory behavior of those who claimed to love liberty while owning slaves. During the American Revolution, Samuel Johnson had voiced the mind of many puzzled Englishmen by asking, "How is it that we hear the loudest yelps for liberty among the drivers of negroes?"

Recent historians have offered a plausible answer to the riddle of how slaveholders could conceive of themselves as champions of liberty. Slavery caused rather than contradicted the masters' love of freedom by holding constantly before them a harsh example of what it meant to be unfree. Slaves and indentured white servants in America suffered "a much harsher, more brutal, and more humiliating status" than servants in England. A plentiful population gave England an oversupply of labor, low wages, and cruel poverty, but it also made hiring more help a feasible alternative to working people to death.

In thinly populated America, by contrast, land was relatively easy to acquire, but getting it to yield wealth was difficult because of the scarcity of labor. As a result, both black slaves and white servants were often driven with extraordinary cruelty. Mostly forgotten today are what can accurately be called the killing fields of seventeenth-century Virginia. There, black slaves and indentured whites, faced with hideous punishments if they resisted, were worked to death raising fabulously profitable tobacco.

But later, in the era of the American Revolution, the idea of liberty swelled in the souls of the slaveholders. In 1787, Jefferson expressed the belief of more than a few that the "peculiar institution" could not forever coexist with freedom. Slavery, Jefferson said, trained whites in the habits of tyranny and made them unfit for freedom: "Our children . . . thus nursed, educated, and daily exercised in tyranny, cannot but be stamped by it. . . . Indeed I tremble for my country when I reflect that God is just."

Jefferson unrealistically hoped that the master class would voluntarily abolish slavery: "I think a change already perceptible, since the origin of the present revolution. The spirit of the master is abating . . . , the way I hope preparing, . . . for a total emancipation, . . . with the consent of the masters rather than by their extirpation."

But any chance for a peaceful end to slavery was cruelly doomed by the rise of the cotton economy. Eli Whitney's 1793 invention of the cotton gin reduced to a machine operation the previously expensive task—even with slave labor—of separating fibers from seeds of short staple cotton, the only variety that would grow in the Southern inlands. Cotton plantations spread rapidly west, frequently numbering their slaves in the dozens and sometimes in the hundreds, creating in slave overseers and drivers the first large group of managers in American private enterprise.

Managing Slaves

As the largest private enterprises of the early republic, cotton plantations presented a managerial challenge and brought into being America's first significant body of management writings, mainly by the slave owners. The planters shared ideas on how to manage slaves, entered essay contests on plantation management, and published scores of articles on the subject in agricultural journals. They soon contradicted Jefferson's view as to the evil of slavery and attempted moral justification of undemocratic top-down power in managing human beings.

The planters eased their moral qualms with assurances that the master's interest was the same as the slave's. Adam Smith had taught that in a free market, self-interest does God's work of maximizing the good of all. The planters extended that idea to include the management of unfree labor. The slaveholder's self-interest ensured, as one of them put it, that

he would fulfill his "duty to know how his slaves are treated, and to protect them against cruelty."

The rare owner honest enough to admit that market forces could make
it profitable to work a slave to death insisted that such was not now the
case. One Mississippi planter pointed out that the rate of return on investment affected the length of useful life it took to yield a profit. If the
price of cotton was high enough, it could make economic sense to "kill
up and wear out one Negro to buy another." But "it is not so now. Negroes are too high in proportion to the price of cotton, and it behooves
those who own them to make them last as long as possible."

Owners more frequently claimed that the need to keep slaves productive ensured gentle management. "If the master be a tyrant," wrote a Mississippi planter in 1849, "his negroes may be so much embarrassed by his
presence as to be incapable of doing their work properly." The writer
could have supported his assertion as to the discouraging effect of
tyranny with quotations from newspaper advertisements for runaway
slaves: "His back very much scarred by the whip"; "Randal, has one ear
cropped"; "I burnt her with a hot iron, on the left side of her face."

Guru owners cautioned that not just physical but also verbal abuse
worked against the master's self-interest. "Anger begets anger," cautioned
a Virginian in 1852, adding that "a low tone of voice is recommended in
speaking to negroes." This insightful gentleman also warned that skillful
human relations are no substitute for material incentives: "No negro . . .
will be faithful who has his absolute wants unsatisfied; I mean food and
clothing."

Cotton planters mustered confidence in their own righteousness by insisting on the moral degradation of blacks, who were therefore justly en-
slaved. Not white slave owners but "Negroes are by nature tyrannical in
their dispositions; and if allowed, the stronger will abuse the weaker." As
natural tyrants, blacks had to be held in bondage in order to protect the
weak among them from the strong.

Like all tyrants, blacks were lazy and dishonest. "The only way to keep
a negro honest," said one owner, "is not to trust him." Another thought
that the ordinary slave's "most general defect . . . is hypocrisy," leading

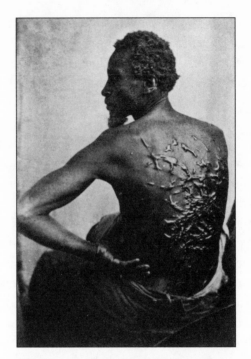

PHOTO 1.1   "Gordon," whose owner
apparently had not heeded the advice of
writers on the management of slaves to
apply the whip calmly and judiciously.

him to "play the fool's part" in "neglect of duty." It followed that "[t]he
most important part of management of slaves is always to keep them
under subjection."

Godlike power over other human beings can only be justified by godlike virtue, for which the owners did not hesitate to strive. Discipline, one
advised, should be administered not in a vengeful spirit but with divine
self-control over base passions like anger: "[E]ven in inflicting the sever-
est punishment, do so in a mild, cool manner. . . . When you find it necessary to use the whip (and desirable as it would be to dispense with it
entirely, it is necessary at times), apply it slowly and deliberately and to
the extent you are determined in your own mind to be needful before
you begin." Anger and a violent temper "reduce the man who uses them
to a level with the negro."

The master made himself capable of impartial justice by cool self-control—a common ideal in today's management ideology, and rightly so, provided it is combined with humbling recognition that the ideal is unattainable rather than with hubristic confidence in the morality of the master, whether a slave owner or a manager.

The owners had a captive audience for their self-righteous moralism, because they often hired white overseers to assist them. The 1850 U.S. census reported that 18,859 Americans earned their living as slave overseers, probably the largest group of salaried managers in the world at the time.

Few managers since could have had it worse than the overseers. Usually aspiring to having farms of their own, they had little real chance of joining the planter class. Stuck in dead-end jobs, sometimes illiterate, often given to drink, and usually uncouth, overseers seemed, as one planter put it, "the curse of this country . . . the worst men in the community." Socially unacceptable to the owners' families and living on rural plantations that offered no other free companionship, overseers were often single men and desperately lonely. Notorious for their sexual exploitation of slave women, some overseers nevertheless limited their diversions even there out of concern for the effect on their workers' morale. "I think I shall Have to get me a wife," reflected one overseer. But "where shall I find hir[?] Ladies seem to Be as scarce as chicken teeth in this vicinity."

The overseer had responsibility for crops, slaves, animals, barns, equipment, and ultimately the safety of a white family far outnumbered by their human chattel, whose true thoughts and resentments were impossible to know. "I don't get time Scarcely to eat or Sleep," complained one plantation manager, adding that the need for "strictest vigilance" over the slaves made a day off from the plantation a rarity.

Job insecurity added to the overseer's misery. The planters used fear to manage overseers as well as slaves. One planter opined that "when a manager goes on a place where he expects all his energies will be taxed to the utmost in order to remain even one year, he immediately girds himself to be up and doing." Not surprisingly, planters found that overseers "all seem to wear out after a while" and needed "changing" at frequent intervals.

With only a short time to make a mark, overseers sought quick results, recklessly working slaves and land whose depletion then became an item in the planters' indictment of them. The overseers doubted the owners' sincerity in calling for careful handling of slaves and land. The planters, land rich and cash poor, always wanted a large crop, which led the overseers to deride them as short-sighted "Colonel Cottonbags." As one overseer wryly noted, in "a favorable crop year, *the master makes* a splendid crop; if . . . an inferior crop be made, it is the overseer."

Owners often micromanaged overseers and violated their own admonition that master and manager "should always pull at the same end of the rope." Masters sometimes undercut overseers' authority on the basis of "negro news" from trusted slaves. One planter announced that he would "not encourage tale bearing" but in the next breath added that he would "question every negro indiscriminately whenever he thinks proper." Slaves of course used the opportunity to put owner and overseer at odds.

Some slaves were similarly caught in the middle because the management ranks of the Old South included blacks. Supervision of the slave workforce was too big a job to be performed entirely by owners and overseers. Therefore, slaves themselves were given whips to wield over other slaves. Large plantations had a number of black drivers reporting to the overseer, whereas the small farmer who could not afford an overseer might put all his slaves under a driver who reported directly to himself. As many as two-thirds of slaves may have labored under the immediate supervision not of whites but of blacks.

Planters knew that black drivers might be torn between loyalty to their fellow slaves and their "duty" to their owners. To get the drivers to manage upward, the planters provided material incentives, including cash bonuses, better work assignments for family members, and better clothes, food, and housing. They also appealed to the drivers' "pride of character" with incentives such as a horse-drawn cart to drive to market.

Owners sometimes used the idea that blacks were natural tyrants to justify violating a basic principle of management hierarchies—loyalty up is earned by loyalty down. One Mississippi driver served faithfully for thirty years only to have his daughter sold away. Remarkably, he managed to procure his freedom and tell his story on abolitionist platforms in the North. Mississippi newspapers reacted furiously and reported that the ex-driver's owner had to "curb his sanguinary temper to prevent him from exercising cruelty on his fellow servants," who viewed him "as a *bug bear* or *Negro devil*, whose very name would terrify the unruly into obedience, . . . a blood-thirsty tyrannical Mahometan Negro, the most cruel and vindictive wretch that ever existed."

Subsequent accounts have tried to clear the black drivers of the charge of cruelty, but the evidence is thin on both sides. According to one of the best histories of slavery, the art of being a driver was to temper the cruel injustice of the situation with whatever fairness was possible: "They had to demand a certain level of discipline and performance. . . . When they did not get it they used the whip. . . . The difference between a good driver and a mean one, from the slaves' point of view, centered not on whether or not he commanded hard work—he had to—but on whether or not he proceeded according to . . . evenhandedness, a decent respect for individual weakness and unfeigned illness."

By this account, the drivers managed with common sense and in something of the spirit that the guru owners prescribed for overseers, creating whatever justice was possible within the limits of an inherently unjust system. Caught in an appalling web of power and required to exercise it on those below, the drivers surely understood their compulsory society better than those above them, understood how much it depended on power, how little on moral authority.

Managing Women

The coming of the machine age, which placed less of a premium on physical strength, might well have been expected to ease the subjection of women. That seemed at least to be the case in early nineteenth-century America when women became the first factory workers. But the New England women who escaped the control of fathers, husbands, and brothers by going to work in textile factories found themselves governed by a new group of men—corporate managers.

The Americans who invented the factory sought not to improve the situation of women but only to circumvent the English monopoly of machinery for manufacturing textiles. In the late eighteenth and early nineteenth centuries, thanks to the Arkwright frame and the power loom, John Bull had become the richest nation by clothing the world in inexpensive cotton, grown in America but spun and woven in England.

The American economy got a boost in 1790 when an English mechanic named Samuel Slater disguised himself as a farm boy and slipped out of the country, violating laws aimed at keeping skilled mechanics at home. At Pawtucket, Rhode Island, he rebuilt the Arkwright frame from memory.

America got the power loom two decades later. Francis Cabot Lowell, an enterprising Boston merchant, journeyed to England, ostensibly for his health. He memorized the structure of the looms from his visits to Manchester mills. Returning home, he obtained a corporate charter for the Boston Manufacturing Company to produce textiles and in the process created fortunes for himself and his investors, mainly family and friends who called themselves the "Boston Associates."

Lowell's success lay in his decision to spin as well as weave. Integration of the two processes gave him a cost advantage over English manufacturers, who, despite their invention of textile machinery, had undertaken no organizational innovations. The English spun and wove in separate plants, under separate ownership, just as they had done in the era of hand production.

By integrating spinning and weaving, Lowell inaugurated the century and a half during which Americans led the world in managerial and organizational know-how. The water-powered mill he built at Waltham, Massachusetts, rationalized production, lowered costs, and according to some historians was the world's first factory.

Lowell's organizational innovation—the integrated factory—made him initially dependent on women workers. Because the Waltham factory both spun and wove, it operated on an unprecedented scale and needed a large workforce. Slater at Pawtucket and his numerous imitators in southern New England found workers for their spinning mills by hiring whole families—the basic unit of labor in the surrounding agrarian economy. But Lowell could not have lured a sufficient number of families to his large Waltham factory. And young, single men—the most mobile part of the laboring population—were needed on farms. Young, single women were the only available workforce.

To make New England farm families willing to send their daughters to the factory, Lowell had to create "arrangements for the moral character of the operatives employed." He built large boardinghouses and employed respectable matrons, often widows, to run them. With their reputations intact, the "factory girls"—actually young women, often in their early twenties—would be able to return home to marry after a few years of work, with their saved earnings serving as an attractive dowry. Farm girls, attracted not only by the high wages of $1.85 a week and up but by the chance to enjoy some personal independence before marriage, flocked to live "on the corporation" (which they conceived of more as a place than a firm).

So successful was this system of transforming farm girls into factory workers that the Boston Associates transported it intact to subsequent, larger mills at the falls of the Merrimack River. There, in the 1820s a new industrial city sprang up—Lowell, Massachusetts, named in honor of Francis Cabot Lowell, who had died in 1817—with numerous large boardinghouses and a dozen or more factories staffed by thousands of women.

For young New England women, factory work became an uplifting rite of passage, a little like going to college today. Exchanging their homespun shawls and country twangs for store-bought bonnets and the "city way of speaking," they subscribed to circulating libraries and paid for lectures by such visiting literati as Ralph Waldo Emerson. They also published a celebrated magazine, *The Lowell Offering*, in which they expressed their love of "freedom and equality" and their delight in being "independent of everyone!"

From the 1820s to the 1840s, the city of Lowell served as one of the emblems of American democracy, drawing visitors from home and abroad. Pretentious social observers saw the red-brick mills, six stories tall and topped with white belfries, as cathedrals of industry. Inside, the clacking din of throstles and looms deafened the ear, but the long symmetrical rows of machines, their wooden frames painted a brilliant metallic green, pleased the eye. To European visitors, the factories, spewing out calicos, symbolized new world efficiency—"the American System of Manufacturing."

But the most attention went to the women workers. They seemed to embody the spirit of Liberty, whose iconic representations, as later in the Statue of Liberty, were always feminine in the age of democratic revolutions. When President Andrew Jackson visited Lowell in 1833, the factory women paraded 2,500 strong in white muslin dresses trimmed with blue sashes. Marching past Old Hickory, they saluted him with a wave of their green parasols while the aged president bowed himself into exhaustion and swore them "very pretty women, by the Eternal."

Charles Dickens agreed. Touring Lowell in 1842, he took hope from the women's healthy visages that industrialism did not have to lead to working-class misery as it had in England. Dickens was astounded by the white curtains and potted plants the women had placed in the factory windows, by their devoting their few free hours to reading and self-improvement, by their pooling of money to buy pianos for their boardinghouses, but above all by the absence of misery in their expressions. He found not "one young face that gave me a painful impression; not one young girl whom I would have removed from those works if I had had the power."

Yet working conditions were probably far from as good as visitors believed. Long hours attending to the pulsing beat of machinery brought throbbing headaches to many of the women. The mills' dank, fetid air—kept moist to hold newly spun threads intact, saturated with cotton dust and, after dark, fouled by fumes from oil lamps—caused nosebleeds and asthma. Some women talked of "going home to die" of tuberculosis contracted in the factory.

The social observers who rushed to Lowell for a portent of the American future would have done better to ignore the democratic spirit embodied in the women workers in favor of the top-down power of the male managers. The owners—merchants with affairs of their own—relied on hired managers, or "mill agents," whose numbers grew rapidly as the textile industry expanded. Lowell alone spawned a dozen or more corporations, each of which needed an agent for its mill. Assisted by a superintendent of production and a paymaster, the mill agent oversaw half a dozen "overseers," one for each floor of the factory. Because each overseer had a "second hand," one mill could easily have a dozen managerial positions. By the time of Andrew Jackson's visit, Lowell must have had more than 100 managers striving along an ascending "career path."

Mechanical know-how and supervisory skill qualified a man—never a woman—to move up this management ladder. From the beginning, the mills had some male workers who ran the repair shop, staffed the "watch force" (security), and did the heavy labor in the mill yard. Out of this pool of male operatives a few were promoted to supervisory positions in women's departments such as spinning, weaving, winding, warping, and dressing. Occasionally, a skilled mechanic became rich as a result of the mill owners' practice of rewarding key employees with an equity stake. But few workers climbed all the way to mill agent because that position required enough education and social standing to be comfortable in reporting to the patrician shareholders.

Kirk Boott, the original mill agent in Lowell, fit comfortably with the owners' conservative values. Although he was an American citizen, Boott had served as an officer in the English army and, according to an associate, had learned "engineering at a government establishment in England." Like other Anglophiles among the American merchant class, Boott was disgusted with his native country for declaring war on Britain in 1812. Still, he returned to the United States, where he found a market for his skills in the new textile industry. The Boston Associates hired Boott to build and run their first mill on the Merrimack River, where the city of Lowell came into being. Boott's military experience enabled him to boss the workers, and his engineering training qualified him to dam a stream to drive a waterwheel and power a factory.

The haughty Boott ruled Lowell, as one of the factory women reported, like a "great potentate" and "exercised almost absolute power

PHOTO 1.2   Kirk Boott, the unpopular mill
agent in Lowell who disliked the rising
spirit of democracy in America.

over the mill-people." Riding horseback through the city, he used his
whip on boys in the street who annoyed him. He built an Anglican
church in Lowell and paid for it by garnishing the workers' wages,
though few of them were Anglican faithful. But there were limits to what
even Boott could get away with, as when on a Fourth of July he flew the
Stars and Stripes beneath the Union Jack, until an indignant crowd
changed the order.

While the factory women favored the rising glory of democracy, the
owners and managers clung to an older, hierarchical notion of social
order. They lamented, for example, the fact that good wages enabled the
factory women to dress far above the level of the ordinary farmer's daughter, so that clothes no longer provided a ready marker of a woman's social
class. The workers, for their part, resented the lordly attitude of the
agents and envied their fine homes, surrounded by well-tended gardens
and set apart from the workers' boardinghouses.

The women saw the agents as "over-bearing tyrants" and believed the overseers were made of the same cloth. Most overseers had begun as factory hands and often had lower social origins and less education than the women they supervised. Yet the overseers imitated the agents' aloofness. It was no more easy then than now to bear an uncouth boss who confuses position and power with personal sublimity. When a worker married an overseer and began to put on airs, her erstwhile comrades labeled such bosses' houses "Puckersville."

At least the women were physically safe. This was no small matter, because in the family-staffed Rhode Island and Connecticut spinning mills, overseers sometimes claimed the authority of a husband and father, with the right to strike women and children. At Lowell, a worker comforted herself, "To strike a female could cost any overseer his place."

But the workers were not exempt from verbal abuse. The overseers' faultfinding often resulted in tears. An early industrial guru, visiting Lowell, hinted that he found undue harshness there. James Montgomery of Scotland visited New England to tour its mills, and his resulting *Carding and Spinning Master's Assistant* (1832) cautioned that a mill agent's responsibilities and anxieties can easily "ruffle the temper" and urged them not to be "tyrannical."

Managers of textile workers seem to have put much less emphasis on workers' morale than did the slave overseers of the South. Manuals for mill agents focused mainly on maintaining and operating the machinery, with only incidental attention to managing the workforce. The factory overseers probably felt little need to think about human relations because they used machinery to drive the workers. A slave in a cotton field might feign and malinger, but broken threads and fouled looms quickly identified laggard machine operators. All of the attention to motivation with which the Southern master class attempted to extract work from slaves seemed unnecessary in Northern textile mills.

Good wages, not benign management, maintained social harmony at Lowell. When prosperity declined, contention rose. New mills came on line in the 1830s, increasing the supply of textiles and lowering prices. In

1834, Lowell's various boards of directors colluded in a joint order to mill agents to reduce wages by 25 percent.

The infuriated workers resented not only the reduced pay but also the insult to their proud sense of themselves as free Americans. Invoking the spirit of 1776, they vowed to resist attempts to "enslave us" and to act in "the spirit of our Patriotic Ancestors" who "preferred privation to bondage."

Eight hundred of the women walked off the job. They violated sexual decorum by holding street rallies and speaking in public, according to a newspaper account, "on the rights of women and the iniquities of the 'monied aristocracy.'" The mill agents, alarmed at the "amizonian [sic] display," hurriedly paid off the leaders in the hope that they would leave for home, which some did. The majority soon returned to work.

Two years later, the Lowell women struck more successfully against a raise in their charges for room and board. Their numbers doubled this time to between 1,500 and 2,000 strikers, and they stayed out for weeks rather than days. Again placing themselves in the tradition of the American Revolution, they pledged to resist the owners as strongly as their fathers had defied "the lordly avarice of the British ministry." The corporations surrendered and revoked the fee increases for room and board.

The frustrated factory owners turned their attention to increasing productivity through the "speed-up" and the "stretch-out"—either speeding up the machinery or stretching the workers to cover more machines. Over the years, the workday at Lowell was extended from eleven to thirteen hours, and some workers claimed that management stretched out the last hour by slowing down the clock.

One overseer lamented the new spirit of antagonism and blamed the mill owners for forcing the ordinary supervisor to be "apparently harsh and unmindful of those employed under him." Owners quelled overseers' consciences by paying "premiums" to those with the most productive departments, an incentive for hard driving of workers that the factory women unsuccessfully protested. As conditions grew harsher, women still constituted a large part of the factory workforce, but fewer of them were native born.

Irish immigrants, their numbers surging in the late 1840s as potato crops failed in their homeland, soon provided the Lowell mills with a more manageable workforce. For the Irish, home may also have been a farm, but it was famine ridden and thousands of miles away, not the sort of refuge that had given New England women the security to fight for their "independence."

The story would soon be much the same throughout industrializing America as immigration eased the shortage of labor, tilted the balance of power away from workers, and subjected white men as well as women and slaves to management control.

Managing Men

As the factory spread from textiles to other products such as axes, shovels, shoes, clocks, locks, and guns, the factory workforce became predominantly male. Not only did immigration lower the cost of male labor, but many of these industries involved skilled use of hand tools, traditionally a male preserve and an important element of production long after the coming of factory organization. Machine tools such as the filing jig and the drill press were in their infancy and only slowly evolved toward cutting tolerances that made interchangeable parts feasible for all metal products. As late as the 1840s, gunsmiths still used hand files to fit many parts individually.

Running factories with large numbers of men brought a seemingly natural tendency toward military-style management. Early manufacturing organizations aimed primarily at the same goal as armies—command and control of men. Nowhere was this more true than at the federal armory at Springfield, Massachusetts, which made many of the weapons with which the new nation protected its independence and expanded west.

Managing gunsmiths posed a far greater challenge than supervising textile workers. Machinery drove the Lowell women, but many of the men at the Springfield Armory still worked by hand and eye, filing and fitting metal parts. Foremen had to control and drive the 250 workers engaged in more than 100 different jobs at the Springfield Armory.

Colonel Roswell Lee, commanding officer of the Springfield Armory, developed foremanship to a new level, amounting to a breakthrough in managerial practice. To track production and prevent theft and waste, Lee had his foremen keep records of tools and materials issued to each worker such as files, steel, wood, and coal. And each armorer put his individual mark on his finished work, enabling the foreman to compare a worker's output with the volume of tools and materials he had received. The foremen, according to an 1819 army report, forced the workers to pay for any "deficiency" between supplies issued and work produced.

In contrast to the Springfield workers and their military management, workers at the nation's other major armory at Harpers Ferry, Virginia, were an unruly lot. Situated dangerously close to the frontier at the time of its founding in the 1790s, the Harpers Ferry armory owed its location to the patronage of President Washington, a passionate advocate of economic development in the upper Potomac Valley, where he and his associates had land and canal investments. Something of a political boondoggle at its conception, the Harpers Ferry Armory would be mismanaged for half a century.

Gunsmiths at Harpers Ferry believed their metalworking skills entitled them to a high degree of autonomy. They thought of themselves not as workers to be driven by foremen but as fine craftsmen to be directed by master artisans, as if they were medieval guildsmen. As in medieval workshops, social life and work life intertwined at Harpers Ferry. Workers took frequent breaks to commune over a dram of whisky or to bet on a cockfight in the armory yard.

But unlike medieval craftsmen, the Harpers Ferry armorers worked for a giant organization, Uncle Sam. Taking advantage of their employer's deep pockets, workers sometimes sold their government-issued tools and always claimed their full pay regardless of short hours and absenteeism.

The Ordnance Department therefore transferred Colonel Lee from Springfield to Harpers Ferry for a couple of brief stints in the late 1820s. Forbidding gambling and alcohol on the armory grounds, Lee punished unexcused absences with dismissal and levied fines for "lost" tools.

But Lee soon returned to Springfield and left the job of enforcing these regulations to a civilian named Thomas Dunn, whose hard-nosed management style cost him his life when a dismissed armorer shot the new superintendent in his office. Dunn's civilian successors remembered their manners and returned the armory to its old, easy ways. In the 1830s, Andrew Jackson rewarded loyal Democrats with armory jobs. Managed by political hacks, Harpers Ferry had no chance of improvement until power shifted in Washington.

The 1840 election of a Whig president, William Henry Harrison, brought managerial reform under military aegis. Harrison put Harpers Ferry under Major Henry Craig, who was appalled to find that, as his civilian predecessor understated it, the armory was "to some extent controlled by the workmen." Craig reinstated Lee's prohibitions of gambling and alcohol, then compounded the injury by lengthening the work day to ten hours, even though the armorers had grown accustomed to half that. Insisting that ten hours was no hardship in an era when private manufacturers demanded twelve, Craig added insult to injury by installing a clock.

The armorers protested as free Americans against having to work, as they saw it, under martial law. The Army Ordnance Department replied that the need for good order applied to all production, whether military or civilian, "especially when the operations are partly performed by machinery, as they are at the Armories." The unconvinced workers went on strike and sent elected representatives down the Potomac to Washington to present their grievances to President Tyler (Harrison having died of pneumonia shortly after his inauguration).

But Tyler had bigger questions on his mind than the situation of his frontline employees. A Virginia slaveholder, erstwhile Democrat, and the first vice president elevated to the White House by the death of an incumbent ("His Accidency," the resentful Whigs called him), Tyler was busily awakening the sectional antagonisms between North and South that a generation later would bring Civil War. Promising the armorers that there would be no reprisals for their strike, the president sent them back to their anvils to "hammer out their own salvation."

The United States—casting covetous eyes on Texas, Mexico, and Oregon—knew that resistance might greet its impending drive to the Pacific and deemed weapons more important than the happiness of the men who made them. Soon after the strikers' return to Harpers Ferry, President Tyler signed an act of Congress permanently placing national armories under military control.

—◦—

Railroads, the era's transforming innovation, also used military-style management, complete with line-and-staff hierarchies, organization charts, and downward flow of authority. Military terminology—"division," "dispatcher," and "semaphore"—abounded on the railroads, and in the early days employees were even disciplined by "court martial." By the 1850s, managers of the main trunk lines controlled thousands of miles of track. The daily frenzy of divisional offices, coordinating crews, engines, cars, stations, sidings, and fuel depots had something of the high drama of a battlefield headquarters.

As Daniel McCallum, president of the Erie Railroad, put it, "The enforcement of a rigid system of discipline in the government of works of great magnitude is indispensable to success." On a single-track line curving through hilly country, a crew that broke the rule against waiting on sidings for oncoming trains could cause a collision. An oilman who failed to lubricate wheel bearings could bring a train to a grinding stop in the wilderness, tying up for days the entire line and the capital invested in it. A ticket clerk filching pennies, if imitated by his brethren up and down the line, could mean the difference between operating at a profit or a loss.

Because control of workers was paramount, railroad Hammurabis wrote detailed codes of conduct. A Baltimore & Ohio manual, for example, spelled out rules for the conductor's relations with passengers. While greeting passengers, seating them, making sure that each took only one seat, getting them to keep their feet off the seats, adjudicating between two passengers claiming the same seat, keeping away "newsboys and *other annoyances* [prostitutes?]," and advising passengers on "coaches, omnibuses, the 'through car' in Baltimore, meals and baggage wagons," the conductor was "*to be always in a thoroughly good humor and polite to everyone he meets*; to be cleanly and tidy about his person" and dressed "as a gentleman."

And those were just passenger relations. Other written rules guided the conductor in governing the train's crew, anticipating the need for extra cars, lighting oil lamps at night, stocking tools in case of breakdown, running the train on time, checking the accuracy of station clocks, thwarting deadhead riders by marking numbered tickets with the individualized hole of his paper punch, and carrying cash in double-keyed lockboxes to prevent employee theft.

While each B&O job—engineer, brakeman, and so on—had its own specific regulations, there were also generic rules for all employees such as the prohibition of alcohol: "No man who uses intoxicating drinks at all can thus rely upon himself, or be relied upon." The nineteenth-century temperance movement was built on an alliance of employers and evangelicals, the two overlapping groups both interested in getting the well-oiled American *demos* under control.

To make sure the rules were obeyed, every railroad employee reported to a superior with authority to hire and fire. "Each officer," according to McCallum of the Erie, had the power "to appoint all persons for whose acts he is held responsible, and may dismiss any subordinate."

Still stronger discipline, probably the harshest ever applied to wage earners in America, fell on the 15,000–20,000 imported Chinese laborers who, just after the Civil War, cemented the union by building the transcontinental railroad. Sometimes held against their will and flogged to work, they demanded, in their one recorded strike, that their supervisors not "whip them or restrain them from leaving the road when they desire to seek other employment."

A folklore account of a legendary construction supervisor named Strobridge on the Central Pacific, the western end of the transcontinental, has the style of what Mark Twain called "a stretcher." But the man really existed and the attitude attributed to him accurately represents the spirit of the ordinary "mule-whacker" toward Chinese labor: "He had a mild but firm way, which was in the form of a pick handle . . . he could spot the ringleaders at one glance and would bring his persuader into action and was not particular where it landed."

The Central Pacific president, Leland Stanford, glossed matters more benignly, reporting to shareholders that the Chinese were more "prudent and economical" than white men and therefore "contented with less wages"—a good thing, too, because the labor agents who procured the workers from China collected and distributed their pay, stealing some of it in the process.

Similarly harsh discipline helped lay the track for the eastern end of the transcontinental, the Union Pacific, under the direction of General Jack Casement, who had honed his management skills on Civil War battlefields. Photographed near a construction train on high plains resembling the Russian steppes, the bearded Casement in his fur-trimmed coat looks like a tsarist autocrat lording over the workers in the background. A viewer might well think he was building the Trans-Siberian, but he was wielding American management power with the bullwhip in his hand.

◂○▸

The post–Civil War railroad network and the telegraph wires strung along the tracks made the United States the world's largest free market. In a legal sense, of course, the United States had already been a free-market nation for more than half a century. But the railroads turned legal fiction into economic reality, replacing the mainly intraregional trade of the antebellum era with a truly national market. Train and telegraph moved goods and information across the country at speeds not much slower than today (with the obvious exception of air freight). Economies of speed made possible economies of scale, bringing the rise of mass distributors and mass producers. These new corporations built hierarchical organizations of managers to coordinate their vast operations, lowering costs and tremendously increasing American wealth and prosperity.

The downside from the point of view of democracy was that as long as a century ago, which was only a century after Jefferson's presidency, millions already worked not as the yeomen farmers Jefferson envisioned but as wage earners at wholesalers like Marshall Fields, department stores like Macy's, mail-order firms (Sears), distillers (Seagram's), petroleum re-

PHOTO 1.3 General Jack Casement, a builder of the transcontinental railroad, holding one of the oldest management tools.

finers (Standard Oil), cigarette manufacturers (American Tobacco), canning companies (Campbell Soups), grain processors (General Mills), meatpackers (Armour), explosives manufacturers (Du Pont), ore refiners (U.S. Steel), machinery makers (Singer Sewing Machines), and electrical manufacturers (General Electric).

But in many of these companies, workers were subject less to the power of management than power wielded by foremen, who often operated much like sergeants, with great power and considerable independence from their superiors. Management at many of these firms paid little attention to control of the workforce. First-mover advantages, capital-intensive barriers to entry, and the high protective tariffs that Northern manufacturers had imposed after Union victory in the Civil War protected many of the new corporations from competition. High costs due to inefficient foremen did not threaten profitability.

Adding to the power of foremen was the fact that the burgeoning manpower needs of industrializing America were met by immigration from Eastern and Southern Europe, resulting in a working class with guttural accents, peasant manners, and liturgical faiths, all off-putting to native WASPs. Managers were ill equipped to handle such a workforce and gladly left matters in the hands of foremen who hired, fired, and disciplined workers at their complete discretion and without appeal. Sometimes, a foreman was an inside contractor, supplying a company with a gang of laborers who were *his* employees to treat as he saw fit.

The qualifications for a foreman's job included not just skill and knowledge but also strength and brutality. A veteran of the late nineteenth-century bricklaying trade reported that a foreman had to be able to "lick any man on the job, and he did it, occasionally, to prove it! In how many cases in your life have you ever seen a little, small fellow a foreman? He had to be twice as good as a big fellow to be foreman."

Corruption often augmented the foreman's power, especially in the new mass-production industries—oil refining, food processing, steelmaking, and the like. In those industries most work was unskilled. The authority to hire and fire unskilled workers with few job alternatives enabled foremen to sell jobs and extort bribes from employees. Because their positions offered a chance at lucrative graft, foremen not infrequently paid to get their own jobs, if not with money then with connections, nepotism, or in industries employing women, sexual favors.

Whatever the coin in which they purchased their jobs, foremen soon recovered their investment. A study of Pittsburgh steel companies done in the early twentieth century found that foremen routinely sold jobs paying a few dollars a week for $5, $10, or even $25: "The grafting system has its roots partly in the fact that the Slav is willing to work for less than an American and partly in his ignorance . . . . The newcomer is given to understand that it is the custom to sell jobs in this country, . . . the price is paid, . . . and the man goes to work."

Nor did the extortion end once the job was landed. Workers not uncommonly had to "treat" their bosses to a drink or a dinner on payday or else give them cases of beer and boxes of cigars. Some foremen had only to make it known at work that their larders were empty at home for new supplies to arrive, with the shopkeeper's bill paid in advance.

Workers got something back for their bribes—a measure of control and power over their working conditions. Why should foremen, collecting their perquisites from the bottom up, be overly concerned with management's objective of maximum profit? Even foremen who did not exact monetary tribute often engaged in a de facto alliance with workers against managers, whom they often kept ignorant as to the inefficiency of the factory. Foremen sustained their power not just through brutality and corruption but by giving workers some measure of protection against managers' and owners' interest in the most work for the least pay.

Although most managers were content to let sleeping dogs lie, one instinctively combative and power-thirsty boss—Frederick W. Taylor—aimed to bring foremen to heel. Thomas Jefferson's principles of bottom-up democracy may have won out in culture and politics, but at work Americans were about to get a dose of the top-down power that Alexander Hamilton believed essential to social order.

2

The Demon:
Frederick W. Taylor

A Battle for Speed

PRUSSIA, PROBABLY BERLIN. 1869.

Two teenage brothers—on a grand tour of Europe of the kind fashionable for wealthy American families in the decades after the Civil War—are out for a walk by themselves. Civilians in the land of Bismarck are supposed to step aside for soldiers, but the two sauntering American teenagers refuse to yield to an oncoming trooper. Locking arms, they crash into the spike-helmeted Prussian and knock him down. He rises and hands the boys his card, which they interpret as a challenge to a duel. The younger brother, thirteen-year-old Fred Taylor, tears up the card, and they stroll coolly away. So the story went in Taylor family folklore.

The story cannot be accepted at face value, because Frederick Winslow Taylor was its source. All his life the inventor of "scientific management" stretched the truth when he did not make up the facts to suit himself. Yet even his outright lies have a self-aggrandizing authenticity. The story of the downed Prussian soldier—true or false—captures Taylor's idea of himself as the iron-willed hero subduing the rank and file.

For 100 years now, Taylor has rightly symbolized cruel management power. Driving workers as if they were mindless machines, he aimed to extract their last ounce of energy. Devoid of human sympathy, he was a fist-shaking, foot-stomping tyrant with a power-hungry ego that often hurt his own cause. Full of priggish self-righteousness, he held others to high standards of integrity despite his own mendacity.

And that's just the beginning. According to more recent critics, Taylor created dead-end factory jobs that "de-skilled" workers. His treatment of men as machines supposedly led American industry, especially the automobile industry, into noncreative stagnation by the 1970s.

In short, Taylor is mostly remembered today as an example of how *not* to manage. That is unfortunate. It prevents today's managers from learning the many important lessons that he still has to teach, especially the importance of top-down power.

More than anyone else, Taylor created modern management and gave it its central importance in economic life. For two generations, managers around the world openly looked to Taylor as their intellectual master. Even now that he is considered mostly an embarrassment in the history of management, profitable businesses follow his pioneering emphases on efficiency, low costs, and pay for performance. To dismiss his top-down methods out of democratic prejudice and dislike for his atrocious personality is to miss an opportunity to understand some longtime sources of productivity and success.

Taylor's use of top-down power helped enrich the United States during the late nineteenth and early twentieth centuries. His system of full and fast employment of capital-intensive machinery worked well during the second industrial revolution, the century of heavy industry from about 1870 to 1970 that was characterized by railroads, automobiles, airplanes, and mass manufacturing. Scientific management could and often did lead to abuse of employees, but so can every other management scheme. Taylor's lesson for managers today is less that top-down power can be abused than that it has its uses.

In some ways this tightly puckered control freak exemplified managerial integrity. He did not dispute the biblical idea that work became part of human life only after Adam and Eve got evicted from Paradise. Knowing that people labor mainly out of earthly necessity, Taylor used money as his principal performance incentive. He did not try to manipulate workers' psyches or to substitute spiritual rewards for higher pay. Acknowledging that employees worked for their own self-interest, Taylor asked no one to love the company.

But he was not a saint by anyone's standards, and especially not the standards of the Philadelphia family of well-bred Quaker and Puritan stock into which he was born in 1856. His pious parents aimed to make him a gentlemanly lawyer, not the cursing factory boss that he became.

Returning from the grand tour of Europe on which thirteen-year-old Fred claimed to have knocked down a Prussian soldier, Taylor's parents enrolled him in Phillips Exeter Academy as preparation for Harvard and law school. At Exeter, however, he suffered crippling headaches that one biographer attributes to astigmatism and another to neuroticism. Taylor had his own explanation. He had studied so hard that "I . . . broke my eyes down." Even dropping out of school became grist for Taylor's self-created legend of the hard driver.

Abandoning plans for a legal career, the young neuralgic found an apprenticeship in a Philadelphia hydraulic works—a pump factory—owned by a family friend. In the next four years he learned two trades—machinist and pattern maker—despite the rigorous demands of those occupations on the eyes. Then he moved on to a journeyman's job at Midvale Steel on the outskirts of the city.

Although Taylor claimed that illness drove him to the factory, he also saw bright prospects in heavy industry. He was not alone. Other upper-class youth sought machine-shop jobs in order to learn the arts and techniques of their era's new economy.

Variously characterized as the Age of the Railroad, Age of Steam, or Age of Steel, Taylor's time might also be called the Age of the Machine Shop. Coal, steel, and steam were known in ancient times but did not enrich the world until the nineteenth century when "tool steel" of unprecedented hardness began to cut other steels to thousandth-of-an-inch precision. From the lathes, presses, and borers of the era's machine shops came pistons, blades, and tubes for the engines, reapers, and rifled cannon that multiplied humanity's capacity to create and destroy.

Taylor saw early that the way to wealth in the machine age was to raise productivity. In 1879, not many months after going to work at Midvale

Steel, he was promoted to gang-boss over the lathe operators. He determined to prove his mettle by getting out more work. To try to increase output would certainly provoke his men. But Taylor, who as a boy had supposedly downed a Prussian trooper with impunity, would admit to no fear of a fight.

Taylor's energy and ambition were apparent. His fierceness was not. Twenty-three years old, fresh complexioned, five feet seven inches tall, and 145 pounds in weight, the bantam foreman probably seemed foolhardy, not formidable, to his men. They were badly mistaken.

The lathe operators, as Taylor told the story, warned their new boss, "Now, Fred, you know the game. . . if you try breaking any of these rates you can be mighty sure that we'll throw you over the fence."

The ugly game that the Midvale machinists wanted their new foreman to play was to maintain the lie that piece-rate pay gave them an incentive to work hard. Wrong, wrong, wrong, as every foreman knew. If workers raised their output, management almost invariably "broke the rate." As pay per piece fell, workers ended up having to maintain the new high pace to earn the old daily wage. It was as if Sisyphus, besides never quite getting to the top of the hill, had to push a heavier rock on every try. Naturally, pieceworkers stuck together and held down production.

Savvy foremen did not rock the boat. Nineteenth-century managers tolerated much in foremen but not inability to control their men. But Fred Taylor, unlike other foremen, had job security. His well-to-do family was socially connected to William Sellers, president and partial owner of Midvale Steel.

Emotional unintelligence also explained Taylor's impending battle. Other bluebloods dirtied their hands in nineteenth-century factories as preparation for a career in the executive office, but only Fred Taylor went to war with his men. The other shop-floor scions probably saw the sensible fairness of the men's plodding pace in response to the fraudulent incentive of piece-rate pay. But Taylor, with his self-righteous lack of empathy, believed that the shirking workers were cheating him and the company. Claiming the moral high ground, he told the lathe operators that though he had played their game as a journeyman, he was a foreman now and would keep faith with the company by getting out all the work he could.

He focused on individual operators, showing them how they could run their machines faster. But as soon as he turned his back, they slowed down. Taylor fired them and combed the plant for intelligent, quickly trainable replacements. But no sooner were the new men ready at their lathes than they succumbed to the threats of the veterans and broke their promise of faster work.

Then Taylor lowered the piece rate before rather than after the speedup. Now his men could either work more or earn less. The choice was theirs—present pace or present pay, but not both.

The machinists fought back with "accidents." Lathes broke daily, the result, said the men, of the high speed insisted on by their "fool foreman" who was also a "nigger-driver." Taylor, unable to prove sabotage, nevertheless levied heavy fines for breakage.

He got "friendly" warnings—veiled threats—that he was in danger. After work, to reach his parents' plush home in the suburbs, he liked to walk along lonely railroad tracks, a route his "friends" urged him to avoid. Anyone, he replied, who attacked him would find it a matter of "bite, gouge, and brickbats."

After three years of bitterness, Taylor prevailed, doubling his men's output. But victory was not sweet, or so he claimed thirty years later when he turned the story into a morality play for a wide audience that thought of him as a high-minded social reformer. A life of "continuous struggle with other men," he opined, "is hardly worth living," an opinion Taylor could have documented with his entire career.

More honestly, Taylor said he had learned that crushing his men was an impractical management style, unusable by a gang-boss without his social status. Ostracism that would have brought a working-class foreman and his family to heel had no effect on the upper-crust Taylor. And the company would have long since fired, as not worth the ruckus, any foreman lacking Taylor's social connections.

He drew a conclusion that would have served as premise for a less combative personality. The way to raise productivity was to fix the piece-rate system so that more work really did earn more pay.

Why did management almost always defeat its own incentive scheme by breaking the rate? Taylor decided the problem was that managers had no idea what a full day's work really was. They set the rate so high that hard workers could earn "too much"—wages so far out of line with the market as to embarrass management and force a pay cut.

The first step was to figure out what a full day's work was. Then the company could reward full output with higher earnings, but not so high that they would have to be cut. Deciding that management needed to know each job as well or better than the men who did it, Taylor aimed to move knowledge away from workers.

Midvale's president consented to Taylor's request to hire a couple of college graduates to study workers' potential output. Equipping his new assistants with stopwatches, Taylor had them measure the men's time, not only in operating a lathe, jig, or press but also in the complex task of setting up work in the machine. Breaking the job into component parts, Taylor's aides timed each step. Adding up the component times gave the right time for the job without "soldiering," or loafing between steps.

Then Taylor set new rates. Under the old system, Midvale paid lathe operators fifty cents to cut an axle for a railroad car, each man turning four or five a day for $2.00 or $2.50. But his stopwatch studies convinced Taylor that ten axles was reasonable. He set a rate of thirty-five cents per axle, which would yield a wage of $3.50, a large increase in daily pay but not so far above the market rate that management would later have to cut it.

To prevent a slacker from turning just seven axles, three less than a full day's work but enough to match his pay under the old system, Taylor created the "differential" piece rate. Only "first-class" machinists who did a full day's work of ten pieces would get the thirty-five-cent rate. "Second-class" men who turned nine pieces or fewer got a different, lower rate of twenty-five cents, yielding a day's earnings of $2.25 at most.

Taylor believed himself a profound psychologist by virtue of his capitalized precept that "Men will not do an extraordinary days work for an ordinary day's pay." But he never considered the effect of a bad day on the morale of a "first-class" worker. Missing the quota by just one piece, or 10 percent, would lower the man's pay by 35 percent, from $3.50 to $2.25. Still, Taylor never indulged in the claims of later "humanist" psychologists that money is a minor motivator.

According to Taylor, the differential piece rate worked splendidly at Midvale, raising both productivity and pay. Maybe it did.

Taylor's repellent personality makes it easy to miss the fact that his system really could benefit workers as well as capitalists. Since a lathe did not ask for more money for faster work, its cost could be spread across more units of production, allowing both more profit and higher pay, as Taylor illustrated with data from Midvale:

Ordinary piece-rate		*Differential piece-rate*	
Man's wages	$2.50	Man's wages	$3.50
Machine cost	$3.37	Machine cost	$3.37
Total cost per day	$5.87	Total cost per day	$6.87
5 pieces produced		10 pieces produced	
Cost per piece	$1.17	**Cost per piece**	$0.69

A 40-percent increase in pay (from $2.50 to $3.50) resulted in a 41-percent decrease in unit cost (from $1.17 to $0.69), thanks to a 100-percent increase in production (from 5 pieces to 10). Taylor's trinity was pay, profit, and productivity.

Taylor seldom used the language of teamwork, less in vogue in his day than ours, but he shared its wishful hope that everyone could be on the same side. And everyone would be if they did as he told them. The Prussians had nothing on Taylor.

The Method in His Madness

Taylor's speedy nervousness and dictatorial temper perfectly equipped him for life in the machine age, which valued men who could take charge and make things hum. He probably missed the irony, but he understood the fact that labor-saving machinery gave manufacturers more rather than less reason to work employees to the breaking point. High-speed "throughput" raised return on capital invested in machines. Because the machines had to be driven hard, so did the men who ran them.

Many Americans experienced from different vantage points a bit of Taylor's nervousness as they beheld the gargantuan power, profits, and problems of the new industrial corporations. Externally, their market dominance seemed a threat to consumers, small business, and free markets. The corporations' deep pockets, with which they purchased the support of state legislators, congressmen, and senators, seemed a threat to democratic government. Internally, the new firms challenged managers' ability to coordinate vast resources—employees in the thousands and capital in the millions.

From all perspectives, the challenge of the new corporations seemed to be control, a felt need of every human being and the craving of every neurotic. Fred Taylor, self-constricted and fond of bossing others, was perversely well adapted to his time and place.

Today's psychologists and neurologists use computer metaphors to explain that some people are not "programmed" or "wired" to read the feelings of others. In even the most intensely social situations, they give emotion no weight and respect only cold reason. Taylor seems to have been such a straitened soul.

Although Taylor was descended from a noble line of Quaker abolitionists, his family's religious instruction misfired, producing in him fierce self-righteousness with men rather than humility before God. His father warned that "where your conscience doubts," it is best to "walk carefully and slowly." But Taylor always ran rather than walked, and the records of his adult life indicate no qualms of conscience. Whatever uprightness he had came not from pious self-doubt but from rigid self-control.

Machinery interested Taylor by its promise of control in his personal life no less than in industry. Troubled in youth by nightmares, he woke from horrors on his back, so he slept in a contraption of leather straps and wooden points that kept him prone. In an age when men wore buttoned shoes, he saved a minute a day by slipping into "gaiters."

Out of his passion for golf came Taylor's most notorious invention, a two-handled, Y-shaped putter with which he faced the hole and stroked the ball croquet style from between his legs. Better aligned with the hinge of the human shoulder than the traditional putter, Taylor's forked wand more often put the ball on line to the cup. But the authorities at St. Andrews saw his quest for mechanical advantage as foul play and declared his putter "beyond the pale" as he mournfully reported to friends in 1909. (He evened the score with the genteel duffers by making himself an expert on grass and helping to create the fast greens that torment their descendants today.)

Fortunately for Taylor, he worked in factories where concern for production and profit, not sportsmanship, ensured proper appreciation for a good machine and its control over wayward nature. At Midvale Steel in the 1880s he invented new grinders, borers, tool feeders, turning devices, and as pièce de résistance, a mammoth steam hammer, the world's largest by a factor of three. The superiority of Taylor's hammer lay in its flexible parts. Unlike the machines of Midvale's competitors, his hammer did not eventually shake itself to pieces from the reverberations of its seventy-five-ton blows.

Taylor's mechanical inventions—like his later management innovations—lowered costs by raising the speed and precision with which metal could be fed into a machine and cut, lathed, stamped, drilled, bored, or pounded into its desired shape. Midvale's top management could scarcely have missed Taylor's large contributions to the company's bottom line. In less than a decade, he rose from journeyman to chief engineer, in charge of all the plant's machinery.

Success only fueled the rage with which Taylor pushed for higher productivity. He imposed dozens of regulations to achieve it, decreeing, for example, that at the start of every job workers should lubricate their lathes—a fifteen-minute chore for a machine with scores of oil holes. The men resisted; they thought they knew from personal experience that the machines did not need oiling so often. Taylor probably never explained to them that in the economics of machine production, it made no sense to save a few minutes of lubricating time at the risk of burned bearings and long downtime for repairs. He kept a fierce watch and reacted to violations of his edicts with abusive fury, goddamning his men to their faces as cowards, quitters, and yellow dogs.

In his steel mill swagger Taylor found a typical antidote for the late-nineteenth-century epidemic of WASP self-doubt. Through self-affirming lust for conquest, the ruling class sought renewed confidence in its own vitality. Effete Brahmins felt false nostalgia for chivalric virtues, college men sought in football a substitute for the hardening experience of war, and Theodore Roosevelt led the charge up San Juan Hill. Taylor thus cast himself as the shining knight of the factory, robustly outdoing immigrant Hungarian, Serb, and Croat workers who put fear of racial decline into the clammy Anglo-Saxon elite.

In a thinly disguised bit of autobiography at a Harvard Business School lecture near the end of his life, Taylor described a young managerial hero whose best foreman, using jointed rods, failed to clear a clogged drain beneath a steel mill floor. Digging up the drain would mean shutting the mill for days. Instead, the manager—Taylor—"crawled in through the black slime and muck . . . . Time and again he had to turn his nose up into the arch of the drain to keep from drowning. After about 100 yards, however, he reached the obstruction, pulled it down, and when the water had partly subsided backed out." Allowing for Taylor's usual, grotesque exaggeration, the story conveys the zest he found in factory work. He never regretted passing up law school.

Yet the age of academic credentials for the middle class was coming on apace, so Taylor covered his bets with an 1883 degree in mechanical engineering from Stevens Institute in Hoboken, New Jersey. How he did this is a mystery. Apparently, he attended no classes and took only an occasional examination. Family connections probably played a role. As Taylor told the story, he completed the four-year curriculum in just two and a half years by studying far into the night while laboring ten hours a day, six days a week at Midvale Steel—one more piece in the self-made myth of the Herculean Taylor.

It was not classroom knowledge but shop floor experience that led to Taylor's most important contribution to management, his reform of foremanship. He intended to prevent foremen from colluding with workers to slow the pace of production as they had done in his early days at Midvale. Only with foremen subjected to the top-down power of management could the plant be run at high speed and low cost.

Taylor rationalized Midvale's operations by abandoning its *"military type of organization,"* to which he objected not because of its authoritarianism—he was a martinet himself—but because it gave foremen the all-encompassing authority of sergeants. In the pre-Taylor era, foremen's responsibilities were so general that qualifications for the job included, he said, brains, education, technical knowledge, tact, energy, grit, honesty, judgment, and health, "and if such a man could be found he should be made manager or superintendent of a works instead of a gang-boss."

With their many responsibilities, foremen could not possibly do their primary job of keeping men and machines constantly employed. Foremen ran production, controlled quality, kept cost records, hired and fired, advised journeymen on difficult jobs, disciplined wayward workers, routed tasks to each machine, and maintained supplies. No wonder machine shops often ran at much less than full capacity, incurring costs not only for lost wages but for "overhead charges on machinery and plant, which go on all the time, whether tools are working or idle."

Foremen were also too distracted to maintain order, on which efficiency depended. In the pre-Taylor factory, noted one observer, "spoilage and breakage were high, the stockroom was crowded with obsolete material, needed supplies were constantly running out, shipments were delayed." Often, foremen did not remove old equipment as they added new machines but jammed them together until the aisles were so narrow that for simple jobs, boys were preferred to men. The disorder cost time, and time was money.

Taylor attacked disorder with the same fury that he turned against recalcitrant workers and jammed machines. Loathing the chaos of what historians call the "first factory system," Taylor replaced it with his "second factory system," aimed at organizing operations with machinelike precision.

PHOTO 2.1   A machine shop of Taylor's era before and after scientific management.

His main reform was to replace general foremen with "functional fore-men," four of whom would work on the shop floor—a *"Speed Boss"* to drive the men, a *"Gang Boss"* in charge of tools and materials, an *"Inspector"* to check quality, and a *"Repair Boss"* to maintain the machinery. Speed from smooth operations was the job of them all, not just the speed boss.

Four other functional foremen worked in the "Planning Department" located in the middle of the shop floor. They did the intellectual work for which the old general foreman had had too little time. The *"Time and Cost Clerk"* enforced the piece rate. The *"Order of Route and Work Clerk"* planned the flow of train wheels, cannon barrels, or whatever devices the shop was making so that all the machines were kept busy. The *"Disciplinarian"* decided "when the best results will be accomplished by a 'jolly,' or when sternness is a necessity." Most important of all and most threatening to workers was the *"Instruction Card Clerk."*

The instruction card clerk wrote elaborate orders onto job cards, telling machinists "where to start each cut, the exact depth of each cut, and how many cuts to take" as well as "the speed and feed." Over the years, Taylor had conducted thousands of metal-cutting experiments and learned how to calculate the machine settings for different variables—cutting angle, shape of the tool head, type of metal from which the tool was made, type of metal being cut, and the strain that could be tolerated by a particular machine's weak belt or strong gears.

A mathematically gifted assistant named Carl Barth transposed all this information onto elaborate slide rules. The ordinary wooden slide rule—a common calculating tool in factories until the age of the computer—had just one slide. Barth's had five slides to accommodate all the variables involved in determining machine settings. Using a Barth slide rule, the instruction card clerk could calculate in less than a minute the settings that might have taken an hour for a skilled machinist to figure out by trial and error.

Critics then and later objected that Taylor's detailed instruction cards deprived the machinist of skill and sociability. The worker just set the machine as told, made the cut, and took down the instruction card for his next job from the bulletin board above his bench. Gone was the social contact with other men the machinist had enjoyed in work lulls under the old system. Gone too were his dignity and job security as the intellectual element of his trade was transferred to a drone with a slide rule in the planning room.

Worse still, the man at the lathe might earn higher pay than he had before, but he was not the same man. With the thinking done in the planning room, men of lesser skill could replace master machinists. These new men got significant pay increases but earned less than the highly skilled workers they replaced.

All these criticisms of Taylor's system were sadly true, but also beside the point. Machinists could scarcely claim to be fine artists. Machine tools had come into existence a century earlier so that workers incapable of hand filing and hand fitting could compete with skilled smiths in manufacturing metalware. Only as hand skills were forgotten did operation of lathes and presses come to be understood as a skill itself. Taylor more than his critics labored in the American tradition of building machines and systems that relatively unskilled workers could operate at high productivity and low cost.

Taylor created new jobs for unskilled workers. If the machinist was to keep his expensive lathe running at the most productive rate, he could not be wasting his time searching for tools. By hiring clerks and couriers to keep track of tools and carry them to the machinists, Taylor made it possible for an operator to stay at his lathe steadily turning out the highest possible number of pieces across which to spread the machine's cost.

To further speed machinists, Taylor relieved them of responsibility for maintaining tools, which he placed in the "tool room." Formerly housing only expensive items, the tool room now kept and maintained nearly all equipment. By making sure that a clamping bolt, for example, did not have a damaged thread requiring a wrench rather than a man's fingers to turn it, the tool room staff helped the machinist work at top speed.

Under Taylor's system, the tool room itself became a complex organization. Cutting heads alone, with their different shapes ground to different angles, were too numerous for casual handling, and then there were the drill bits, borers, hammers, gauges, chains, straps, clamps, blocks, bolts, nuts, and washers, all of many different sizes. Taylor arranged these thousands of items in logically ordered bins, trays, drawers, cabinets, and racks, with an elaborate system for checking them in and out. Once returned, each tool was inspected and if necessary reground, rethreaded, or reset to ensure efficient use by the next man, which meant that the tool room had to have its own workmen and benches.

For each job, the Planning Department made up a list of tools for a clerk to collect in a wooden box. A "tool messenger" carried the box to the machinist, so he had all the tools needed when he turned to the instruction card for his next job.

Efficiency was one thing; paying for it another. Employers eager to increase speed and output were often dismayed when they engaged Taylor in his later career as a consultant and learned how many supervisory and support staff were required. Orthodox doctrine held that the most efficient plants had the highest ratio of "producers" (production workers) to "nonproducers" (managers, foremen, clerks, messengers, and so on). Taylor heretically but reasonably claimed that adding nonproducers raised efficiency and lowered costs. The proper level of staff was whatever number it took to keep capital-intensive machinery running full and fast.

Taylor's system offered workers a greater chance of advancement. By increasing the number of foremen and managers, he made it possible for more workers to clamber onto the bottom rung of a career ladder. The fact that "the man with the slide-rule . . . was able completely to distance the skilled mechanic" not only lowered costs but expanded the number of white-collar workers.

But those left behind on the factory floor experienced a huge loss not only in dignity and skill but in power. No longer could they form alliances with foremen against management to hold down the pace of work. Foremen and planning room clerks, working with production quotas and slide rules provided by management, were themselves now much more tightly supervised.

Taylor's tightening of the factory's top-down hierarchy left workers exposed to the risk of increasing tyranny. He felt absolute in his power because, as one of his machinists remembered him often saying, "I have you for your strength and mechanical ability, and we have other men paid for thinking." That machinist left to start his own shop. But not everyone could be self-employed in a mass-production economy. Taylor's reforms ensured that Americans would enjoy less and less Jeffersonian freedom at work.

In return for workers' lost dignity, freedom, power, and skill, Taylor promised higher pay, but his system had a mixed record on that score. Daniel Nelson, one of Taylorism's most thorough scholars, has found that where workers "earned higher wages" they "favored scientific management." But many Taylorized factories did not deliver higher wages, just more work. Taylor gave power to managers, and they often used it to raise profit but not pay.

Yet for those who shared Taylor's better angel, the ingenious artificer who got joy from the machine, be it a lathe or a company, his system no doubt created some collegial warmth. Taylor's reforms gave such men self-enlarging community in working with like-minded others, the kind of personal growth that today's gurus hawk by the truckload and that can nonetheless be real and rewarding.

Also real and useful in corporate life was the fraternity of power that Taylor helped to create. He strengthened companies' internal coherence by multiplying managerial positions, increasing their ability to reward able employees with the satisfaction of bossing erstwhile comrades. To lathe operators who lost status as they set their machines according to their instruction cards, Taylor held out the compensating possibility of power. A machinist might move to the planning room, where he would no longer live in subjection to the slide rule but would wield it over others. Taylor alone scarcely created management, but his power-hungry personality epitomized its nastiest motive.

The Lambs of Bethlehem

Taylor's upward path at Midvale Steel was blocked in the late 1880s when the company was acquired by a father and, unfortunately, a son who was obviously destined for ultimate control.

Taylor found a new job because armaments contracts at Midvale had alerted naval officials to his ability. An ex-secretary of the navy, William Collins Whitney, multimillionaire intimate of the Rockefellers and Astors, was searching for a manager for a factory with a new papermaking process on which he had bought the patent. Whitney offered Taylor triple what he was making at Midvale, plus stock options. Taylor moved to Madison, Maine, where he hoped to make a fortune.

He lost his shirt. His riches-to-rags story, as usual, must be accepted with a pound of salt. According to him, the new papermaking process was not as good as promised, and the investors had so poorly planned and built the factory that most of his time went to physical repairs. He had invested much of his savings in the project and in 1893 got out, not with the bonanza he had expected but with a huge loss that, fortunately for him, his well-heeled parents made up.

From this experience Taylor acquired a dislike of financiers. Given his arrogance, he had had to learn the hard way that managers as much as workers may be lucre's slaves. He recaptured his independence with a new career as a consultant, telling others how to manage instead of doing it himself.

In five years, Taylor had many small jobs and four-month-long contracts in far corners of the industrial landscape, bringing him into close acquaintance with the boardinghouses of the Northeast and Midwest. Reorganizing an electric-motor factory in Johnstown, Pennsylvania; installing piecework at a ball-bearing plant in Fitchburg, Massachusetts; designing an accounting system for a Wisconsin factory, Taylor gathered and sowed the seeds of scientific management. Like consultants today, he learned from a client as much as he taught, then carried his new knowledge to another firm, where he learned yet again.

Eventually, he had a stable of more or less official disciples who worked as consultants and helped spread his hard-won knowledge. By World War I, tens of thousands of workers labored in factories run by the principles of what even Taylor, with his purist standards, would have admitted was Taylorism.

When possible, he eased worker resistance by not installing the piece rate until after he had reformed foremanship and rationalized operations.

With the planning room in place and the tool room reorganized, he could simultaneously speed up production, cut the piece rate, and raise wages, just as he claimed in his idealistic pronouncements.

At least as often, Taylor's consulting pushed him back toward the brutality he had used as a young gang-boss at Midvale Steel. Clients in trouble might have no money for retooling, no time for elaborate reorganization. Then Taylor cut costs the cruel way, with a speed-up and lower piece rate that increased production and profit at the expense of workers, especially if they were unskilled, easily replaceable, and therefore defenseless. Such cruel shortsightedness left him frustrated—more by the shortsightedness than the cruelty—at not being able to do the wholesale reorganization that brought maximum efficiency.

He got his chance to do it right in a big way at Bethlehem Steel in 1898, after the company was suddenly deprived of its unconscionable profits on iron cladding for battleships. During the runup to the Spanish-American War, muckraking newspapers reported that the steelmaker charged Uncle Sam three times as much as the Russian czar for armor plate. The public raged, Congress threatened action, and Bethlehem cut prices. Higher profits would have to come from lower costs.

Who better to lower costs than Taylor? Bethlehem officials had read and been impressed by a paper Taylor had published explaining his differential piece rate. They contacted Taylor who, in preliminary discussions, did his best to prepare the Bethlehem president, Robert Linderman, to do the job right. Emphasizing the need for a long planning process and sweeping organizational changes before the company would be ready for the piece rate, Taylor warned that he would not only cut costs but pay workers more. He came to Bethlehem on his terms.

Bethlehem Steel, situated on the Lehigh River, fifty miles north of Philadelphia, seemed an ideal candidate for Taylorism. The plant's machine shop, probably the world's largest at 1,250 feet in length, was a splendid must-see for patriots eager to see the technology driving the emergence of the United States as a world power. Visitors flocked to the quarter-mile vista of train tracks and overhead cranes for moving giant cannon barrels cut by immense lathes and borers. Despite its impressive scale, the machine shop was the plant's worst bottleneck, with a slow work pace and foremen guarding their turf.

Taylor had an ally in a Bethlehem vice-president, Russell Davenport, a former colleague at Midvale Steel. Taylor moved to take control of the plant by persuading Linderman to create a new position, superintendent of manufacturing, and to give it to Davenport. Through Davenport, Taylor appointed dozens of new "functional" foremen, according to principles that he explained in a talk to Bethlehem's top management. Lacking "perfect men," the company should not give foremen general authority. But within their functional specialties, foremen should have great responsibility. A manager should not require "that everything that occurs in his department 'pass over his desk.'" By relying on regular reports and operations data to identify problems, managers would enable functional foremen to run the plant more efficiently than under "direct control."

Soon, of course, there was trouble. Taylor had to ask Linderman to raise the new foremen's pay in recognition "of the opposition they have met at almost every turn, and the unpopularity which this has produced."

The real problem was power, not popularity. Taylor may have failed at the start to get the Engineering Department, which was responsible for plant and equipment, put under his ally Davenport. Or else Linderman did not back up Davenport. Either way, the Engineering Department ignored Taylor. He asked for overhead mains to deliver soda water that would cool the tool heads to allow them to cut faster. But a year later, only 12 of the shop's 236 machines were water-cooled. Taylor's increasingly plaintive missives to Linderman lamented working "without the help of the Engineering Department."

Fortuitously, Taylor made a discovery—high-speed steel—that would let him speed up the machines without water cooling. Trying to determine the right alloy for the machine shop's cutting tools, he "dressed," as the hardening process was called, a tool by heating it to a temperature far beyond which steel was normally softened rather than hardened. The serendipitous result was a superhard steel, holding out the possibility that cutting speeds could be doubled, which would halve both labor and capital costs.

Taylor's discovery of high-speed steel paradoxically slowed him down. He insisted that the Bethlehem machines be prepared for high-speed operation before he would install the piece rate for which he was hired. Some machines, unable to stand the vibration and stress of high speeds, would have to be replaced. Others would need rebuilt gears or stronger belting.

The chance to get rich from high-speed steel further slowed Taylor's reorganization of Bethlehem. He spent time patenting his discovery, selling the American rights to Bethlehem, and filling the purchase orders that poured in from around the world. Keeping the international rights for himself, he traipsed off to Europe to market high-speed steel at the Paris Exposition of 1900. Crowds gathered at his demonstration booth to see the glowing, amber-red nose of the tool braced against the whirling metal while white-hot chips flew off the lathe. Returning to Bethlehem in the fall, he found management increasingly restless for progress in lowering costs.

The biggest success Taylor could claim at that point was not in the Bethlehem machine shop but in the company's far less important loading yards. There he had created his famous "science of shoveling." Noticing that laborers used the same shovels on coal as on much heavier iron ore, Taylor experimented to find the ideal shovel load. He found that the average worker moved the most material with a scoop that held twenty-one pounds, so he issued big shovels for rice coal and small ones for iron ore, both designed for a twenty-one-pound load. Production, he claimed, more than tripled while costs fell and wages rose. If true, it was scientific management at its best.

But it may not have been true, given the untruths in Taylor's most famous story of all, also drawn from the Bethlehem yards. Millions of excess "pigs"—bars of iron thirty-two inches long, four inches wide, and four and one-half inches high—lay piled in the plant's yards while their value rose during the Spanish-American War. In the spring of 1899, the company began to sell its surplus iron, which meant laborers had to carry the ninety-two-pound pigs up gangplanks and load them onto railroad cars. Years later, Taylor told the story of his involvement in this loading operation as his main example of scientific management. But his version of the story was mostly fantasy.

The average worker loaded twelve tons of pig iron a day, when, according to Taylor, forty-seven tons was possible! He claimed to have collected data that, in the hands of his mathematical assistant Barth, yielded "the law of heavy laboring." The "law" revealed—unremarkably one would have thought—that the heavier the load a man is under, the less time he can stand it. A man handling pig iron works most efficiently, Taylor said, if he is under load only 43 percent of the day and resting for the other 57 percent. It sounded as if Taylor nearly quadrupled productivity by shortening work time to less than half a day.

According to Taylor, a thrifty and industrious "little Pennsylvania Dutchman" whom he called "Schmidt"—his real name was Henry Noll—was picked out to prove the law of heavy laboring:

"Schmidt, are you a high-priced man?"

"Vell, I don't know vat you mean."

"Oh, come now, you answer my questions. What I want to find out is whether you want to earn a $1.85 a day or whether you are satisfied with $1.15. . . ."

"Did I vant $1.85 a day? Vas dot a high-priced man? Vell, yes, I vas a high-priced man."

"Oh, you're aggravating me. Of course you want $1.85 a day. . . . For goodness' sake answer my question, and don't waste any more of my time. Now come over here. You see that pile of pig iron?"

"Yes."

"Well, if you are a high-priced man, you will load that pig iron on that car to-morrow for $1.85 . . . ."

"Vell, den, I vas a high-priced man."

Taylor justified this "rather rough talk" as "appropriate and not unkind" with a man "so stupid and so phlegmatic that he more nearly resembles in his mental make-up the ox than any other type."

The next day the bovine Noll ("Schmidt") worked "when he was told to work, and rested when he was told to rest," and loaded forty-seven and one-half tons. After that, Taylor reported, it was easy to enlist others so that "all of the pig iron was handled at this rate, and the men were receiving 60 per cent more wages than other workmen around them."

But a report written at the time by two of Taylor's assistants shows that much of the story was untrue. Reading Taylor's later account, one imagines that Noll's supervisor forced the dim brute to sit down 57 percent of the day, husbanding his energy in order to work more efficiently the other 43 percent of the time. Taylor did not explain that because Noll was only "under load" when carrying a pig to the railroad car, the trip back to the pile to get another counted as "rest."

Noll's supervisor did not hold him back but drove him on at several times his normal pace. Twice a minute, eleven hundred times a day, the 135-pound Noll planted his feet beside a ninety-two-pound pig, squatted to grasp it by the ends, heaved himself upright, lugged the bar fifteen or twenty feet up a gangway, pitched it into a railroad car, and raced back down to get another. Much larger men came nowhere close to matching Noll, whose physical coordination must have been a marvel of mechanical efficiency.

Taylor's claim that Noll's example had made it easy to recruit others was also untrue. Noll did not even participate in the initial experiment, whose subjects, according to Taylor's aides, were ten "large powerful Hungarians." Exhausted by the work, the Hungarians tried to go back to the day-labor gang. The plant's assistant superintendent recommended mercy, but Taylor insisted that all ten be fired.

Not surprisingly, it took two weeks to recruit a second piece-rate gang. Noll was one of this new group of five workers, two of whom, "much fatigued," quit after one day. Soon there was just Noll. At least forty more tried the work, but only two others equaled Noll's heroic performance.

Cruel as the true story was, it nevertheless showed that Taylor's use of top-down power got results. He exaggerated the increase in productivity, but he did raise it, disproving "the old idea that each workman can best regulate his own way of doing the work."

But his success in improving the productivity of shovelers and pig-iron loaders was scarcely enough to satisfy Bethlehem's increasingly impatient management. Mucking around in the loading yard, Taylor charged $35 a day plus the cost of his assistants to speed up men making a dime an hour. The big savings were to be made by speeding up the machine shop, bringing higher return on capital-intensive equipment. Yet Taylor, who rivaled Cromwell in thoroughness, insisted on waiting for complete reorganization and retooling before he would begin to introduce the piece rate.

Meanwhile, he had charged Bethlehem close to $100,000 for consulting fees for himself and his half dozen assistants. Bethlehem also bore the cost of Taylor's experiments with high-speed steel, his replacing or rebuilding of expensive machines, his elaborate reorganization of storage, his construction of a new planning office, and so on. By the spring of 1901, according to management's reckoning, Bethlehem had spent $1,100,000 on Taylor's system. A few years before, Congress had considered building a new armory similar to Bethlehem and estimated the cost at $4,000,000. In short, Taylor had spent one-fourth of the price of a whole new plant, yet was nowhere near done with the reorganization of the machine shop for which he had been hired.

The situation deteriorated rapidly in early 1901 as Linderman ordered Taylor to focus on installing piece-rate pay in the machine shop: "[C]onfine your entire time and attention to the work which was expected of you when you came to this Company."

Taylor, whose game was to exert power, not submit to it, replied by asking in effect to take over the entire plant: "I respectfully request that the various officers of the Company be instructed to carry out all orders."

"I beg to advise you," Linderman answered, "that your services will not be required by this Company after May 1st, 1901."

It would be comforting to conclude that Taylor's Bethlehem failure proves that harsh discipline is futile and that running a human organization as if it were a machine just jams up the works. But the problem at Bethlehem was not his cruel people-handling. He allowed his discovery of high-speed steel to slow him down and thus exhausted the patience of the company's managers. Whenever Taylor retained the support of management, both before and after Bethlehem, he succeeded. Defeat at Bethlehem came from Taylor's having too little top-down power, not too much.

When he later achieved fame outside the corporate world, he would draw on his Bethlehem experiences to support his advocacy of management power. But he would find his ideas a hard sell in a democratic society.

Fame and Fall

Taylor was the first guru to achieve national recognition, not just in business but also with a broader public that for a brief time saw him as a man with a message. Middle-class social reformers who had never set foot in a factory bought his act as a noble friend of workers whom he really held in contempt.

After Bethlehem, Taylor lived in a seemingly selfless way, which later made him an attractive figure to idealistic reformers. Rich from high-speed steel, he liberated himself from the control of paying clients. By mail, he answered inquiries from around the country and gave advice gratis. If a company wanted to pay for on-the-scene help, Taylor recommended one of his disciples.

Visitors flocked to hear him expound his ideas. Twice a week, Taylor received up to thirty guests in a lecture room he had fitted up in his Philadelphia mansion. After his two young sons handed out pads and pencils, he instructed the audience to write down questions rather than interrupt him, then launched into a two-hour stream of anecdotes about his factory feats. Finally, he called for questions, treating them as hostile challenges to beat back and hammer down. The tactful learned to preface their inquiries with deference: "Could you expand on what you were saying about . . . ?"

He sometimes followed his lectures with tours of two Taylorized factories near his home—the Tabor Company, a producer of power-molding equipment, and Link-Belt, a manufacturer of chain drives. Taylor had an ownership stake in these companies, so his system of top-down control had met no resistance from management. Instruction cards, stopwatches, and other Taylorist trappings left no illusions about workers' autonomy. "The processes and [human] relations," noted a visitor to Link-Belt, "were

PHOTO 2.2   The cool gaze of a hard man,
Frederick W. Taylor.

as mechanical as the Taylor system could make them." Yet this observer, a neutral labor economist, not one of Taylor's flacks, praised Link-Belt for the "better than average earnings" of its 900 workers, showing that scientific management sometimes kept its promise of higher wages as well as higher profits.

A tour of the Tabor plant won over Edwin Gay, the first dean of the Harvard Business School, which opened its doors in 1908. Taylor saw propaganda possibilities at Harvard and urged Gay to hire his assistant Barth as a professor. Gay did not come up with a job for Barth, but he injected Taylorism into the HBS curriculum. Besides making scientific management part of the required first-year course, Gay also set up a "laboratory" at a nearby manual training school where Harvard students could get shop experience, probably a concession to Taylor's insistence that factory rough-and-tumble bred better managers than classroom decorum.

New business schools such as Harvard had embarrassingly little systematic knowledge to teach and desperately embraced Taylorism to fill class time. In 1910, Dartmouth's new Tuck School based its curriculum on scientific management because, said the dean, Harlow Person, Taylor's "was the only system of management which was coherent and logical, and therefore *was* teachable." Student attention could be concentrated on instruction cards, slide rules, and time study, lending business schools a facade of science and academic rigor.

Taylor's system burst out of academic cloisters and came to national attention in 1910 when the B&O, the Pennsylvania, and other railroads asked the Interstate Commerce Commission for higher freight rates to cover a pay increase for workers. Shippers and consumers of course opposed higher rates. In this well-publicized "Eastern Rate Case," the railroads enjoyed an initial public relations advantage, protecting their workers' pay raise against selfish customers. But Louis Brandeis, "the people's lawyer," would relieve consumers of the charge of being anti-labor by invoking Taylorism. Through scientific management, Brandeis would say, the railroads could lower prices while increasing profits and pay.

Brandeis had become one of the nation's best-known lawyers through pro bono work in public interest cases, which had taught him the importance of good public relations. Having earlier heard about Taylor from a business client, Brandeis now traveled to Philadelphia to meet him, probably to see if he would make a good expert witness. Taylor subjected Brandeis to his regular two-hour lecture and hushed the future Supreme Court justice with a reproving finger whenever he tried to interrupt with a question. Brandeis called Taylor's followers to testify, but not the master.

The ICC hearings created widespread interest in "scientific management," the name for Taylorism that Brandeis decided was most attractive and which stuck. Many people already loathed the railroads as rapacious monopolies. To the charge of shameful greed, Brandeis added the tarnish of inefficiency, creating a newspaper headline by having one of Taylor's imitators testify that bad management cost the railroads $1 million a day. The ICC denied the railroads their rate hike on the grounds of bloated profits, not scientific management, which the commission called a mere "theory." But the public credited Taylor with the victory.

Middle-class reformers, eager for both social justice and corporate prosperity, embraced what Brandeis called Taylor's "gospel of hope." Muckraking journalists, normally hostile to business interests, gushed over the prophet of scientific management. Ida Tarbell, Rockefeller's nemesis, interviewed Taylor and warmed to his "idea that the mission of industry was to produce abundantly in order that all might enjoy abundantly." Ray Stannard Baker, another well-known muckraker, called Taylor a "rare high type of American," a "public servant in the best sense" who would "show us new ways of commanding our environment."

Press coverage of Taylorism created a national efficiency craze, the first of many twentieth-century management fads to spill over into the general culture. Former president Theodore Roosevelt, an advocate of making corporations into instruments of national strength, joined the chorus, singing the praises of efficiency. Office workers, librarians, housewives, hospital nurses, schoolteachers, and many others were soon doing their best to add a mite more productivity to the American economy.

Meanwhile, Brandeis had moved on, leaving Taylor to mismanage his own public relations. Editors clamored for something by Taylor. He complied with a series of articles for the *American Magazine,* which were subsequently collected in his famous and, in some circles, infamous book, *The Principles of Scientific Management* (1911).

Taylor had chosen the *American Magazine* over the more prestigious *Atlantic Monthly* because he believed the former offered a better chance to reach "those doing the practical work of the world." But factory managers were rushing into scientific management, with no need of Taylor's writings to entice them. By writing his book in a rough-mannered style that he thought managers would like, Taylor alienated the audience Brandeis had prepared for him—reformers and, as Taylor dismissively said, "professors and literary men, who would be interested more in the abstract theory."

His clumsy telling of the story of Noll ("Schmidt") defeated Taylor's pose as a friend of the working class. Angry letters to the editor of the *American Magazine* pointed out that although Noll's productivity had quadrupled, his pay had only risen by half. Taylor sensibly replied that not only Noll's increased effort but management's had raised output and that a "third great party, the whole people, the consumers" must share the gain through lower prices. But sweet reason was never Taylor's forte. Blaming "the literary classes" for the idea that it was not in the workers' interest to increase output, he wrote off the opinion makers who might have upheld scientific management's favorable public image.

Meanwhile, Taylor found a new enemy in the labor movement. He conceded that labor unions were a "proper and legitimate answer" to the evils of the pre-Taylor factory. But in the theology of scientific management, everyone was on the same side, so the "necessity for the labor union . . . disappears." Unions, Taylor said, "are in many, if not most, cases a hindrance to the prosperity" of employees.

Samuel Gompers's American Federation of Labor started an information campaign against Taylorism while looking for the best ground on which to fight. Gompers found his opening in government arsenals, whose adoption of scientific management enabled him to carry the battle into the political arena. Sympathetic congressmen began to argue against government use of a system that "reduces the laboring man to a mere machine." Taylor's PR problem now went far beyond his own gaffes.

Feeling the pressure, Taylor bungled the implementation of scientific management at the U.S. Arsenal at Watertown, Massachusetts. The poorly managed arsenal regularly incurred costs far above those of private arms contractors, making it a perennially cited example of government inefficiency. In 1909, the army brought in Taylor's aide, Barth, who made good progress for two years by following the deliberate pace prescribed by Taylor, completely reorganizing the machine shop and only then installing the piece rate that raised both production and pay.

But by 1911, Taylor was worried about the next year's election, in which he feared organized labor would try to make an issue of the government's use of scientific management at Watertown. To ensure "during election time next year, that the workmen at the Watertown plant would be with us heartily instead of against us," Taylor urged Barth to make it possible for workers outside the machine shop "to earn higher wages."

In other words, Taylor urged violation of his own dictum that reorganization came first, then the piece rate. Barth set up a generous premium for extra work in the foundry, quickly raising the molders' pay. But Taylor and Barth evidently neglected to tell arsenal managers that the goal was to buy the molders' political support. During a Barth absence, a couple of managers started stopwatch timing with the clear goal of cutting the men's new high earnings. The workers of course objected, and one of Barth's assistants handled the protests ineptly, bringing on a walkout. It was a public relations disaster for Taylor, who liked to boast that there had never been a strike under scientific management. The army, unable to find replacements for the skilled molders, had to give in to the strikers.

Meanwhile, the International Association of Machinists had launched a nationwide campaign of letter writing to congressmen and senators, complaining of working conditions at the Watertown Arsenal. Con-

PHOTO 2.3 Workers at the Watertown Arsenal about the time that a strike there started Taylor's reputation on its downhill slide.

gress appointed a committee, ostensibly to investigate the situation at Watertown but really, Taylor feared, to condemn scientific management. He worked behind the scenes to rally friendly witnesses and then, in January 1912, made the mistake of testifying to the committee in person.

The committee chairman, William Wilson, a former coal miner and future secretary of labor under Woodrow Wilson, shrewdly gave Taylor his head. For four days, he talked for hours at a stretch while the committee chuckled at his grotesqueries:

> . . . the ordinary pig-iron handler is not . . . well suited to shoveling. He is too stupid; there is too much mental strain . . . required of a shoveler.
>
> You gentlemen may laugh, but that is true, all right.

Wilson would have none of Taylor's pretense that he put managers and workers on the same side. Managers had the dangerous power to serve their own interests when they set the piece rate. So Taylorism, like all corporate management, violated the democratic principle that power is not to be trusted: "Under our laws no judge would be permitted to sit in a case in which he had a personal interest."

By the fourth day of Taylor's testimony, hostile congressmen openly baited him, giving the bully in him more of his own medicine than he could stand. In the final ugly hour, he dissolved into rage that Wilson expunged from the record. Taylor's kindest biographer reported, "With flushed face, he hurled denunciations at his opponents and made accusations which . . . he could not prove. For a time it appeared as if blows would be struck." So shaken that he nearly broke down afterward, Taylor had to be escorted to his train out of Washington.

In the public arena, Taylor had passed in a seeming flash from prophet to pariah. Congress, in 1914, attached a rider to the Army Appropriation Act forbidding time study of work. Because a different bill funded the Watertown Arsenal, scientific management continued there. But organized labor had achieved its goal of being able to say that the U.S. government banned Taylorism.

Pneumonia killed Taylor in 1915, at the age of fifty-nine. In the three years since his implosive congressional testimony, he had cut back on public appearances, ostensibly to care for his ill wife (after his death, she recovered and lived a long life). Frank Copley's admiring official biography of 1923 failed to rejuvenate his public image and served only as raw material for John Dos Passos's cruel portrait of Taylor, in his free-verse novel of 1933, *The Big Money*, as a small mind who missed the big picture right down to the end:

> . . . when the nurse
>> went into his room to look at him at fourthirty,
>> he was dead with his watch in his hand.

Taylor met defeat not as a management pioneer but as a social prophet. Naive middle-class reformers had briefly bought Taylor's delusion that in his system, managers are on the same side as employees and can be trusted to do justice to them. But few workers had ever been deceived. Once organized labor found a way to trigger a political investigation, it had little trouble revealing the lie.

Those who wanted to put the best face on management power soon realized that they needed some other accommodation with a democratic society than Taylor's false claim that top-down power could be trusted. Dean Gay at Harvard surely winced when Taylor, near the end of his life, frankly explained his method: "I have found it necessary almost invariably to talk but little to men, but to go right ahead and *make* them do what I wanted them to do." Gay remained committed to Taylorism, but the Harvard Business School eventually deemphasized top-down power and even questioned its reality in favor of the politically more acceptable idea of bottom-up management, a story told in Chapters 5 and 6 of this book. Not power and productivity but "humanism" became the business schools' path to social respectability.

But behind factory walls secure from academics, congressmen, and reformers, scientific management not only survived but thrived. In the years after Taylor's death, dozens, perhaps hundreds, of management consultants followed in his path, spreading his methods far and wide in American industry. For example, just three of Taylor's followers—Henry Gantt and Frank and Lillian Gilbreth—consulted in total for something like 100 companies. Gantt and the Gilbreths owed some of their considerable influence to their softening the unnecessary harshness of Taylor's system, as the next chapter shows. But they mostly clung to his insistence on managerial control as the basis of efficiency. Scientific management, sometimes shorn of its more sadistic elements, sometimes not, lived on with the critics who would have mattered most to Taylor—factory managers eager for full and fast operations. Professors, politicians, and do-gooders could say what they liked, but Taylor's system of top-down power worked well, especially in the hands of his saner successors.

3

The Engineers:
The Gilbreths and Gantt

A Cheerful Bricklayer

CAMBRIDGE, MASSACHUSETTS. 1898.

Bricklayers are putting up a 250-foot smokestack, a common sight in fin-de-siècle America, as rapid electrification feeds demand for coal-burning power plants and giant flues. What makes this scene unusual is the uninvited arrival of one of Frederick W. Taylor's agents, who asks permission to time the masons for a book he and Taylor are writing on the construction trades. The contractor, Frank Gilbreth, grants permission but thinks it wrong to use workers' present performance as a standard. They could do better by improving their technique through what he eventually called "motion study." He would become Taylor's disciple but would later alienate the master by improving on his system.

A far more genial and likable man than Taylor, Gilbreth naively believed that his personal decency extended to everything he touched. But a good heart does not protect the powerful against doing bad things. Gilbreth invented motion-saving techniques that, far more than Taylor's stopwatch, treated workers like machines. Gilbreth justified imposing robotic motions on human beings by claiming that his speedups saved more time for "happiness minutes."

In short, he was a cheerful naïf—a type not unknown in management consulting ever since. His undiscerning good nature enabled him to put a more human face on scientific management and made him one of Taylorism's most successful apostles. Not that Gilbreth was unintelligent. He was bright and superbly energetic. But he could not see broadly or deeply, hard as he tried. Personally generous, he saw no reason why he should not have and use power. Moral self-assurance and good spirits worked well for him and, unfortunately, are still the principal qualifications of some gurus.

Thirty years old in 1898 when Taylor's man showed up at his smokestack, Gilbreth was already known as Boston's fastest builder. He would seal his reputation for speed in 1902 when he built the Lowell Laboratory for the Massachusetts Institute of Technology, driving the foundation's 1,300 pilings, clothing the iron frame with 1 million bricks, installing electrical, plumbing, and heating systems, and finishing the interior down to plaster and paint, all in just ten weeks!

In search of speed, he invented devices worthy of Taylor. For example, the "Gilbreth Scaffold," mounted on jacks, raised bricklayers as fast as the wall they built. The scaffold had a two-foot-high bench on which hod carriers set stock, ending masons' six millennia of inefficient stooping for brick and mortar.

But Gilbreth managed his men far more generously than Taylor. Construction workers—often native born and unionized—would not tolerate hard driving. Instead of demanding speed, Gilbreth told his foremen to promote "athletic contests" by dividing workers into teams "of different nationalities . . . . If this is not feasible, put the tall men on one bed and the short men on the other, or the single men against the married men."

His common touch came from growing up in a Boston boardinghouse run by his widowed mother. He applied to MIT and was accepted but in the end passed up post-high school study for a bricklayer's apprenticeship to help his mother financially. When he became a contractor, he pursued new building methods not only to save money but out of longing for the social status of an engineer.

Later, as a management consultant, Gilbreth compensated for his lack of a college education with ludicrous scientific and literary pretensions. Claiming to have made world-shaking discoveries, he dubbed them with

PHOTO 3.1   The Gilbreth Scaffold. Bricklayers were jacked up as fast as the wall they built.

zany neologisms. Analyzing all human motion into seventeen elements—search, find, grasp, and so on—he called them "therbligs" ("Gilbreth" spelled backward, almost). His horribly written books read like catechisms, answering numbered questions in prose both peppy and strangled, sprinkled with clotted Latinisms.

The same fatuousness earlier caused him trouble as a contractor. In the boom years of the early 1900s, he expanded throughout the Northeast and Midwest and even to England, until he employed 10,000 men building dams, power plants, office buildings, factories, and an entire company town with a paper mill, houses, and stables. Why not a city? After the San Francisco earthquake in May 1906, Gilbreth rushed there to help rebuild, announcing himself with a sign on Market Street "sixty feet long and thirty feet high—unparalleled, a corker, the talk of the town." But locals resented him, spread rumors that cost him jobs, and made sure he was last in line for materials. Defeated in the West, he arrived back in the East just in time for the recession of 1907 to shrink his prospects.

That same year, in search of lower costs, he got himself introduced to Taylor. A bad judge of character, Gilbreth took an instant liking to the demon. To friends he would point out the Engineering Societies Building in New York and say, "Here on this spot I met a very great man." Taylor already knew a bit about his new admirer, having published a *Treatise on Concrete,* which described a gravity-fed mixer of Gilbreth's without mention of its inventor's name or patent. Gilbreth, either ignorant of this piracy or somehow forgiving it, made the pilgrimage to Taylor's Philadelphia mansion, heard the canned lecture, and decided to try scientific management in construction.

He turned to his new wife for help. With a widowed mother to support, Gilbreth had remained single until his mid-thirties, then married the cultured Lillian Moeller, who offset his gaucheness and also contrasted with him in appearance, her seeming fragility accentuated next to his well-fleshed frame and oversized head. Lillian, evidently less delicate than she looked, bore a huge brood, two of whom grew up to write a comic memoir of Gilbreth family life, *Cheaper by the Dozen* (later a popular movie), that described the children's being raised by the time- and motion-saving principles of scientific management.

Lillian, unlike Frank, was well educated. A Californian, she gave up graduate study in English at Berkeley to marry Frank but later earned a Ph.D. from Brown University for her dissertation, *The Psychology of Management.* Published in 1914, her book argued that workers' interest was a key element in productivity. A better judge of people than her husband, Lillian accompanied him on his first visit to Taylor's mansion and immediately disliked the egotistic tyrant.

Yet she was attracted to Taylor's lifestyle. Dissatisfied at having her husband "entertained in the club rather than the home," she saw consulting as a path for social ascent. Frank Gilbreth, eager to be done with construction, needed no convincing.

And management consulting opened doors for Lillian in an era when few women in business worked above the level of typist. The Gilbreths'

PHOTO 3.2   Frank and Lillian Gilbreth with some of their dozen children, raised by the efficient methods of scientific management.

home became their office. Lillian would be deeply involved in all of Frank's management projects.

Frank and Lillian learned Taylorism by applying it to bricklaying, simultaneously improving it with "motion studies." Their "Gilbreth packet system" delivered every brick to the scaffold right side up. Formerly, a mason took a brick from a hod's jumbled pile and looked for the slightly wider top that was laid along the string, with the bottom falling inward. But taking a brick from a neatly loaded packet, the mason knew he had it by the top. So he could give his attention to the trowel in his other hand, as Frank recommended, and "pick up both [brick and mortar] at the same time."

Gilbreth's men feared a traditional speedup—more work for the same pay—and went on strike against his innovations. At a union assembly, he insisted on his generous intentions, declaiming that he would "raise the pay of bricklayers throughout the United States." He got the masons to try his system on a daily wage until they saw they would earn more on piece rate. Some laid 3,000 bricks per day, triple the old record.

Yet little came of the Gilbreths' innovations. Bricks are laid more slowly today. Despite the Gilbreths' common touch and lack of Taylorist brutality, they imposed inhuman, robotlike movements impossible to sustain in the long run.

The Gilbreths eventually took less interest in construction than in management. In 1910 when the Eastern Rate Case brought Taylorism into the headlines, Frank testified before the Interstate Commerce Commission. He dramatically scooped law books off the hearing room shelves and used them as ersatz bricks to illustrate savings from scientific management.

Taylor, impressed with Gilbreth's public relations skills, commissioned him to write a text called *Primer of Scientific Management*. Gilbreth also represented the movement at academic conferences, including one where he upstaged the anarchist Emma Goldman. She had rushed to an organization chart at the front of the room and denounced the injustice of workers carrying layers of management above them. Gilbreth sprang to the easel and turned the chart upside down, implying that management supported the workers. "Never," reported an observer, "have I seen a better piece of repartee."

Gilbreth began bringing Taylorists together for informal meetings at Keen's Chop House in lower Manhattan. It was the beginning of the Taylor Society, which survives today as the Society for the Advancement of Management.

Yet Taylor, who recovered his Philadelphia propriety once his factory days were done, disdained Gilbreth's "emphatic" manner. How embarrassing to have an uncouth bricklayer as his most visible disciple.

Gilbreth probably further offended Taylor by installing scientific management at the New England Butt Company in Providence, Rhode Island, faster than the demon thought it could be done. His common touch with employees made it possible for him to reorganize the company in thirteen short months, even though Taylorist orthodoxy held that it took three years to bring workers along.

New England Butt made braiding machinery for manufacturers of thread, string, twine, wire, steel cables, electrical insulation, and lace for women's clothing. Gilbreth saw that assembly of such a wide array of machines could be sped up by using instruction cards and other methods that Taylor had developed for machine shops.

But unlike Taylor, Gilbreth could work fast because he won workers' cooperation. An employee later remembered him amusing the workers by starting the company's reorganization in the office, telling all the managers that they had to follow his system. And he involved workers with a "home reading box" of books and magazines from which they could learn about management.

Gilbreth partially compensated for his imposition of cramped motions by pioneer work in ergonomics that workers appreciated. He built tall stools for high workbenches, put springs on chair legs to neutralize machine vibrations transmitted through the floor, and placed cuspidors as near as possible to workers to reduce their fatigue from spitting. Because of Gilbreth, "fatigue study" became a major field of industrial research.

Taylor praised Gilbreth's work to his face but kept him off the shortlist of consultants he endorsed to install his system. To make matters worse, Frank and Lillian opened a summer school in scientific management that Taylor probably saw as competition for his own lectures. Borrowing a room from a Providence music school, they named it "Taylor Hall" and invited managers and professors in an attempt to bridge the divide between academia and the factory. Lillian taught the psychological aspects. Frank led tours of New England Butt. Prominent psychology professors such as G. Stanley Hall of Clark University and Hugo Munsterberg of Harvard visited the Gilbreths to study their techniques, and Frank was soon a featured lecturer on the college circuit.

Frank's innovative use of movies ran up against Taylor's distaste for "damned improvements" in his system. Gilbreth filmed assembly workers, then asked them to join him in a search for wasted motions. By including in the background a clock with a large second hand, he tracked time on every frame of film with far more accuracy than Taylor's stop-watch observations.

Later came Gilbreth's hideously named "stereocyclechronograph." At-taching tiny lights to assemblers' hands and tools, he took a timed expo-sure of their work with one of the stereoscopic cameras popular at the time, yielding a three-dimensional image with tracks of their motions. From these photographs, Gilbreth built wire models of assembly workers' hand motions and used them to teach workers "the one best way."

Taylor professed disinterest. "Showed micromotion film to Taylor," reads a note in Gilbreth's diary, "and told him I was surprised he could not see its meaning. He acted so I saw he was hurt so I changed the sub-ject." Eventually Taylor would claim his system had always included mo-tion study, in effect denying Gilbreth's contribution.

Gilbreth finally figured out that Taylor was no friend. He resented Tay-lor's 1912 congressional testimony. There, the demon described the Gilbreth Scaffold as though he inspired it, but Frank had invented it long before he had ever heard of Taylor. Then in 1914, Taylor advised a dis-satisfied client of Gilbreth's to drop him and supplied a replacement. Gilbreth stopped communication after Taylor's "act of war."

Taylor died the next year, leaving Gilbreth as scientific management's most visible spokesman, not only in the United States but in Europe, where Taylorism was soon a staple of industrial life. In France, the Napoleonic business schools, Grandes Ecoles de Commerce, which had previously focused on finance, began to teach scientific management. In England, a well-publicized visit by Taylor in 1910 had provoked a hot public debate about his methods, but the technical press mostly accepted scientific management as the wave of the future.

Germany could ill afford to be left behind. In 1913, a delegation from the American Society of Mechanical Engineers, including both Gilbreths, visited Germany to meet with the counterpart Verein Deutscher Ingineur. The Americans found German factories no competition for Taylorist effi-ciency in the United States.

Frank got contracts to install Taylorism at companies like Auerge-sellschaft and Zeiss. The outbreak of World War I in 1914, with the

United States neutral, did not deter him. Comforting himself that he worked on lamps and lenses, not weapons, Gilbreth traveled several times to Germany in 1915.

Gilbreth believed Germany was the perfect country for scientific management. Surely a German elevator operator who switched off the light when no one was in the car could be taught that he wasted motion by exiting the cubicle to bow passengers on. Gilbreth tried to turn Prussians' parsimony against their wasteful punctilio. In factories, he tossed pfennigs onto the floor. As scandalized workers scooped them up, he lectured them on "the enormous waste going on around you." A sucker for picayune conscience, he rooted for Germany early in the war.

After U-boats made transatlantic travel dangerous, he focused on the war from America, committing himself to the "crippled soldier" problem. He had seen the maimed return from the front in Germany and tried to prepare for the same eventuality in the United States by creating new occupations like dental hygienist. Disabled veterans, instead of languishing wastefully, would conserve teeth with pumice and a stick, a job Frank claimed could be "done by a one-armed, one-eyed, and totally deaf operator."

When the United States declared war in 1917, Frank—by now anti-German—got himself commissioned as a major. A wiser man—almost fifty, greatly overweight, with seven children and still counting—would have stayed at home. But Gilbreth went off to Fort Sill, Oklahoma, to enliven training films, in the words of a coworker, with "'hate' pictures showing the atrocities of our opponents." He had a high time until, in February 1918, he contracted pneumonia that left him with a weakened heart and only six years to live.

Back in the consulting game after the war, Frank reduced motions at American Radiator, cut in half the time it took Regal Shoe salesmen to fit customers' feet, and sped up women wrapping soap bars for Lever Brothers.

He also resumed his work internationalizing the management movement. In 1922, when the new Republic of Czechoslovakia asked Washington for help from American management experts, Frank visited the

Masaryk Academy of Work in Prague. In 1924, he lured American gurus there with an International Management Conference that went so well that it was repeated several times in other European cities in the 1920s and 1930s. But only Lillian represented the Gilbreths at Prague in 1924. Frank had died of heart failure a few weeks earlier.

Frank Gilbreth turned his clownish facade into an advantage by pioneering the "You-can-trust-me-because-I'm-an-honest-goof" school of management. He got results by giving Taylorism the appearance of more decency and humanism than it had in fact. His personal exuberance and generosity made it possible for others, maybe even for workers, to mistake cramped motions for progress toward a better society. Gilbreth's more dignified friend and ally, Henry Gantt, would reveal more clearly the dark potential of managerial high-mindedness.

Bonus Pay and Bad Accounting

BETHLEHEM STEEL. MARCH 1900.

Henry Gantt observes to the head of manufacturing that the men at "No. 8 hammer" pound ingots into plate with "skill and rapidity . . . to challenge the admiration of anybody." A bonus "double their daily rate," Gantt suggests, will make them work even harder, setting an example of "the right kind of spirit" for the rest of the shop.

Gantt, who had assisted Taylor in his failed attempt to reorganize Bethlehem Steel, had a less punitive spirit than his boss. Even though Gantt thought the men running the steam hammer could work faster, he called their present effort admirable. Instead of a differential piece rate to punish laggards while rewarding high producers, Gantt used only the positive incentive of a bonus. His method worked well at Bethlehem.

Bonus pay became Gantt's method and eventually the method of many American manufacturers, making rationalized factory operations more bearable and profitable for millions of twentieth-century American workers. Gantt, forgotten today, deserved his wide reputation in his own time as the guru who made scientific management more practical and decent.

PHOTO 3.3   H. L. Gantt.

Gantt's personality combined outgoing warmth with the stereotypical engineer's emotional blockage. Guarded with strangers, he was informal with friends, who knew him as "H. L." or "Duffy." Younger friends like the Gilbreths called him "Father," in recognition of his status after Taylor's death as America's best industrial engineer.

Beneath the surface warmth, unacknowledged anger burned in Gantt, probably the result of a hard childhood in a fallen family. Born in the opening weeks of the Civil War to a Maryland plantation owner, he lost his patrimony when Union victory freed his father's slaves. With his mother reduced like Gilbreth's to running a boardinghouse, Gantt learned discipline from the military regimen of a charity school near Baltimore, then worked his way through Johns Hopkins.

After a stint of schoolteaching, he earned a master's degree in engineering at Stevens Institute. Then, in 1887, he got a job at Midvale Steel, where Taylor put him to work finding "economical methods" to run the factory.

As with Frank Gilbreth but with far less justice, Taylor sometimes depreciated Gantt to others. A great deal less uncouth than Gilbreth, Gantt nevertheless brought out the innate snob in Taylor. Despite only a five-year age difference, Gantt and Taylor used "mister" rather than first names for each other throughout a relationship of nearly thirty years.

Gantt launched himself as a consultant at about the same time as Taylor and worked with him often. But unlike Taylor, Gantt had human feelings and a conscience. He suffered personal anguish at the injustice, lost jobs, and waste caused by bad management. Joining Taylor in a failed 1897 attempt to save a ball-bearing factory in Fitchburg, Massachusetts, Gantt grew bitter when the owners shut down the plant rather than making the investments he recommended to cut costs and achieve competitiveness.

When Taylor invited him to Bethlehem Steel, Gantt may have shared his boss's hope that they had finally found pockets deep enough to do the job right. But they did it wrong, because Taylor expanded the job, insisting on retooling to accommodate his discovery of high-speed steel. By spring 1901, even Taylor knew he was in trouble and needed quick results, so he accepted Gantt's suggestion to speed up the lathe operators with a bonus. Rather than wait months for retooling and a new piece rate, Gantt just raised the target and promised a fifty-cent-a-day bonus to those who met it.

Gantt's bonus worked well. A machine shop boss reported that Gantt's positive incentive, without Taylor's cruel punishment of laggards, "inspired the confidence of the shop hands." Downtime fell. To earn their bonuses, operators had to keep the machines turning, so they practiced good maintenance. Soon the entire shop went over to bonus pay and production soared. But it was too late to save Taylor, who was dismissed on May 1, 1901, while Gantt stayed on.

Gantt's success with bonus pay rested on Taylor's reforms. A Bethlehem report lauded the shop's slide rules, instruction cards, and well-organized tool room. When the workers balked at the amount of time allowed for a job, the planning room staff played the role Taylor had envisioned for his functional foremen by going "out into the shop" and showing "that the time was ample, by doing the work well within the limits set."

But because Gantt had set the bonus before time study, he departed from Taylor's treatment of workers as mindless machines and relied on them to accomplish the speedup. Bonus pay, as a Bethlehem manager said, forced the individual worker to "utilize his brains and faculties to the fullest extent . . . as every move must be made to count."

With the bonus motivating workers, foremen could stop driving the men and give attention, Gantt said, to those "who most needed" it. A Bethlehem official claimed that the foreman became the men's "friend and helper," a refrain Gantt often repeated.

This was surely not all true. Foremen got a bonus for each of their men who "made task" and another if they all did, providing incentives for hard driving. Still, Gantt moved scientific management toward a milder use of top-down power by eliminating Taylor's negative incentives and allowing workers to decide how to do their jobs.

But Bethlehem Steel soon changed hands. Charles Schwab, the new owner and a traditional hard driver, dismissed Gantt. Returning to consulting, Gantt in the next fifteen years worked for more than fifty companies where he used bonus pay and called for workers' participation in deciding how to do their jobs.

A mistake Gantt made in 1904 at Sayles Bleacheries, a Rhode Island textile manufacturer, confirmed his belief in the importance of engaging workers' hearts and minds. Moving too fast against employee opposition, he provoked a strike and was fired. Workers, he decided, had to be taught to welcome new methods by making learning itself one of their skills: "Unskilled workmen . . . who have become skilled in one kind of work, readily learn another." If Taylor de-skilled workers, Gantt aimed to re-skill them to heighten their adaptability and willingness to learn.

When Gantt sent Taylor a draft of an article that included these ideas, Taylor objected to publication. Gantt went to print anyway, prompting Taylor's warning that "if we expect to have weight with people outside, we must make it appear, in all cases, that we are in absolute agreement." Gantt did not agree, and their relationship cooled. Taylor stopped recommending him to clients, but Gantt kept his consulting business going on his own.

Despite Gantt's idea that workers should think and learn, he was just as much as Taylor a believer in top-down power, sometimes even just as much a bully. Gantt's biographer tells of a foreman who had "turned in several particularly indefensible orders." Gantt, consulting, had no authority to fire the man. So he "cornered him . . . and said: 'If I had written out orders like these, I would resign. Yes,' striking one fist into the other palm, 'I would resign at once.' The machinist quit." Another time, when a naive new employee asked for a raise, Gantt leaped onto a desk and shouted to fifty or sixty others, "Here's a man who has worked for us one week and wants a raise in pay." The man slunk away.

Like Taylor, Gantt egotistically believed himself, not entirely without reason, the exclusive possessor of world-enriching knowledge. He pioneered the "learning-curve" strategy—now often credited to the Japanese—of using low prices to take market share and gain manufacturing knowledge that drives down costs, making possible still lower prices, higher market share, and bigger profits. Too many businessmen, Gantt lamented, clung to the "theory . . . that a high selling price is necessary to large profits."

Where Gantt really differed from Taylor was in his social conscience. With bile accumulated in his youthful struggle out of poverty, Gantt hated financiers who withheld capital, hampering production and keeping the world poorer than it had to be. Just as bad were the bookkeepers who hid the plutocrats' sins.

Obscurantist accounting that covers up bad management is scarcely unique to our time. The accountants of Gantt's era, according to him, served the needs of "financiers, whose aim has been to criticize the factory and to make it responsible for all the shortcomings of the business." They did not let the production manager "present his side of the case."

Intellectually, accountants still lived in the pre-industrial world, where the cost of a basket was labor plus straw. Mass production of steel took not just men and ore but a blast furnace. When demand for steel fell, the mill owner could buy fewer materials and lay off workers—the same as in basketry—but the blast furnace stayed put. Whether a steel mill ran full or stood partly idle, accountants included all of the capital sunk in the plant when they calculated "overhead cost per ton." Why, Gantt asked, should a ton of steel bear the cost of equipment that sat idle while the steel was being made? He saw such faulty accounting damage and even destroy companies.

A hypothetical example will have to serve because Gantt did not go into details. Suppose a manufacturer of typewriters—a leading-edge product a century ago—introduced a new model. Projecting sales of 40,000 units per year, management invested $2,000,000 in new manufacturing equipment that was expected to last five years and therefore depreciated at $400,000 per year. The ordinary green eyeshade figured equipment cost at $10 per typewriter ($400,000 divided by 40,000 units).

But the new model flopped, selling only 20,000 units per year. The company cut direct costs by laying off workers and buying fewer supplies. However, the cost of the new machinery could not be cut, even though it was now sitting idle half the time. The accountant now attached the $400,000 of sunk capital to 20,000 units, raising equipment cost per typewriter from $10 to $20 ($400,000 divided by 20,000 units). Because the cost of making typewriters seemed to have risen, management raised the price, starting a vicious cycle of fewer sales, higher costs, higher prices, and fewer sales.

As the company's bottom line moved south, top management found a scapegoat in the manufacturing department, with its ever-rising costs. Gantt argued that instead of attaching the cost of the idle equipment to products, the accountant should subtract it from profit in order to point an accusing finger at the top managers who had made the bad investment in the new typewriter. Just as important, then the accountant would still calculate equipment cost at $10 per typewriter, guiding the company to hold prices steady instead of raising them and losing even more sales.

Gantt had seen companies stop production on parts they made for their own use because bad accounting convinced them they could buy the articles for less from an outside supplier. Such accounting, carried to its logical conclusion, meant that "the manufacturer would be buying everything before long, and . . . give up manufacturing entirely." The Fitchburg,

Massachusetts, ball-bearing plant Gantt failed to save in 1897 was "put out of business by just this kind of logic. It never started up again."

Bad accounting did immense damage during the mergers-and-acquisitions mania of the late 1890s and early 1900s. A handful of successful companies like Du Pont and General Electric got created in the frenzy of consolidation, but many more, their names now justly forgotten, failed to generate the higher earnings that the mergers, according to the deal makers, were supposed to bring. The bankers who made the senseless deals got paid for their services out of the heavy debt with which they saddled the new companies. The firms' accountants attached the cost of servicing their debt to their products, showing higher costs and making them believe they had to raise prices, starting a downward spiral in sales. Many failed.

Manufacturers sometimes made the same mistake on their own, without help from financiers. Expanding till they had machinery idle, manufacturers attached the cost of the inactive equipment to their products. Calculating that their unit costs were rising, they raised prices, then helplessly watched sales and profits plummet, driven down by an accounting system that mysteriously defeated production know-how. "Many manufacturers have made money in a small plant," Gantt warned, "then built a large plant and lost money for years afterward, without quite understanding how it happened." Gantt therefore proposed to put cost accounting under the control of engineers: "This is primarily the work of the manufacturer, or engineer, and only secondarily that of the accountant."

Power to the engineers! But how would they get it? Who would uproot the greedy financiers and accountants who enriched themselves by reducing humanity's ability to produce wealth? Gantt, whose own slave-holding family had been brought low by the Civil War, hoped that accountants and financiers, the new exploiters of humanity, would be toppled by a war to make the world safe for democracy.

Financiers' Failure to Make the World Safe for Democracy

Gantt saw an affinity between production and democracy because both were threatened by "plutocracy." He was not alone. Many citizens of the era distinguished between productive industry and parasitic finance as they debated capitalism versus socialism and felt their way toward the middle ground of a managerial society.

Around 1916, Gantt began to read the economist Thorstein Veblen, whose *Theory of Business Enterprise* (1904) mused over conflicts between finance and production in wonderfully mordant prose, implying madness in bankers' "chronic derangement . . . and misdirected growth of the industrial equipment." Veblen's *Imperial Germany and the Industrial Revolution,* published early in World War I, credited the Reich's successful industrialization to militarists who empowered production-oriented engineers rather than profit-minded businessmen. Germany briefly became the American intelligentsia's favored model for beating up on the American business system, much as with Japan in the 1980s. According to Veblen, at the same time that the Junkers put German industry under the control of "the technological expert," American industry "was drawn in under the rule of the financial strategist." Gantt's view exactly.

But Gantt was not pro-German. While the United States was still officially neutral, Gantt saw Germany as an "OUTLAW which must be suppressed by the civilized world." Even before the outbreak of World War I, he had cited German realpolitik to make the point that "large corporations are not very much more squeamish." German barbarism and American business fell on one side of Gantt's moral divide, engineers on the other.

Gantt got political inspiration from Charles Ferguson, one of many minor messiahs swarming the literary landscape and calling for strong political leadership. Like-minded litterateurs included the publicist Walter Lippmann, who proposed that government experts guide the unwashed masses. Herbert Croly, founding editor of the *New Republic,* said the country needed "some democratic evangelist—some imitator of Jesus." That the engineer was, if not the second coming at least the angel of wealth, according to Ferguson, the "economic discovery that Germany had made."

Ferguson, a clergyman and author of yards of uplifting tracts, was the reputed alter ego of Colonel House who was alter ego to President Wil-

son. Who better, Gantt must have thought, to help him organize a political movement to win for engineers their rightful place as managers of
American industry? He put Ferguson on his payroll.

In Ferguson, Gantt bought a vision of a coup d'état by engineers who
need not "wait for the crowd to say what it wanted. Crowds never say."
Instead of asking for "consent of the governed," production managers
could assume the people's agreement to a wealth-producing government
"not out to master men—but materials."

In short, Gantt got himself tangled up in some of the worst ideas of the
time, especially the elitist liberalism that the Wilson administration used
to stir up war fever. Wilson, elected on his promise of a "New Freedom"
from corporate giantism, had delivered antitrust laws and the Federal Reserve Act. But he had no mandate for war, toward which American economic ties to England slowly pushed him. The president fell back on his
reform credentials and called for a "war to make the world safe for
democracy." Gantt, like many reformers, took the bait.

In the idea of a war for democracy Gantt found an outlet for his frustration with financial sleight of hand that ruined factories. Like many political naïfs of the time, he believed that war would force the country to
address his pet grievances. The pressure of wartime production would
expose the financial buccaneers, inefficient managers, and incompetent
accountants who plundered American industry.

With full production needed for war, surely the government would
put the engineers in charge. Even before the war, business botched the
ramp-up of weapons production Wilson had called for in his "prepared-
ness" campaign. Gantt saw "incompetency in high places" and called for
action against profiteers who had no idea how to maximize production
for national defense. Taylorism, he decided, had erred by focusing on the
inefficiency of workers, not managers. Taylor had created efficient factories but left incompetent managers in the front office.

Incompetent management happened because "industrial control is too
often based on favoritism or privilege." The business system would only
be fully productive *when industry becomes democratic.*" Industry had to be
gotten out of the hands of the parasitic elite, be they German generals or

American financiers. By giving power to engineers, America would both raise production and promote democracy.

Other engineers shared Gantt's fervor, delighting in politicians' heated emphasis on the importance of war production. Ferguson reported that "palaver about the war in the New York engineers' clubs . . . veered away from the orthodox Wall Street view." America's safety lay in empowering producers, not profit seekers.

With Ferguson's help, Gantt created a political organization for engineers called the "New Machine." It arose out of a "schism" in the American Society of Mechanical Engineers (ASME). Long involved in management studies, ASME had concerned itself mainly with worker productivity. But the New Machine aimed to reform managers, not workers, by winning political power for engineers. During the winter of 1917, Gantt claimed swollen attendance at the New Machine's weekly meetings—there were probably no more than a hundred people present—at the Engineering Societies Building in New York.

Exciting as it was to talk about taking over the government and giving bankers the boot, the engineers had no idea how to stage their putsch. Then in February 1917, the well-connected Ferguson got a letter from Woodrow Wilson's secretary, passing along the president's suggestion that engineers prepare for war by surveying the country's industrial capacity. Ferguson probably wrote the reply, but Gantt signed it, urging Wilson to "call upon us . . . to establish first in New York and then in other cities, a political institution . . . to improve the normal operation of the business system."

Gantt and Ferguson advised the president that by putting the engineers in charge, he would close "the gap between business and politics." The corporation was "at bottom a civil polity," and "the invisible government should be made visible." The president should deliver industry from the control of "idlers and wastrels" and hand "it over to those who understand its operations."

All of society should be governed like a factory. In speeches and newspaper articles, Gantt had spoken contemptuously of the "debating-society theory of government," which confused democracy with "doing as one pleases" and in which decisions were made "not according to the laws of physics but by majority vote." To the president, Gantt and Ferguson explained that democracy lay in full production, not antiquated civil liberties: "[T]he idea of politics devoted to subjective rights and careless of the earth-struggle will in due time pass out of the mind and memory of the race." A White House secretary probably filed Gantt and Ferguson's letter without letting it get near the president's desk.

After Congress declared war in April 1917, Gantt abandoned politics, confident that the need for production would bring engineers to power in industry. But Wilson, who had been elected as an opponent of corporate bigness, feared the production increases that Gantt desired. Wanting "as little disturbance of . . . our normal economic fabric as possible," the president cautioned against any tendency "to create new plants or enlarge old ones." Rather than expand industry, Wilson wanted to divert existing capacity toward war. The president seemed to think economic growth was a greater peril than the Hun.

Contrary to Gantt's expectations, the war did not ally Wilson with industrial engineers against financiers. The president relied for wartime economic advice on the same quick-buck artists who were the bane of Gantt's existence in peacetime. Wilson maintained a facade of public control of the economy by creating government boards such as the Fuel Administration and the Railroad Administration. But he staffed them with financial types who rushed to Washington to serve both their country and their egos as "dollar-a-year men." Gantt believed they were overpaid.

At the top of the pile was the War Industries Board run by Bernard Baruch. A Wall Street speculator and Wilson loyalist, Baruch worked along the lines the president preferred, aiming less to increase production than redirect it toward war. Relying on his reputation as a capitalist freebooter to win cooperation from fellow robber barons, Baruch did not set the price on ship plate, for example, but asked Henry Clay Frick to decide what was fair, "not as a steel man but as a citizen."

Baruch's methods ensured that the war would only increase Gantt's frustration at industrial inefficiency. The historian of the War Industries Board summed up its members as "a patrimonial band of loyal followers, a partisan, political directorate, and a group of gentry-professionals." They were men, Gantt complained, "of the 'business' type of mind who have made their success through financiering, buying, selling, etc."

Compounding their sins, the dollar-a-year men brought their accountants to Washington. "Convinced that record-keeping was the main aim of business," the bookkeepers slowed rather than sped production. While the army and navy called for ships and shells, trucks and tanks, the pencil pushers, Gantt said, "busied themselves with figures . . . , apparently quite satisfied that they were doing their part."

Gantt had pitched in to war production with a frenzy, only to run into bottlenecks created by the dollar-a-year men. Working at first on rifle procurement for the army, he grew distracted to the point that colleagues reported him walking down Pennsylvania Avenue, discussing some production problem without realizing he was not on the sidewalk. Everywhere he found the same obstacles as in peacetime, above all the same obfuscating accountants and slippery bankers. The frustration brought him close to paranoia. "I am alone," he declared. "Everyone seems to be working against me."

Just as in peacetime, accountants ignored production managers, especially the need to keep them "continually advised . . . and to point out where the shortcomings are." Bookkeepers took weeks to deliver their numbers, leaving managers without the daily information they needed to spot problems.

To speed information, he created the "Gantt Chart," still a widely used project management tool. Easy to make and easy to read, Gantt's chart met the need for fast reporting on rifle production. The army's instructions for completing the charts emphasized "Time: The One Constant Is Time."

The Gantt Chart represented equal lengths of time, usually a day, with vertical columns of equal width. At the end of the day, a factory manager drew a horizontal line partway or all the way across the column to show how much of planned production had been achieved. If output was 100 percent of the amount planned, the line crossed the entire column; if 75 percent, the line went three-fourths of the way across. Instead of complex cost data to be slowly sifted by accountants, the Gantt Chart graphically represented one simple calculation—the day's output divided by the amount scheduled.

From armories and machine shops across the United States, the Gantt Charts flowed to Washington. Ordnance officers could glance quickly across a week's worth of columns to see, in Gantt's words, how well each of the nation's production managers "was performing the work assigned to him." Progress or, more important, "*lack of progress*, could be seen at once. No other government department had at that time so clear a picture of its problem and the progress being made in handling it."

Some of Gantt's postwar bitterness probably stemmed from the failure of his charts, later prevalent in private industry, to find wide application in war production. The dollar-a-year men took no heed of an adviser to the Ordnance Department who recommended using the charts to coordinate the entire war-production effort: "[T]hese charts assembled in one clearing office would give the data necessary in order *to make the whole program of war production move with fair uniformity.*"

Gantt took his charts and moved on to the Emergency Fleet Corporation to work on shipbuilding, another fouled up war-production program. Tracking production in shipyards was harder than in armories. A manager who wants to know how many rifles his plant made today just has to count. But it takes many days to build a ship. If a shipyard reported at the end of the day that it had built one-hundredth of a ship, no one could be sure the figure was right. What constitutes one-hundredth of a ship? Laying the keel? Erecting the bridge? Yet Gantt could not wait months to find out whether shipyards were meeting their targets. Shortfalls had to be found and fixed immediately.

Because every part of the ship was riveted, Gantt hit on "rivets driven" to measure productivity. Each day foremen submitted counts of rivets driven to shipyard managers, who then recorded the totals on Gantt Charts and sent them to Washington. There, slowdowns could be spotted right away instead of waiting for a missed delivery to indicate problems.

Counting rivets also raised morale. Citizens concerned about replacing ships lost to German U-boats followed newspaper reports of rivets driven. Rivalries sprang up between shipyards, and riveters worked as if they were the home team. The main national event on the Fourth of July 1918 was the launching of ninety-five ships.

Yet the government's shipbuilding program was a failure, having lost many months to bureaucratic infighting in 1917, prior to Gantt's arrival at the Emergency Fleet Corporation. By September 1918, only 500,000 tons of new shipping had been built, less tonnage than U-boats sank in a single month. As with much of the war effort, diversion of existing capacity had won the day. For example, Great Lakes freighters had been cut in half, enabling them to fit through the canal locks bypassing Niagara Falls. Towed to the Atlantic and welded back together, they ferried soldiers and supplies to Europe.

When peace came, however, Bernard Baruch and the other dollar-a-year bunglers emerged as heroes and touted victory as their doing. Gantt tried to set the record straight in his 1919 book, *Organizing for Work*, which argued that the war's brevity had masked the fact that "our industrial system has not measured up as we had expected. To substantiate this we have only to mention airplanes, ships, field guns, and shells." Production fell short because of the dollar-a-year men and their financial mindset. Among the "higher officers" of the Emergency Fleet Corporation, for example, not "a single person" had worked in production in civilian life. The dollar-a-year men "simply did not know the job."

Gantt believed that Taylorism's focus on the performance of workers rather than managers helped get Baruch off the hook for his sorry wartime performance. No wonder the dollar-a-year men took no interest in Gantt's Charts, which measured performance against goals. The plutocrats "were much better satisfied to report what they had done, rather than to compare it too closely with what they might have done." Scientific management let the dollar-a-year men claim credit for a victory they actually impeded.

Then, in 1919, the year of the Red Scare, Gantt hoped that fear of Bolshevism would focus American plutocrats on producing tangible wealth instead of paper profits. Pointing to the Russian Revolution, he warned businessmen not to "risk any such attempt on the part of the workmen in this country." Defying public opinion, Gantt sympathized with Lenin for his goal of a just society "which should not be dependent on the exploitation of one man by another." Soviet commissars would later reciprocate Gantt's friendly feelings by buying 100,000 copies of a book explaining his charts and using them to help organize Russia's five-year plans. Yet Gantt doubted that the Soviet experiment would work. Marxist politicos, not engineers, were running Russia.

Gantt finally gave up on politics. Deciding that a more productive society would have to come from capitalism, he urged businessmen to give up financial buccaneering because "social purpose" and "democratic methods" were more profitable. "Democratic methods" meant giving "each man the full reward of his labor." "Social purpose" meant creating real wealth instead of jobbing stock.

He was ready with an answer to the obvious question: Why are democratic methods not widely used in business if they make the most money? Bad accounting hid industrial inefficiency, enabling selfish financiers and incompetent managers to claim their unjust rewards while cheating the rest of society.

In accounting reform, Gantt saw the promise of justice and democracy. Accurate cost records would make possible high pay for productive workers. Managers who made bad investments in excess capacity would get what they deserved when the books revealed their responsibility. Knowledge of which managers used capital efficiently would ensure that top jobs go "to those who know what to do and how to do it." They would know to treat workers as minds, not machines, giving morale a boost that would be "reflected in an improved and increased product at a lower cost." Thus would begin a virtuous circle of ever-higher pay, ever-higher profit, and "that industrial democracy which alone can afford a basis for industrial peace."

In other words, Gantt remained politically naïve, if not about Woodrow Wilson at least about corporate power. Better accounting might lead to more profitable investments and operations, but it would scarcely ensure that power be used to satisfy conflicting notions among owners, managers, and workers as to just division of industry's rewards.

Nowhere did Gantt's confusion of democracy and production show up more clearly than in his postwar clinging to Veblen's idea of the superior virtue of German industry. Unlike American financiers, German militarists forced "business and industry to see that men were properly trained and that their health was safe-guarded . . . with the result that a kind of industrial democracy was developed under the paternalistic guidance of an autocratic military party." Only Gantt's personal decency suggests that had he lived to see it, he would not have idealized as democratic the Nazi ramp-up of production in the 1930s.

Gantt died of food poisoning at the end of 1919, cutting short an interesting chapter of his life. He had gotten himself connected to the New School for Social Research. Its faculty would include Thorstein Veblen, who had helped inspire Gantt's critique of the business system. Gantt had planned a new reform organization focused on getting managers, not politicians, to make the world safe for production.

It is tempting, but would be mistaken, to see Gantt as a stereotypical "techie" cursed with a feeble social imagination. He saw more deeply into his times than many. His methods of bonus pay, training, and participation moderated the inhuman side of scientific management and made it more bearable for many twentieth-century American workers.

Perhaps a good amount of the injustice Gantt tried to correct—managers' immoral use of power for their own advantage instead of to create wealth—is tragically inevitable in a corporate economy. Clearly, Gantt's erstwhile solution of top-down political power for engineers would be a nightmare. And his close friend, Lillian Gilbreth, would learn that the seeming alternative of cooperative, bottom-up management was ineffective in the largest economic crisis the United States ever faced.

Lillian Gilbreth, Herbert Hoover, and American Individualism

WASHINGTON, D.C. MARCH 4, 1929.

Just a decade after Gantt gave up on political power for engineers, Lillian Gilbreth sat in a VIP seat at the Capitol's east portico and witnessed an engineer being sworn in as president of the United States. Her presence at Herbert Hoover's inauguration was almost inevitable, given her re-

markable feat of achieving national prominence in the engineering profession in the five years after Frank Gilbreth's death.

Because few 1920s companies would hire a lone woman consultant,
she ran a management course in her house and found a few firms willing
to send trainees. For half a dozen years the course enrolled increasingly
well, drawing both managers and academics, until engineering and business schools spotted the market and began to offer executive education.
By then, she had made a connection with Macy's, introducing scientific
management to the store while serving as an informal liaison between
male managers and the mostly female workforce. Specializing in "fatigue,"
she tried to serve both employers and employees by making workers more
efficient but also less tired.

By 1928, when the Republicans formed the National Committee of
Engineers to Elect Hoover, Lillian was the obvious choice to head the
women's branch, an important job because women had gotten the vote
eight years earlier. Building a national organization of engineers' wives to
support the Republican candidate, Lillian made the alliance personal as
well as political, striking up a friendship with both Hoover and his wife,
Lou. Lillian therefore sat close by, while an enthusiastic nation, thanks to
radio, listened to Hoover's lofty inaugural address.

The sorry state of Hoover's reputation when he left the White House
makes it easy to forget that when he entered, he enjoyed unparalleled
confidence. That he was not a politician but an engineer and manager explained his remarkable popularity. The late 1920s was the height of "New
Era" prosperity, when the corporate economy seemed to have come of
age, making Americans masters of their economic fate as long as they ran
the industrial machine intelligently. Hoover, the "Great Engineer," as the
newspapers called him, seemed to know which levers to pull.

Yet he also symbolized continuity with older American values such as
individualism, volunteerism, and opportunity. Orphaned as a boy in
Iowa and educated at Stanford on a scholarship, Hoover had made a fortune as a mining engineer in Australia, China, South America, and Europe. Living in London at the outbreak of World War I, he had taken
charge of getting Americans safely home from Europe and then organized

food aid for Belgium under German occupation, saving many thousands of lives.

When the United States entered the war, Hoover went to Washington to head the Food Administration and conserve grain to feed European allies, not through rationing but through voluntary restraints. With the slogan "Food Will Win the War," he put "the stamp of shame on wasteful eating." Restaurants stopped serving wheat products, and children ate "patriotic potatoes" instead of bread. A popular 1918 Valentine's Day card read, "I can hooverize on dinner . . . but I'll never learn to hooverize on loving you." After the war, Hoover cemented his can-do reputation by organizing food relief for Europe.

During the 1920s, as secretary of commerce, he thrust his department, previously known for "turning out the lighthouses at night and putting the fish to bed," into air travel, radio, oil reserves, labor relations, and a hundred other issues relevant to the New Era economy. His crusade for cooperative standardization in American industry eliminated huge amounts of waste and made him a hero to the Taylorists. Any American who has ever tried to change a light bulb in Europe, where types and sizes of sockets seem to proliferate of their own accord, can appreciate the American debt to Hoover.

Hoover stood for progressive management and agreed with the emphasis on workers' minds and morale that had been pioneered by Gantt and the Gilbreths. The question as to whether democracy or autocracy was more efficient depended, Hoover said, on "whether people can be organized from the bottom up or the top down."

American Individualism, Hoover's widely read book of 1922, announced that the old virtues of initiative, self-reliance, and community spirit were alive and well in corporate America: "The encouragement of solidarity in all grades of [corporations'] employees . . . [and] the sense of mutuality with the prosperity of the community are both vital developments in individualism."

After Warren Harding died in 1923 and Calvin Coolidge took over, Hoover treated the sleepy new president with disdain and seemed to many Americans the country's real leader. He was so obviously the right man for the White House that his 1928 campaign slogan was a rhetorical question: "Who But Hoover?" He won the election by the largest popular majority in American history until, four years later, Franklin Delano Roosevelt trounced Hoover by an even bigger margin.

Hoover brought to the White House a managerial emphasis on bottom-up cooperation that would become characteristic of the management movement in the 1930s. Like many later proponents of cooperation, Hoover lost sight of Taylor's emphasis on top-down power that Gantt and the Gilbreths had sensibly preserved even while encouraging worker participation. He was scarcely the first or last manager to underestimate the importance of top-down power, but he may have paid the most dearly for his mistake.

Hoover had forebodings. Before his inauguration, he told a newspaper editor that he feared "the exaggerated idea the people have conceived of me. They have a conviction that I am a sort of superman . . . If some unexpected calamity should come upon the nation . . . I would be sacrificed to the unreasoning disappointment of a people who expected too much."

Lillian Gilbreth certainly had high expectations. A week after the inauguration, she wrote to the new president promising to hold her organization of engineers' wives together to help his administration. In return, she expected to see government action to support more efficient, less fatiguing management of women workers. Hoover's private secretary responded with alacrity, assuring her that "[w]hat you say regarding . . . women workers, has been noted."

But instead of leading progressive reforms as he hoped to do, the Great Engineer had to deal with the 1929 Wall Street crash and the onset of the depression. A former CEO rather than a politician, Hoover had never previously held elective office and utterly lacked the skill to rally the country in the crisis. With national production and income reduced by one-half and with one-fourth of the workforce unemployed, Hoover relentlessly proposed the sort of cooperative, bottom-up solutions that work best with a CEO "leading" the way. He urged people to have confidence and go out and spend. But Hoover was president of the United

States, not a CEO. Citizens and companies refused to follow their leader's urging that they spend their way toward a bottom-up recovery.

Meanwhile, Hoover refused to use his power. When he was commerce secretary in the 1920s, he had developed farsighted plans for New Era America to manage its way through troughs in the business cycle by increases in government spending. But he had anticipated nothing like the depression and refused to incur the debt it would have taken for the government to spend the country back to full employment. Instead, Hoover asked Lillian Gilbreth and others to get Americans to increase their spending voluntarily.

Appointing the President's Emergency Committee for Employment (PECE), Hoover made Lillian Gilbreth a member and charged the group to persuade citizens to open their wallets and purses. Because women did the vast majority of retail purchasing, PECE organized a Women's Division, with Gilbreth in the lead, to push for higher household spending. She threw herself into the job with enormous energy, but like many members of the committee, she shared scientific management's enmity for waste and could not enthusiastically endorse a free hand with money.

Fearing to promote profligacy, PECE rejected a campaign to encourage patriotic Americans to "Buy Now." The committee feared that using a "patriotic appeal" to encourage spending "might not be wise." PECE was at least certain that there was no harm in buying "goods which, under normal circumstances, would be bought." So the Women's Division came up with a compromise slogan of "wise spending" that in practice implied no more spending than usual, and maybe less.

Gilbreth's nationwide radio talks may have done more harm than good, given the prudence with which she appealed for "wise spending." She advised each American to first consider whether she was "one of the group who should save or of the group who should spend." Only the latter optimistic souls—their numbers surely shrank as they considered Gilbreth's question—should try to lift the economy by opening their purses. Her unintentional but clear message was that women worried about the depression should squirrel away money in their mattresses.

Under Gilbreth's lead, the Women's Division of PECE supported a "Spruce Up Your Home Campaign" that was supposed to create work for carpenters and painters as well as manufacturers of building supplies. But wait! First, the housewife should do "a survey of your own home to see what things need to be done there." And she should ask herself if the proposed project would add to the efficiency of the home. If the housewife wasn't sure, Gilbreth suggested writing to the Commerce Department for a pamphlet called *Care and Repair of the Home,* never mind that it wasn't ready yet.

Gilbreth recommended to local women's clubs and other organizations a list of activities that if followed to the hilt would have made the whole country seem like one of those managerial organizations we know too well today, so sick with frenzied meetingitis that it cannot focus on its purpose. The country's women would have been lecturing, discussing, surveying neighborhoods, stocking library shelves with how-to literature, and doing everything but spending.

Gilbreth's efforts, however, were considered a triumph. Her courage and dedication were unquestionable, and she no doubt did a bit of good with her appeals to well-off women to buy Christmas presents early, not to fire servants, and above all to "Give a job!" She tried to martial consumer power by advising women shoppers to follow "your dollar back through the retail stores to the industries" in order to support companies doing their best to hold employment and wages at pre-depression levels. Some companies that cut wages consulted with her on how to do it, and she urged that the biggest percentage of cuts fall on the best-paid employees.

In short, her work was as good as could be expected from anyone operating in the idealistic mix of bottom-up cooperation and efficiency characteristic of Hoover's attempt to fight the depression. Considered a star of the Hoover program, Gilbreth was sometimes suggested for a cabinet appointment. Had it happened, she would have been the first woman cabinet member. In 1931, when Hoover disbanded PECE, he made a point of sending her the first of his thank-you notes to the committee's members.

Although Hoover finally admitted the necessity of involving the federal government in unemployment relief, he did it mainly through financial aid to states, in order to prevent people from developing a direct dependence on the federal government. Only his crushing defeat in the election of 1932 gave the American people a leader—a democratic politician rather than a manager—who used government power to help them.

In retrospect, Hoover could probably be made to look wise, especially in our time when it has taken great effort to wean the country from welfare. But that would miss the most important lesson of his ultimately failed career as a manager. Only the threat of the enemy without and patriotic war fervor made his cooperative principles work when he was Food Administrator in World War I. When the challenge lay within the country and among divided interests, as it did during the depression, voluntarism and bottom-up strategies might have supplemented but could not substitute for strong use of presidential power.

Lillian Gilbreth resumed her work as a management consultant with enormous success, making herself "the first lady of American engineering" over the next thirty years. Gradually, she found opportunities to work not just on women's issues but on general management for companies like Dennison Manufacturing and IBM. The American Society of Mechanical Engineers eventually awarded her and, posthumously, Frank Gilbreth its "Gantt Medal" for contributions to management.

Although Lillian Gilbreth has been much written about, her personality comes through least clearly of all the major figures in the management movement. Perhaps her shadowy quality comes partly from lack of pretentiousness. Not self-righteous like Taylor, not wanting political power like Gantt, she does not seem even to have imitated her husband's well-publicized claims of generosity. Not on record as ever having claimed righteous superiority either for herself or for managers, she seems to have spared the executives with whom she worked any pretense of moral leadership.

Feminist historians have recently suggested that women, who have had little power, may be more realistic about it than men, who often claim to use power softly and morally. Perhaps, then, Lillian Gilbreth eventually found it easier to make an accommodation with power than Hoover did during his failed, bottom-up attempts to relieve the depression. Yet another woman, Mary Parker Follett, would do still better by giving managers the best advice they ever got on the use of power.

PART 2

------◄o►------

HUMAN RELATIONS

Management as Moral Leadership
of Bottom-Up Power

B Y THE 1920S AND 1930S, MANAGERIAL POWER WAS SO WELL
established, thanks in no small part to Taylor, that increased intellectual energy could be invested in justifying management in a democratic society. Management gurus increasingly minimized top-down power and even profit as forces in corporate life. Managers, they claimed, would help build human community in factories through therapeutic skill and moral authority. A new metaphor came into fashion—the corporation not as a machine but as a living organism. The manager would no longer be conceived of as a mechanical engineer running the organization like a giant machine but as a psychologist, therapist, or moral leader of employees. So began the human relations movement in American industry.

This transformation in management was in part a response to an early twentieth-century crisis of confidence in democracy that resulted from rapid social change. The filling of the manpower needs of the second industrial revolution by a burgeoning workforce of immigrants—some of whom brought radical political ideologies with them from the Old World—inspired xenophobic fear of the lower social orders by the established classes. During the depression of the 1930s, therapeutic management seemed a way to stave off working-class revolution. Managers skilled in human relations would give the dangerous classes the stabilizing sense of community they had lost in the uprooting experiences of immigration and industrialization.

But in the 1940s, management gurus embraced democracy. During World War II, which even more than World War I was a war of production and attrition, a sense of community and social coherence among the population at large became all the more important. Some of the new corporate human relations techniques came into play on the national level in order to manage morale both in the armed forces and on the home front as the country fought antidemocratic evil abroad.

The era's confusing confluence of democratic sentiment and advanced social science provided an opportunity for human relations theorists to show management how to throw off its antidemocratic, un-American incubus. Management by therapeutic skill and moral leadership seemed to fit better with American values than did top-down power. No one at the time spotted the risk that the gurus might carry the idea to extremes, deceiving themselves and even real-life managers into believing that undemocratic power was not an essential part of corporate management.

Mary Parker Follett, the subject of Chapter 4, was the most balanced of these gurus. Understanding the inevitability of power, she nevertheless did not overestimate it but brilliantly analyzed its limitations and the reasons those who lead must also follow. Her idea was that the corporation has the potential to achieve some of the same kind of spiritual unity among employees that an individual human being can achieve within himself or herself. Needless to say, this idea cannot and should not be perfectly realized. But the philosophical insights that led Follett to this idea were sounder than the bases of today's confidence in corporate culture, values, shared visions, and the like as ways of joining employees in a common cause. Managers can learn more from Follett than any other guru about how to turn corporations into communities, though to a far more limited degree than she believed possible.

Underestimation of the importance of power in management gets underway in earnest in Chapter 5 with the psychotherapist Elton Mayo. His call for a gentler style of management made especially good sense in what was called "light assembly" of small machinery such as telephones. Light assembly was relatively labor intensive, and therefore the "human factor" had a proportionately greater effect on the bottom line than in capital-intensive heavy industry. It is certainly believable that Mayo's intellectual heirs have something useful to teach about group dynamics in the Information Age. But Mayo suffered from a shortfall in intellectual integrity that let him draw conclusions his evidence did not justify. He claimed that a therapeutic soft style of management does not just help corporate employees get along better with each other but creates a bottom-up community where there is no conflict of interest between managers and workers.

As Chapter 6 shows, it fell to Chester Barnard, an AT&T executive closely associated with the Harvard Business School, to carry Mayo's reasoning to its logical conclusion. If output soars because humane managers have put workers' interests first, there is no need for top-down power. Managerial authority, according to Barnard, is an illusion that serves employees' psychological need to escape responsibility for their work. Barnard compensated managers for his denial of their power by claiming a new kind of superiority for them—moral superiority. The skillful manager does not boss employees but leads them, inspiring their cooperation through the display of exemplary moral courage in accepting responsibility.

By substituting bottom-up community for Taylor's top-down power, the human relations gurus gave management a better face for a democratic society. But ever since, we have had to ask this question: How large or small a relation do their ideas bear to corporate reality?

4

The Optimist: Mary Parker Follett

A Self-Made Woman

OXFORD UNIVERSITY. 1926.

Participants at an English management conference eagerly wait to hear from Mary Parker Follett, an American woman winning renown as a management theorist on both sides of the Atlantic. But one member of the audience, Lyndall Urwick, awaits her words reluctantly. His boss, Seebohm Rowntree, an English candy manufacturer and admirer of Follett, has insisted that he come. When Follett rises to speak, Urwick is unimpressed and does not relish meeting the "gaunt Boston spinster."

But in the evening they are introduced, and she charms him in "two minutes flat" with her sparkling conversation. She had, he would later say, "[c]leverness with no conceit, pity without patronage, sympathy with no superiority, interest without intrusion, it was a marvelous equipment . . . . She had a mind like a steel blade, but it was carried in a velvet sheath. And she never drew it save when she was alone."

Urwick, who eventually became England's most prominent management guru, took the lead after Follett's death in preserving her writings. A survivor of horrific combat during World War I, he thought Follett's ideas could be used not just to manage companies but to keep peace in the world. She was "one of the makers of life. Centuries hence . . . [her] ideas will remain the first intimations of that great science of human organization which men will build against the ultimate disaster."

PHOTO 4.1   Mary Parker Follett in the
late 1920s.

Many who knew Follett agreed with Urwick that she was one of the
lights of her time, both a shining personality and a brilliant social theorist. Eduard Lindeman, a once famous writer on social problems, spent a
week at a conference with her and called it "the most exciting intellectual
event" of his life. Follett, he said, was "the most highly sensitized person
I have ever known" and one of the "great thinkers" on the "conflict between a willful individualism and a compulsive . . . collectivism."

A rare surviving photograph of Follett shows an alert smile, suggesting
the lively personality to which her friends attested. Insightful courage
and expressive style still shine in her writings: "Experience may be hard,
but we claim its gifts, because they are real, even though our feet bleed
on its stones."

Out of painful experience with barriers of gender and family, Follett contributed original insights and brilliant ideas to political science, social theory,

and business management. An optimist, she missed the corrupting noxious-ness to which corporate life often descends. But she understood the plus side, the reward of working with others. She gave as good an explanation as anyone ever has of why people do sometimes grow in a group. Her fault was that in hoping such personal growth could spread throughout society, she overestimated management's ability to contribute to American democracy.

It took a quarter century of struggle in a constraining organization—her family—for Mary Parker Follett to create herself. In the 1920s and 1930s, when she counseled corporate managers about the relation be-tween freedom and discipline, about the interdependence of leaders and followers, and about integrative methods for resolving conflict, she drew on knowledge painfully won in her difficult youth.

Born in 1868 and raised in Quincy, Massachusetts, Follett was familiar with business success. The thriving, economically diversified town of Quincy was known for building ships, manufacturing shoes, and quarry-ing granite for churches, courthouses, and gravestones across the country. Mary's grandfather had his hand in whaling, a slaughterhouse, a general store, a bank, and an insurance company. Serving the town as a select-man, surveyor of highways, and overseer of the poor, he conducted "pub-lic affairs," according to his obituary, "as he would his own business, owing no man anything."

The life of Mary's father contrasts sadly with her grandfather's success. Charles Follett shows up in genealogical records as a bootsmith. His army enlistment paper says he was a mechanic. Quincy city directories call him a clerk. In the rapidly mechanizing shoe industry, he may have pro-gressed from craftsman to machine tender to office worker. Evidently he did not earn enough money to own a house, at least not a house of suffi-cient quality for his wealthy wife. The 1884 city directory lists him as a "boarder" with his father-in-law.

Charles's one success had been simple survival in four years of Civil War combat, including Grant's murderous 1864 campaign from the Bat-tle of the Wilderness through Cold Harbor to the Siege of Petersburg. He peers out of a later photograph with hollow eyes, suggesting more than words the cost of war.

Spiritually wounded people often identify with children, who in turn sense sympathy in adult sufferers. Charles Follett closed ranks with his unprepossessing daughter against those who did not understand that the seemingly weak and unattractive have much to offer. Proud of Mary's intelligence, he had her show off her prowess at mental arithmetic. Perhaps he taught her the consolation of quiet religion, a side of her that in adulthood only her closest friends knew. His death when she was sixteen may have been an unspeakable loss. Her management writings sometimes use examples drawn from her family but never refer to her father.

Her father's death cost Mary an ally in her quiet struggle against her mother. Elizabeth Follett, a local socialite in Quincy, may have felt it a cruel blow to have an unattractive daughter, bright but bookish and plain, unlikely to do well in the marriage market. Did Mary show signs of lesbianism? If so, what would have been the effect on the family in a world that did not speak of such things? Was she cruelly forced to play the unlikely role of debutante, waiting for beaux who never came? For four years after her secondary school graduation at sixteen, Mary endured no forward movement in her life and surely much frustration.

Elizabeth's inheritance from her prosperous father allowed her plenty of money to care for her children. But Mary—judging by a friend's testimony in adulthood—believed her mother failed to rise to the challenge of leading her family. Mary managed finances, supervised the family's considerable investments in real estate, managed collections on mortgages held by her mother, and decided on her own what new properties to acquire. The young woman probably enjoyed the work and certainly learned from it, but it also bound her to her mother. Even before her father's death, Mary was not allowed to join friends in skating or swimming after school but had to go straight home to help Elizabeth. She was caught in the family net.

Elizabeth drew the strings tight through invalidism, which let her claim Mary's attention, sometimes at the expense of her studies. One of Mary's friends later recalled Elizabeth as "tall, pallid, peevish and artificial," but it is not clear what troubled her. Maybe she suffered from the "neurasthenia"—weak nerves—that society physicians of her time diagnosed in wealthy women.

Mary's brother, George, younger by ten years, mimed Elizabeth Follett in lording over his sister. Mother and son were close, both of them with personalities that Mary eventually saw as domineering and self-defeating. George spent his life in Quincy in the insurance business, where he never shone. Mary's knowledge of his tyrannical qualities in boyhood, together with his lack of success in adult life, enabled her later to dismiss the idea, popular in the 1920s, that a dominating personality was vital to business success: "I knew a boy who was very decidedly the boss of his gang through all his youthful days. That boy is now forty-five years old. He has not shown any ability to rise in his business or any power of leadership in his community. And I do not think that this is in spite of his 'ascendancy traits,' but because of them."

Her family history offered Follett a lesson in freedom and fate because she had the courage to learn. More genuinely optimistic than even the cheerful gurus of our time, she would convincingly teach that corporate life can enlarge the spirit. If she overlooked the darker side of what it means to be an employee, she eventually had less difficulty than many later gurus in honestly accepting the fact of power. She satisfied her reformer's urge not by futile appeals for top-down generosity but by trying to integrate the opposed interests of bosses and workers.

That she achieved not just such maturity but anything at all in the world depended also on her having the good fortune of a way out and the will to take it. She had money, which she used to help pioneer one of today's standard escape routes for young women—college. In 1888, four years after her high school graduation, Follett enrolled in the Radcliffe "Annex" for women that Harvard had reluctantly accepted a decade earlier. She took ten years to earn her degree, summa cum laude. Just as important as academic success was the emotional freedom she found at Radcliffe. After "she went to college," Mary's nephew reported, "the bond between mother and daughter was never the same."

Although Mary mainly studied political science at Radcliffe, she was well aware of the exciting battle within the Harvard philosophy depart-

PHOTO 4.2   Mary Parker Follett at her Radcliffe
graduation.

ment between Josiah Royce and William James. Royce, Harvard's leading
idealist, had influenced one of Follett's secondary school teachers, a
woman named Anna Boynton Thompson who entered Radcliffe in the
1880s and may have inspired Follett to do the same. Probably thanks to
Royce, Thompson wrote a book-length manuscript on Johann Fichte, an
eighteenth-century German idealist who also influenced Follett. When a
1920s corporate manager asked Follett to straighten out a tangle between
him and his employees, she "answered him straight from Fichte" and "it
seemed to meet the case."

Follett may have been influenced more by James, whom she quoted
often in her writings. Where the idealist Royce believed the universe was
contained in the mind of God, the empiricist James dispensed with superhuman principles of unity and explained even human consciousness
as a relation of experience in this world. Follett's later idea that a corpo-

ration could achieve some of the same kind of spiritual unity as an individual human being seems more in the spirit of James than Royce. She did not rely on some mysterious oversoul but urged people to create spiritual unity by communicating and working together.

She studied more modern philosophy and simultaneously slipped further from her family ties during a year at Cambridge University in England in 1890–1891. In one course she was the only student of the philosopher Henry Sidgwick, a leading influence among European and American political theorists as well as an advocate of equal educational opportunities for women. According to Katharine Furse, the partner of Follett's later years, she would reminisce "with affection and admiration of Henry Sidgwick . . . who seemed to have opened the door of living to her."

The year in England may have opened the door to love with Isobel Briggs, an English woman twenty years Follett's senior. Or they may have met earlier. Briggs had run a school for girls in Boston, and Follett seems to have done some teaching along the way. Within a few years of Follett's return from England, she had set up housekeeping with Briggs, in an apartment at the foot of Beacon Hill in Boston. They stayed together thirty years, until Briggs's death. The late nineteenth-century fashion of "Boston Marriage"—women living in pairs because of the thinning of the male population during the Civil War—would have provided good cover for a lesbian relationship if that is what it was.

Follett seems to have been the dominant partner. One visitor reported that when Mary wanted to speak alone with her guest, she "would simply tell Isobel to go away and sit in her room." Briggs, "often demurring, but amused," went "to her tiny room, asking now and then if she might come back." The two women, the same friend recalled, "worked and played and laughed and discussed and stimulated and criticized one another . . . and one was quite used to being called a silly ass or an awful liar."

Isobel supplied moral support that helped Mary keep free of her mother. "Miss Briggs," reported Mary's nephew, "supplied my grandmother with all the information as to Mary's doings, as Mary seemed too busy."

Escape from small-town spinsterhood to love with Isobel Briggs in a Beacon Hill apartment brightened Follett's worldview and helped inspire her hopeful message that people can grow. The outer evidence would have justified her in thinking of her life as a triumph of courage, energy, and determination. Friends at the time described her as resolute looking, with a firm mouth, blue eyes, and a reddish tinge to her short brown hair.

Her escape, no matter how brave, probably also felt narrow and lucky to her. Lyndall Urwick described her as "always very . . . self-conscious and anxious," and another acquaintance noted a "sensitiveness" that "made her friends suffer." But she turned even low self-esteem to advantage. By underestimating her own achievement in self-creation, she bolstered her confidence that other people could grow.

The Corporation as a Person

Follett eventually came to believe that a corporation at its best is a person. That is, she believed that groups of people are capable of achieving some of the same kind of spiritual unity or personal identity as an individual human being.

Many gurus pretend to plumb intellectual depths, but Follett was one of the rare ones who really did, especially in her studies of philosophy and psychology. She saw that her era's interest in the unconscious was part of a larger cultural change, the collapse of the ancient notion of human beings as transcendental souls. Personality came instead to be seen as a series of thoughts, impulses, and experiences, both conscious and unconscious, and not necessarily well integrated into a harmonious whole.

While Pierre Janet, Sigmund Freud, and Carl Jung led the new thinking in Europe, William James helped move Americans toward the new view of the self as a series of related thoughts and actions. James reconciled religious believers to the loss of the traditional soul by paradoxically using heretical ideas to support theism. If the human spirit can be made not of some mysterious *ens entia* but of related ideas and experiences, so can the divine self. There is a God, said James, or at least gods: "[S]uper-human unities of consciousness exist."

Follett applied James's argument for the existence of superhuman persons to social groups. If related ideas can create the divine self, they can make for larger persons in this world as well. A true "group" is a larger person created through communication. When group members' ideas are as closely related to each other as the ideas that make up an individual person, the group, too, is a person. Pointing out that James had called the individual human being "a complex of experiences," Follett added that "society as a complex of groups includes many social minds."

Both democracy and capitalism had been built on the fallacy that the self achieves its highest form by asserting itself alone against others, against society. No, said Follett, the self reaches its highest level "in and through others." The opportunity for the individual to grow by participating in a still larger spiritual person made the business corporation seem a hopeful institution to her.

These optimistic views grew not only out of Follett's philosophical sophistication but also out of her writings in political science. After returning from her 1890–1891 year of study in England, Follett had set to work extending into a book a paper she had written at Cambridge on the Speaker of the House of Representatives. This was the era when "Czar" Thomas Reed used the House appropriations process to dominate many of the executive departments and agencies, making it debatable whether the president was the most powerful government official. Follett examined whether reforms were needed.

She worked on her book under the guidance of her Radcliffe adviser, Professor Albert Bushnell Hart, one of a new breed of scholars aiming to make history and political science less idealistic and more useful through painstaking empirical research. Follett observed the House in action, interviewed its members, visited archives, and studied old newspapers. It added up to a triumph. Her *Speaker of the House of Representatives* (1896) remains a minor classic, still useful today.

Rejecting proposals for structural change, Follett accepted the Speaker's power: "It would be absurd to retard our development by a too strict adherence to an ideal of democracy impossible for a great nation." Some wanted a constitutional amendment creating a government council involving both Speaker and president, a measure Follett opposed as unnecessary. Nothing prevented the Speaker and the president from working together, when they chose, through "private understanding."

Opposition to structural reform put her in tacit opposition to a future president. Woodrow Wilson, as a young political scientist, had suggested aping the English parliamentary system by drawing cabinet secretaries from Congress. Another future president, however, agreed with Follett. Not yet a war hero, Theodore Roosevelt slaked his thirst for combat by reviewing books. Roosevelt probably intended an attack on Wilson in his praise of Follett's *Speaker* for facing "facts as they are" and not "seeing analogies between our own and the English system."

Follett, author of an important book at the age of twenty-eight, could have looked forward to an academic career if she had been a man, but in the 1890s a woman seeking a teaching job in higher education had slim chances at best. Like many other young women interested in politics and social reform, she went in for urban settlement work. Jane Addams's Hull House in Chicago was the most famous of dozens of such institutions in major cities. Follett attached herself to the Roxbury Neighborhood House in Ward 17, a Boston district of Irish immigrants.

Policemen, one of her associates recalled, did not work alone in Roxbury, but Follett did, learning the neighborhood by speaking with store clerks, workers, schoolteachers, and many others. She started the Debating Club for Boys and advised its members—including James Curley, future mayor of the city—that they had to learn "to think and talk in the perpendicular" if they wanted "to participate in the deliberations of men in civic life." Soon she established an organization called the Highland Union, to offer educational and recreational activities to young men and women.

Needing space, she hit on the idea of using public schools as evening community centers and touched off what eventually became a widespread movement. Seeing community centers as more likely to attract young people than settlement houses, she worked on local committees to promote such a center in a Boston school. It succeeded so well that the state legislature eventually appropriated money for use of schools as community centers across Massachusetts. She described an evening in one of the centers:

> [M]arried women are making clothes for their children with jolly, friendly rivalry . . . others are learning how to make hats (one club offered to make my Easter hat!) others are learning embroidery and Irish lace. . . . in the gymnasium . . . boys are playing basket-ball, and in another room . . . fifty or sixty girls are learning folk-dances . . . Young men in "Junior City Councils" are settling the affairs of the city!

Follett went on to more civic activism. She worked for years with the Boston School Department on a career-counseling program, researching needs for different skills in different industries with the help of Radcliffe students. Eventually, the city funded her ideas and created the Vocational Guidance Department in the schools.

For Follett, the idea of a group as a larger person was not an abstract idea but a description of her exciting and satisfying experiences in working on the civic committees that got community centers and career guidance started in the Boston schools. In an unpublished paper on the community centers, she wrote that "the group, because it means a larger life than our single, separate lives, thrills us and raises us to new levels of efficiency and power. This thrill will come to us just as completely as we learn to identify ourselves with the interest of all."

Her later appeal to businessmen searching for a coherent spirit for their organizations is not hard to understand, even if a little frightening. Her idea of a complete identification between the individual and the group sits well with simpleminded corporate totalitarians trying to foster a "What's-good-for-the-company-is-good-for-me" attitude in employees. Yet she was onto something real in saying that when a group reaches a "composite" idea, different from any with which its individual members began, "we have become tremendously civilized people, for we have learned . . . to say 'I' representing a whole instead of 'I' representing one of our separate selves . . . . We have all experienced this at committee meetings or conferences."

The enthusiastic optimism of her writings is sometimes wearing, but she mixes it with sensible advice about choosing coworkers carefully and making sure they have the potential to become part of a group: "I asked a man once to join a committee . . . and he replied that he would be very glad to come and give his advice. I didn't want him and didn't have him. I asked another man and he said he would like very much to come and learn . . . I didn't have him either—I hadn't a school."

Her effectiveness in civic groups made Follett a logical choice to serve as the public representative on Massachusetts Minimum Wage Boards, created in response to reformers' arguments that predatory wages for women had hidden social costs—prostitution, illegitimate births, and child neglect. These boards regulated women's wages in department stores, laundries, and restaurants and in factories making brushes, candy, and corsets. Standing up to curmudgeon capitalists outraged at government interference, she befriended liberal businessmen such as paper goods manufacturer Henry Dennison and department store magnate Edward Filene. They welcomed government regulation that took competitive pressure off wages.

Then illness brought Follett's two decades of social work to an end. Surgery to remove a diseased kidney led to a long recuperation, during which she had only enough strength to stay home and work at her desk. Over the years, some of her Radcliffe professors had given her "hard words" for taking up social work instead of political science. Now she answered them by writing *The New State: Group Organization the Solution of Popular Government* (1918), which used her social work experiences as a new model of political democracy.

The living room of the Beacon Hill apartment she shared with Isobel Briggs became Follett's study. With some original Millets on the wall amid photographs and mementos of her travels with Isobel, she sat by large windows offering a glimpse of the Charles River and set down her words with exacting care. Isobel assisted by climbing Beacon Hill to withdraw source books from the Boston Athenaeum. Follett, depleting her energy within hours, could not welcome friends into the apartment—formerly almost a Boston salon. "Ordinary living," a friend reported, "was for the time suspended. Everything was burned up in a fierce white creative glow which left her exhausted, physically, nervously, and mentally."

The result was a near great book, tilting against the elitism too characteristic of early twentieth-century American liberalism. Gantt's idea that engineers should run the country was just one example of pre–World War I arrogance by experts and intellectuals. The most famous of the elitists was the brilliant young *New Republic* writer Walter Lippmann, who, like Follett, had studied at Harvard and been influenced by William James. Lippmann called for a "creative statesmanship" to lead America in the spirit of artists and intellectuals. Like Gantt, Lippmann and the other *New Republic* men believed they could achieve political influence through war. When the United States entered World War I, the *New Republic* even claimed that intellectuals had led public opinion to accept the conflict—a demonstration of the creative leadership intellectuals should exert in politics.

Follett knew Lippmann and was friendly with him, but she may also have harbored some envy and jealousy. Her twenty years of creative social work had won no acclaim beyond the city limits of Boston, whereas Lippmann, just out of Harvard, was busily making himself into the nation's most widely read political pundit. In any case, she rejected his elitist arrogance. Instead of Lippmann's "creative statesmanship," she said in *The New State*, America needed a "creative citizenship." The way forward was not through leadership by intellectuals but through small, local groups of the kind on which she had relied to build neighborhood organizations in Boston.

Because of her idea that a neighborhood group could have the same unity as a person, she criticized democracy's traditional machinery of elections and political parties. Members of a party often support the same candidate but for different reasons, making them a mere "crowd," not a "group" unified by ideas. Although she supported the women's suffrage movement of her era, she warned against expecting much from it: "The ballot box! How completely that has failed men, how completely it will fail women."

However, her vision of a new state built of small groups collapsed in the face of the biggest question that confronted her. How could the entire country possibly engage in the "collective thought and collective feeling . . . which produces true community"? Follett proposed an impossibly laborious system of interrelated and pyramided groups. She seemed to imagine everyone spending every waking moment networking. "War," she said, "is a kind of rest cure," compared to the effort involved in her idea of democracy.

But even the biggest corporations are a lot smaller than the country and a lot better suited to her idea of the group as a person. Follett was not yet a management guru, but she had a fair amount of experience working with corporations because she had served on minimum wage boards with progressive businessmen. She knew that a lot of corporate work is done in groups. Corporations come closer than government to the neighborhood groups in Boston that had become her democratic ideal.

Therefore, she used the corporation as *The New State*'s primary example of how a group can be a "real whole." As proof that her idea of the group as a person was no airy ideal, she claimed it already existed in business: "The power of our corporations depends upon this capability of men to interknit themselves into such genuine relations that a new personality is thereby evolved."

In the 1920s, as Follett became involved in management consulting, she evidently became wary of sounding esoteric to a business audience. She dropped specific references to the corporation as a person and said instead that the parts of a business should aim at being "so co-ordinated, so moving together in their closely knit and adjusting activities, so linking, interlocking, interrelating, that [they] make a . . . functional whole or integrative unity." In other words, she tried to teach the idea of the corporation as a person without calling it a person, obliquely assuring businessmen that unity through related ideas was "one of the most profound of philosophical and psychological principles."

Follett's idea of the business corporation as potential person was her most original, but almost totally unexplored, contribution to management. Lack of understanding of her most important concept has made it more difficult to appreciate the full implications of some of her other ideas on integrative decisionmaking, the law of the situation, and leadership. These ideas, in the context of her idea that groups can have some of the same kind of spiritual identity as individual human beings, help to explain how people can work together effectively but with less risk of self-deceiving denials of power than occurs in our contemporary ideas about corporate culture and leadership.

Integration

Follett went into management theory partly out of frustration at her failure to make a mark in political science in the 1920s. Her 1918 work, *The New State*, arguably the most original book on political theory in her generation, was greeted by silence. She had erred in both timing and tone by writing in something of the voice-of-God style that had won Walter Lippmann his first audience during the prewar era of fervid political reform. Her utopian exhortations for citizens to become not just the "group-I" but also the "state-I" fell flat in a war-weary country eager for what President Harding would call "normalcy."

She made one last bid for influence in political science with her 1924 book, *Creative Experience,* which, like *The New State*, criticized liberal elitism in general and the ever more influential Walter Lippmann in particular. The failure of World War I to deliver the more liberal world order Lippmann promised had not discouraged him in his idea that intellectuals should be running things. He wrote an overestimated tract, *Public Opinion* (1922), suggesting that things would go better next time if the government would create "intelligence bureaus" staffed by rarefied experts like him to advise political leaders and to guide the minds of the masses. In *Creative Experience*, Follett sarcastically replied: "[W]e should have only to get enough Intelligence Bureaus at Washington . . . and . . . the people, it is assumed, will gladly agree to become automata . . . in favor of a superior race of men called experts." Yet Follett's *Creative Experience* was instantly forgotten, whereas Lippmann's *Public Opinion* became and remains an important book in political science.

Meanwhile, she was beginning to find an audience among business-men. When the Boston schools adopted her vocational guidance pro-gram, they hired Henry Metcalf, a pioneer in personnel management, to run it. In the 1920s, he moved to New York and ran a series of confer-ences on labor relations with the aim, in Metcalf's words, of helping man-agers to "see industry as a whole and in its widely ramifying interrela-tionships." Follett's message that people can be integrated into social groups that have some of the same personal unity as individual human beings fit Metcalf's educational goal. He invited her often to his confer-ences, for which she wrote some of her best management papers.

The Taylor Society also welcomed Follett's optimistic message. In her prewar work on minimum wage boards, she had probably been one of those reformers who admired the high-efficiency, high-wage face of Tay-lorism. She would therefore not have been surprised that the Taylor So-ciety in the 1920s shed the more oppressive aspects of scientific manage-ment and served as a forum for managers interested in better labor relations. Finding an audience there, Follett decided that, as her later partner Katharine Furse reported, "it was useless to hope that politicians would adopt her methods and so had thrown in her lot with the Scien-tific Management group." Perhaps businessmen would test some of her ideas in their organizations.

The unrealistic hopes for the spiritual unity of humankind that denied Follett a hearing from political scientists found a ready audience in the corporate world, always eager for an all-embracing sense of mission. Utopianism is the very stuff of management fads. Gurus always try to sound tough-minded, but in hindsight it is hard to think of one distin-guished by realism. Follett possessed in spades a guru's basic qualifica-tion—evangelical fervor for a big idea.

In return, corporate executives offered a ready-made solution to the question that had frustrated her in *The New State*—how to unify neigh-borhood groups into a still larger personality. The boss would fuse a firm's multifarious groups into a companywide totality, a classically undemoc-ratic solution to the problem of unity. Follett seems to have accepted the boss's power and maybe by then had caught a glimpse of its tragic necessity. Instead of opposing power, she merely cautioned against its overuse by explaining why repression fails, whether in governing an organization or a personality. Her analysis of why followers must often lead and leaders follow offered deep insights into group coherence and success. The mix of messenger, message, and audience was just right. In her fifties, she had found a career.

Businessmen warmed to her personality and welcomed her advice. Had she lived a century later, she could have made a fortune as a management guru and consultant. Socially idealistic businessmen such as Urwick and Seebohm Rowntree in England, Edward Filene and Henry Dennison in the United States got more than management advice from her. They not only avidly learned new ideas in labor relations and leadership but also acquired, even if only vaguely, her idea of corporations as potential persons.

Dennison, a Framingham, Massachusetts, manufacturer of office supplies and Christmas wrappings, exemplified the kind of liberal businessmen among whom Follett found her audience. From 1911 on, his family had made headlines by instituting a series of steps "giving" their company to workers. Keeping preferred stock and a guaranteed dividend for themselves, they turned over common stock and voting rights to employees. If workers wanted to cash out, they first had to exchange common stock for preferred stock. The idea was to keep common stock and control of the company in employee hands, preventing speculators and others "unacquainted with the business" from getting control "for some other purpose besides the permanent good of the company itself."

Dennison was one of the most socially and politically active liberal businessmen of his generation, on both a local and national level. He had supported Follett in her successful campaign to get the Boston schools to offer vocational guidance. He introduced William Greene, president of the American Federation of Labor, at the meeting where the Taylor Society committed apostasy by acknowledging that labor unions could contribute to management. In the prosperous 1920s, Dennison was a highly vocal supporter of Commerce Secretary Herbert Hoover's visionary idea that the federal government should plan to increase spending in eco-

nomic downturns. And he held to that idea in the depression when
Hoover, as president, abandoned it. During the Roosevelt administration,
as a key member of FDR's Business Advisory Council, Dennison worked
with industry trade associations to lift the country out of the depression
by raising workers' wages and purchasing power. In 1935, when the
Supreme Court declared unconstitutional the 1933 National Recovery
Act that had created these trade associations, Dennison declared the
Court "fascist."

At a time when management was almost exclusively male, Dennison
had no prejudice against women consultants. He sent employees to the
management course Lillian Gilbreth taught alone after Frank Gilbreth's
death and later hired her to improve the efficiency of his sales staff. Follett,
too, seems to have done some consulting work for Dennison's company,
perhaps aimed at improved intragroup relations among the workers.

What Dennison got most of all from Follett was her idea of the corporation as a person, an idea that influenced a book he wrote on management. His inept title, *Organization Engineering* (1931), suggested a mechanical approach, but he objected to conceiving of workers as cogs in a
machine. Influenced by Follett, he thought of employees as parts of a
larger person or at least an "interrelationship," a "living thing, which
grows and changes from day to day" and "brings to birth some small element of essential newness."

Follett in turn drew on Dennison's practical experience to help her express some of her ideas such as "integration," now probably her best
known and most influential idea. Integration is often understood as
something like "win-win," with both sides getting what they desire. But
Follett actually aimed to create a new, unifying desire that, in the best
possible case, integrated the two sides into one person. She used an example Dennison gave her of a disagreement among his managers over
whether to match a competitor's latest price cut: "The solution came
when something quite different was suggested: that we should stand for
a higher quality of paper and make an appropriate price for it."

Dennison also helped Follett develop or at least express the implication of integration for management-worker participation. Just as Follett

had argued that the highest form of participatory democracy was group unity in a "composite" idea, she believed all employees should contribute to management. Thus, she quoted Dennison on the importance of bringing out "every possible bit of ability" in the company, for "the managing ability of all employees is a great untapped source of social wealth."

Conceiving of integration as psychological unification, Follett said conflict should be recognized rather than repressed: "The 'uncovering' which every book on psychology" says is "of the utmost importance for solving the conflicts which the individual has within himself is equally important for . . . business," where it must be remembered that "sometimes the underlying motive is deliberately concealed and that sometimes it exists unconsciously." The organization, like the individual, cannot achieve personal unity and integration until it permits "the whole field of desire to be viewed." Repression of desire only breeds further anger and conflict.

Compromise, the traditional method for resolving conflict, is a form of repression, according to Follett. She had served on a minimum wage board in Boston where factory women paid "$8.00 or $9.00 a week" demanded "$22.40 (for a minimum wage, note), obviously too great an increase for anyone seriously to think of getting, at one time." The women used the time-honored ploy of opening high in the hope of reaching a more advantageous compromise, a tactic that left their employers "far as ever from knowing what the girls really thought they ought to have." Because the women did not express their real desire, there was no integration, just a compromise that left each side dissatisfied.

Integration, by contrast, merges conflicting desires in a larger, unifying idea, providing managers with a way to use conflict constructively. Follett saw conflict as raw material for organizational development and recommended that it be addressed without "ethical pre-judgment; to think of it not as warfare, but as the appearance of difference, difference of opinions, of interests." Through integration of differences, the old conflict is not repressed but is abandoned in favor of a new, unifying desire, leading Follett to the conclusion that "only integration really stabilizes."

As she often did, Follett set the bar too high in describing integration as the only way of achieving stability. Repressive power often works just fine. And between repressing conflicting desires and integrating them, there is a middle path of maturely accepting them. Most people have reasonably stable personalities yet endure conflicting and imperfectly integrated desires. Organizations are unlikely ever to be more psychologically unified than individuals, and to urge such a goal as the only way of achieving stability is probably destabilizing.

If she erred in optimism, it was a matter of degree. Acknowledging "tragedy in life," Follett admitted that not all conflicts can be integrated. It takes goodwill on both sides. And even if willing, she noted, two men in love with the same woman cannot both marry her. Still, she believed that we can "often integrate instead of compromising."

Follett's optimism reflected the typical guru's cheerful bias resulting from too much mingling with the boss. In Follett's case it probably also came from knowing unusually good bosses like the progressively minded Dennison and his English counterpart, Seebohm Rowntree. She dwelled on upbeat possibilities for integration without mentioning the opportunities corporate life offers for vicious tyrants. An employee's anguished feeling of smallness in the role of cat's-paw for a belittling manager, fat and feline in self-conceit—not two men in love with the same woman—is a good example of a corporate problem that cannot be solved by integration. The employee may either have to endure the oppression or quit.

Follett had an outwardly fortunate adulthood, financially independent and engaged in fulfilling work done for its own sake. The family travails of her youth gave her sympathy for underlings, but she had no personal experience of working for a boss to help her understand employees' experience. Although she knew abstractly the attitude of most foremen— "I'm the boss. You do what I say"—that did not change the fact that, as any factory woman could have told her, she didn't have a clue.

If she lacked experience of the vile aspects of corporate life, her philosophical depth at least offered a convincing explanation of the bright side. Work groups do sometimes come together in a way that delights the soul. Follett's explanation—a relation or integration of ideas among group members similar to the connection of thoughts that gives an individual a sense of personal identity—drew on a psychologically realistic approach to the human self and is still unsurpassed. No one has better described corporate joy than as an experience of being integrated into a larger whole. Follett may not have known the shrinking sensation of working for an edgy tyrant or a smug manipulator, but she had a clear idea of how a good boss helps people grow.

Leadership and the Law of the Situation

"The world," Follett told businessmen, "has long been fumbling for democracy, but has not yet grasped its essential and basic idea"—that is, her idea of the group as a larger person. Politicians and political scientists had paid her no heed, but in the 1920s and 1930s, she believed that "industrial organisation is . . . on the verge of making large contributions . . . to the development of integrative unity."

Businessmen liked being told that they were "helping to solve the problems of human organization, . . . and that is certainly the greatest task man has been given on this planet." Her idea that grubby commerce and industry could contribute to a lofty social mission explained why Lyndall Urwick abandoned his English reserve in speaking of Follett. She enabled "those whose lot is cast in business" to "see their work . . . as a definite and vital contribution towards the building of that new social order which is the legitimate preoccupation of every thinking citizen."

Her idea of business as a liberal social model is a little off-putting today, a seeming anticipation of the hubris of contemporary managerialism with its naive belief that corporate capitalism embodies universal truths, its arrogant assumption that every social organization should be run like a company, its careless abandonment of traditional democratic suspicion of power under cover of a soft notion of leadership. Even allowing for the mitigating circumstance that business treated Follett more justly than most of the other social institutions in her life, she was a little guilty of the above charges, especially inadequate suspicion of power.

Yet she offered a sophisticated new model of leadership that reflected the better aspects of corporate life. The corporation *is* a social adventure, and a newer one than democratic political institutions. Corporations, and for that matter Follett, may not be friends of the democratic right to live apart, but people who want to work together can learn a lot from her.

Follett saw that life in an integrated group not only rewards the spirit but also inspires better work, giving corporate leaders a reason to want a group identity for their employees. The manager, she said, "should be leader of a coherent group . . . who are finding their material welfare, their most effective expression, their spiritual satisfaction, through their relations to one another, through the functioning of the group to which they belong."

In her effusiveness, Follett sounds a little like today's bloviators on leadership. But she differed far more radically than later "humanist" gurus from the orthodox doctrine of her time that the leader was a top-down bully. In the 1920s, the old-fashioned notion of the leader as a dominator had gained ground, ironically, due to the increasing sophistication of popular psychology. "Freudian slip" entered cocktail party chatter, and clinical psychologists began to challenge clergy as personal counselors. But the popularizers of psychology (and even most of the savants) had not thought through its implications as thoroughly as Follett. They saw the human self as a series of related ideas but did not consider the possibility of relating those ideas in a larger person than the individual human being. Conceiving the leader as a separate personality who imposed his or her will on others, they tried to measure "ascendancy traits" as indicators of leadership potential and perpetuated the idea of management as psychological domination.

Follett had learned a different lesson from philosophy. The leader does not subdue others but joins them in a larger self. Invoking Emerson's idea that "[w]hoever connects me with the hidden springs of all life is my leader," she also quoted William James on the leadership qualities of the great German idealists: "How did Kant and Fichte and Goethe and Schiller inspire their time with cheer except by saying, 'Use all your powers; that is the only obedience which the Universe exacts.'" So, too, in business, "There is energy, passion, unawakened life in us—those who call it forth are our leaders."

That was a worthy but very lofty goal, as Follett well knew. She claimed to base her idea that generalissimos are not necessarily bullies on her experience in trench warfare. As a social reformer she had worked in "close connection with a Tammany organization" and personally knew a Democratic ward boss, probably the powerful Martin Louiasey, who was said to govern Boston's West End with an iron fist. But according to Follett, he "was not the domineering type." He led not by bullying people but by influencing and being influenced by them. In the spirit of bipartisanship, Follett added that Boss Platt, infamous head of the Republican machine in Albany, also lacked "ascendancy traits" and led "by his power of harmonizing conflicting interests."

But Follett's opposition to domination did not make her a precursor of today's human relations camp, with its manipulative emphasis on recognition and praise aimed at making employees feel big enough to take on the company's problems. Neither did she tout the ideal leader's admirable personal qualities, as do many of today's leadership mavens. Such methods alienate the leader from the group by claiming for the leader either a superior personality or else superior skill at psychological manipulation. In either of these latter-day "humanist" models, the leader puts his or her own personality above others no less than in the earlier model of the leader as a dominator.

Follett advised, "Don't exploit your personality. *Learn your job*." Competence creates charisma, or at least sustains it. Followers want to believe that their leader knows what to do. The manager's main job is neither to bring others into spiritual unity nor bend their will. Not democracy or dictatorship but making money is the goal of a business. The executive's moral authority ultimately rests on the ability to get the job done: "the industrial leader . . . has the power to *draw forth* the forces . . . for a given end."

By focusing on the goal instead of on dominating or manipulating subordinates' personalities, the leader rises above individuality and helps followers do the same. The group gets integrated not as preparation for the job but in the process of doing it. By competent response to the objective problems of the business, the leader makes it possible for followers to obey not the leader but what Follett called the "law of the situation."

The "law of the situation" was Follett's idea for finding some freedom in a corporation, a method by which the boss can "de-personalize" his or her authority. She offered a homely example, a story "told in the life of some famous American that when he was a boy and his mother said, 'Go get a pail of water,' he always replied, 'I won't,' before taking up the pail and fetching the water." The boy rightly resisted action "at the command of a person," which is tyranny. But he got the water "because he recognized the demand of the situation. . . . [T]hat, he was willing to obey." Obedience to a person is slavery, but obedience to a situation is consistent with the democratic impulse toward self-government, which is "the very essence of the human being."

"Orders" alienate employees by denying them self-government. A skillful leader minimizes orders by focusing followers on the demands of the situation: "Our job is not how to get people to obey orders, but how to devise methods by which we can best *discover* the order integral to a particular situation." Once the situation has given its order, "the employee can issue it to the employer, as well as employer to employee."

In other words, followers are often leaders, and leaders followers. Leaders' most neglected skill is "followership." A "partnership of following," said Follett, is the "basis of industrial leadership" for it creates "a common task, a joint responsibility."

Follett's emphasis on "followership" did not make her a proponent of some of her contemporaries' radical idea—whose origins are explored in the next two chapters of this book—that power is bottom up and authority a fiction. When she said that "final authority" is an "illusion," she was denying finality, not authority. Because real-world relations are never one-way, authority is not absolute, but that does not mean it is nonexistent. She was only cautioning the powerful that their followers' obedience is never purely passive. The creative circularity of experience means that there is always a "come-back."

In Follett's time, the upper middle class still had servants, so a cook preparing dinner was a common situation illustrating an employee's "come-back" to her boss. The lady of the house may have decided on a leg of lamb, but the cook, not her mistress, knows what is needed for the sauce. By charging the ingredients to her employer's account at the grocer's, the cook in effect gives her mistress the order to buy them: "My cook . . . points out the law of the situation, and I, if I recognize it as such, accept it, even though it may reverse some 'order' I have given."

The power of the law of the situation could be seen, Follett believed, in its defeat of a president. As a young political scientist, she had disagreed with Woodrow Wilson's ideas for structural changes to improve relations between the executive branch and Congress. Two decades later, with Wilson in the White House, she disagreed with his post–World War I plan for a League of Nations to maintain peace. Follett presciently warned that "we shall never be able to make an international settlement and erect some power to enforce it; the settlement must be such as to provide its own momentum."

Later, in her management writings, she returned to Wilson's failure to lead the United States into his cherished League of Nations. Instead of following the law of the situation, he had tried to impose his personal vision of world government, provoking resentful "followers" in Congress to oppose him. "One of the tragedies of history," according to Follett, "is that Woodrow Wilson did not understand leadership."

Wilsonian idealists, in pleading the case for joining the League, unrealistically called for self-sacrifice and urged Americans to give up some sovereignty for the sake of peace. Follett warned that "all talk of the sacrifice of interests is ruinously sentimental." To achieve peace, "sovereignties must be joined, not sacrificed."

This message could not be more relevant in business today. In employee relations no less than international affairs, appeals for self-sacrifice are a sentimental mistake. Follett detested the sappy idealism of genteel social reformers, pushing their "fallacy . . . that the manufacturer ought to surrender a part of his power in order to gain a spirit of contentment in the factory."

Today's self-deluding managers who appeal to employees to make sacrifices for the good of the company could use Follett's advice to try to integrate. The company has to look out for its interests in profit and productivity. Employees cannot afford to forget that pay and, sometimes, spiritual rewards, are their reasons for working. The best way for employers and employees to come together is not by sacrificing their interests but by integrating them.

If fully integrating employee desires with company goals is not possible, and probably it often is not, managers should forget Follett's idea of integration, invoke power, and say up front, "We'll do it my way." Similarly, her advice to employees to avoid alienation and "labour *with* your leader" as a member of the group only makes sense if the boss is willing to integrate. Otherwise, employees had better forget the group and accept the sad necessity to "follow as one of a crowd."

Follett had been devastated in December 1925 by the death of Isobel Briggs. Whether or not they had a physical relationship, they were lovers for thirty years. A few of Follett's letters survive from this period and attest to her grief. Yet within a few years, she found a new partner in another Englishwoman.

In the autumn of 1928, Follett traveled with friends to Switzerland, an interwar oasis of hopeful internationalism attractive to other Boston reformers like Henry Dennison and Edward Filene. The latter had founded the International Management Institute in Geneva to build on Frank Gilbreth's success, in his Prague conference, at improving the European economy with American management methods. Follett went to Geneva to observe the League of Nations at work and especially its International Labor Office, in which her English friend, Lyndall Urwick, was deeply involved.

In Geneva, she met an Englishwoman, Dame Katharine Furse, as accomplished in her sphere as Follett in her own. Furse had driven ambulances early in World War I and then headed the Women's Royal Naval Service, for which she received the title Dame Grand Cross in the Order of the British Empire. After the war, she headed the World Association of Girl Guides and Girl Scouts.

Dame Katharine later recalled taking the initiative: "Being a real Bostonian with Puritan traditions, Mary would not have made such fast advances but she talked to me of her philosophy . . . [which] seemed to me to be exactly what we human beings needed." Parting in Geneva, the two women arranged to meet in Italy the next spring, and Dame Katharine's memoir of their travels there has the glow of romance. They soon took a house together in London, with Furse living downstairs and Follett above.

Those last years in England were not always happy for Follett, who, according to Dame Katharine, "often suffered physically," probably from an undiagnosed cancer discovered after her death. Yet England offered her an audience. Writers on politics such as Lord Haldane and Bernard Bosanquet had both, a decade earlier, favorably reviewed her *The New State* and now sought her out. Liberal businessmen remained interested in her ideas, and she returned the favor, preferring them to politicians and professors. Businessmen, she said, did not go in for "theorizing or dogmatizing" and were willing to "try new ways the next morning." In 1932, when the London School of Economics opened a Department of Business Administration, Urwick arranged for Follett to deliver a series of inaugural lectures.

The worst year of the Great Depression, 1933, brought her end. Fearing the collapse of the investments on which she lived, she returned to Boston to see the situation for herself. Her brother, who met her at the pier, found her tired and nervous. She visited Radcliffe to discuss changes in her will, leaving more than $100,000 to endow two scholarships named for Isobel Briggs. Then she entered a Boston hospital for surgery to remove her enlarged thyroid. Although the operation was supposed to be minor, she wrote to friends that if she did not come through it, they should know that everything was "all right." She died of postoperative heart failure and was buried in Quincy. The obituary in her hometown newspaper was a little puzzled, aware that Follett had been an important person but not sure why. She would soon be largely forgotten.

In recent years Follett has begun to be rediscovered. Feminist and management scholars are leading a new surge of interest in her. It would be a lost opportunity if these new studies celebrate her for anticipating today's management ideas when she often surpassed them.

Follett's idea of the corporation as a person offers a more genuine model of community than today's concept of corporate culture, so helpful in reinforcing manipulators' belief that they can change people's behavior and values without their knowing it. Her idea of leaders as followers and vice versa does not morally isolate the manager in the way that many of today's leadership gurus do by focusing on leaders' personalities, implicitly separating them from followers. Follett more profoundly explained how integration of interests and desires enables people to grow in a group without unrealistically minimizing the boss's power or overestimating that of employees. Recognition of such interdependence is the basis of whatever genuine leadership it is possible for managers to exercise as a supplement to power rather than as a substitute for it.

To catch up with Follett, we also need to think critically about some of her contemporaries, for our management ideas today are deeply influenced by the human relations movement that was just getting underway near the end of Follett's life. Unfortunately, the leaders of that movement did not build on her ideas but eclipsed them.

5

The Therapist: Elton Mayo

Democracy in Australia

LONDON. SUMMER 1904.

Elton Mayo—the man who will inspire "organizational behavior," now a required course in business schools around the world—forlornly wanders the streets, suffering feelings of failure and worthlessness. Gaunt and angular when in the best of health, the twenty-three-year-old Australian is pitifully emaciated, recovering from dengue fever contracted while clerking for a mining company in Obuassi. Illness in the African gold fields had followed three failed attempts at a medical education. After flunking out of the University of Adelaide in Australia, Mayo had tried the University of Edinburgh and then St. George's Hospital, London, with no better luck.

Having alienated the well-to-do London cousins with whom he has been staying, Mayo has moved to a rented, flea-ridden room near his only human contact, his sister. Helen Mayo, unlike Elton, is successfully studying medicine and will become one of Australia's leading physicians. Evenings, she listens with the therapeutic skill genetic in the Mayo family as Elton, puffing on an ever-present cigarette, pours out his despair.

This lonely, anomic Aussie will become one of the most important social scientists of his generation by creating the human relations movement in American business. He will try to use a therapeutic style of su-

PHOTO 5.1   Elton Mayo, near the end of his career, speaking to executives at the Harvard Business School.

pervision to recreate in factories the communal harmony that he believed industrialism and democracy had destroyed. He will appeal to businessmen by arguing that not Taylorist bossism but soul-salving, bottom-up communities get the most work done. In 1947, in his last lecture at the Harvard Business School, he will declare, "The solitary who works alone is always a very unhappy man."

Mayo broke his isolation in the summer of 1904 by drifting into London's Working Men's College, just a few doors from his rented room. Christian and patrician, the college taught laborers, Mayo later said, to rise above "the indignity and frustration which the . . . new industrial society forced upon workers." Taking an unpaid job teaching English grammar, he held his classes rapt with seemingly brilliant discursions into politics. Through kind empathy for his working-class students, he took the sting out of his right-wing views. Joining the Debating Society, he carried the resolution that "[t]his house welcomes the recent downfall of the Labour Ministry in Australia."

This small success—teaching gratis for a single term—gave Mayo enough self-respect to return home to Adelaide, the capital of South Australia. Two generations earlier, his grandfather, "old Doctor Mayo," had arrived in the colony as a mere ship's surgeon. But he built a thriving medical practice that enabled him to educate his son, George, Elton's father, "at home," as Australians once referred to the British Isles.

George Mayo studied engineering at the University of Glasgow but made his Australian career in real estate, a comedown from old Doctor Mayo's social status. But he could take comfort in his children's professional success, all of them but Elton winning distinction in medicine and law, and one of them even earning a knighthood.

As for the prodigal Elton, he resumed his education at the University of Adelaide. There he found a mentor in Professor William Mitchell, a Scotsman who held the chair—he called it a "sofa" because of its ludicrously broad title—of English Language and Literature and Mental and Moral Philosophy. Mitchell included within philosophy the now separate disciplines of ethics, psychology, economics, and political science. Such breadth had enabled Mitchell's eighteenth-century countryman, Adam Smith, also a professor of moral philosophy, to write *The Wealth of Nations* (1776), justifying free markets in terms of not only economics but also ethics and psychology. By 1900, this integrative social science had begun to break down under the weight of new knowledge produced at leading universities in Europe and the United States. But Adelaide continued to teach philosophy as the mother of knowledge. Mayo's outdated education prepared him to range across disciplines with a buoyancy that businessmen would later mistake for wisdom.

Sponsored by Mitchell, Mayo landed a lectureship at the new University of Queensland, in Brisbane, where he found a wife. Dorothea McConnel, from a wealthy family and educated in Europe, probably felt like Mayo, alienated from Australia rather than prepared for it by her privileges and culture. The marriage contained friction and may not have been the escape from solitude that Mayo hoped it would be.

At the University of Queensland, Mayo endured a heavy teaching load and despairingly suffered the committee meetings and administrative drudgery of building a new university. Only his facile ease with ideas enabled him to follow developments in mental philosophy and to acquaint himself with avant-garde psychologists, especially Pierre Janet.

His one saving contact with the wider intellectual world was the anthropologist Bronislaw Malinowski, who passed through Brisbane in 1914 on his way to follow-up studies of the aborigine with fieldwork among the Mailu in Papua. Mayo hosted Malinowski on that visit and several more, charming him as he did all on whom he cared to expend the effort. The Polish anthropologist declared his Australian host a "real scientific mind . . . absolutely in touch with life."

Malinowski repaid Mayo's hospitality by exposing him to the empirical research taking hold in modern social science as opposed to the armchair theorizing of old-fashioned universities like Adelaide. Forswearing the deductive reasoning by which imperialists and racists located white civilization at the top of a hierarchy reaching down to black barbarism, Malinowski used fieldwork to understand the worldviews of foreign cultures rather than to rank order them. Malinowski's empirical approach encouraged Mayo to take a hands-on approach to psychology.

Mayo became Australia's first practicing psychoanalyst when a Brisbane physician, auditing his psychology lectures, asked for help with a patient suffering from fear of sex and crowds. The patient said his suffering began at seventeen, but Mayo administered a Jungian word-association test, provoking the man to lapse into a story from his eighth year. With the barrier of childhood denial removed, psychotherapy quickly cured his phobias. After this success, Mayo moved on to melancholics, hysterics, and World War I victims of shell shock.

He got his main psychological ideas from Janet's theory of personality dissociation. In a legendary analysis, the French psychologist had discovered that a hysterical patient—"Lucie"—had two personalities, whose contradictory impulses caused aberrant behavior. Mayo believed loneliness caused such dissociation. Lonely people daydream, slip into the mental hinterland, and lose self-control. By substituting society for solitude, Mayo said, the therapist could focus the patient's attention outward, giving back control to the conscious self.

Mayo applied his theory of personality dissociation to his native country, analyzing Australia's severe social and class divisions as if they amounted to one of Janet's cases of hysteria. Mayo believed that Australia suffered more than other modern societies from social division, the nation's identity shattered by too many reveries in the mental hinterland, too much time alone in the outback.

The fundamental fact of Australian history was the country's origin in the transportation of convicts. When the American Revolution denied England the use of Georgia and the Carolinas as a dumping ground for thieves and footpads, human refuse piled up in prison hulks anchored in the Thames. Finally, in 1788, England began to clear the river by sending the First Fleet and its cargo of convicts to Botany Bay. Convicts, a minor source of immigration in America, founded a nation in the antipodes.

From their convict exile came not only Australians' admirable bush comradeship but also, according to one historian, their "defensive, static, levelling, two-class hatred," their "impotent dreams of vengeance," and their "habit of cursing authority behind the hand while truckling to its face." Mayo saw this legacy of servile hatred for the master class as Australians' dominant cultural trait.

He owed his exemption from Australian class hatred to his well-established family and his native city of Adelaide, which held itself above the rest of Australia by its distinction of not having been born in leg irons. Adelaide was settled in the 1830s by middle-class Englishmen aspiring to land and respectability. What nineteenth-century Boston was to the United States, Adelaide was to Australia, the country's best-bred city, living with one eye turned inward and the other toward England. Mayo inherited Adelaide's sense of superiority, which accounts for his self-conception as a paternalistic rather than egalitarian friend of the working class.

But Brisbane, home of the University of Queensland, was 1,000 miles away from Adelaide and its respectable society. In Brisbane, Mayo encountered a raw, working-class ambience, created by immigrants from

Italy, Ireland, Germany, and Russia who mined Queensland's rich deposits of tin, lead, zinc, coal, and copper. Along with the polyglot miners, the working class included sawyers, sheep shearers, and sugar cane cutters. Queensland's agricultural and extractive industries depended on railroads that in turn employed thousands of locomotive engineers, brakemen, and switchmen.

The immigrant workers had brought anarchism, Marxism, and revolutionary syndicalism with them. The Industrial Workers of the World (IWW) had an enthusiastic Queensland following for their idea of replacing government with "one big union." Day laborers, on the move from one job to the next, embraced the "Hallelujah,-I'm-a-bum" strain of Wobblyism. Scientific management arrived in Australia to be greeted with cries for "scientific sabotage." In 1899, Queensland had elected one of the world's first labor governments. The opposing National Party, when in power, sometimes violently repressed the radicals with the support of right-wing paramilitary groups.

Mayo, with his experience at London's Working Men's College, probably seemed well equipped for the ideological heat of Brisbane. Mitchell, his Adelaide professor, assured the Queensland faculty that Mayo would "do much to promote philosophical studies outside the University as well as in it." Mayo lived up to his mentor's promise by founding a successful branch of the Workers' Education Association in Brisbane.

Still, the Queensland proletariat lacked the deference with which English working-class students had treated Mayo. When he took educational proposals to Brisbane trade unions, radicals taunted him with accusations of class prejudice. Standing up to the heckling with witty ripostes, Mayo impressed the workers with his toughness.

Mayo mistakenly saw World War I, which Australia had entered on the side of the mother country, as an opportunity to create patriotic social harmony in Queensland. He boldly obtained an interview with Queensland's socialist prime minister, "Red Ted" Theodore, and urged him to give up the class struggle. In place of socialism, Mayo proposed cooperative syndicalism—that is, industrial and trade associations composed of both workers and employers to forestall revolutionary syndicalism of the IWW variety. The socialist premier politely dismissed the respectable professor and held to his program of business regulation and heavy social spending.

Mayo, retreating to his study, began writing a book warning against the conflict that lay in wait for Australia if capitalists did not abandon their parvenu greed, if workers did not surmount their angry class-consciousness. While he was writing, in March 1918, Queensland voters reelected the Labour Party, despite inflation and job losses that Mayo attributed to government spending and heavy-handed regulation. Explaining the election results as due to Labour's appeal to voters' "phobias" and "neuroses," he excitedly realized that psychoanalysis had political implications and revised his book accordingly.

Published in 1919, Mayo's *Democracy and Freedom* charged that democratic politicians, like psychoanalysts, use word association to tap into unconscious phobias. But unlike the therapist who tries to integrate personalities, the office seeker engages in the "immoral endeavour" of dividing the electorate. With terms like *conscription* and *inflation*, the typical politician encourages voters' neurotic fears "in order to attach them to the social and industrial conditions his own quack remedies profess to cure."

Therapists, not politicians, have the cure for workers' neuroses, an idea that would make Mayo immensely appealing to American businessmen and social scientists. "Society, like an individual, may suffer from 'nervous breakdown,'" he would write in 1922, his first year in the United States. "What else is socialism but a reverie of this type?"

But even in his book on Australia, Mayo argued that big business offered the best chance to recreate the "common social purpose" destroyed by democratic politicians. He believed that the large corporation, requiring "the active collaboration of many professions," amounted in practice to the sort of cooperative syndicalism he had vainly urged on Queensland's socialist prime minister. Managers already practiced "intelligent collaboration" and should try to inspire it in workers.

In his instantly forgotten book, Mayo created the alternative to traditional democratic theory that he would teach to American management in the next quarter century. The democratic idea of protecting the individual against power only bred suspicion and division. Defining the good life as social participation, Mayo envisioned a therapeutic management to cure those whose negative reveries tilted them against a common organizational purpose.

Mayo favored corporate monopolies to promote social harmony. Free market ideologues missed competition's cost in social division: "A monopoly, upon the other hand, could hardly fail to realise, if intelligently handled, that social service was its chief duty." Managers free from competition would see "that the human factor is as important as any other in the matter of industrial organisation."

Corporate oligopoly and monopoly had been developed the furthest in the United States. What could make more sense than for Mayo, the man who understood the social function of big business, to visit America?

Managing American Social Science

In 1922, the University of Queensland gave Mayo a leave for overseas study. He decided on an "assault on London," hoping to find a permanent job there. Short of money, he planned to travel via California and pay for the rest of his trip to England with fees for lectures a friend had arranged for him to give at Berkeley. In the United States, he could observe firsthand the world's largest corporations. Leaving his family behind, he embarked on a bout of loneliness.

On arriving in San Francisco, he learned that the Berkeley lectures had fallen through and, with them, his fare to England. Stuck in the United States with dwindling funds, Mayo lapsed into anomie similar to his London experience of 1904. Filling his days with long walks through the city, he despairingly noted that even the street prostitutes did not try to penetrate the invisible barrier separating him from the rest of humanity.

Using his psychological theories to treat himself, Mayo resisted negative reverie as much as he could and fought off antisocial tendencies by pursing academic contacts. He got himself invited to a conference at Stanford, where he won plaudits for his witty defense of depth psychology against behaviorist attacks. But he got no job offers.

Fortune smiled when, thanks to Australian connections, Mayo lunched at the exclusive Bohemian Club with Vernon Kellogg, secretary of the National Research Council. A graduate of Stanford, Kellogg had worked with his fellow alumnus, Herbert Hoover, on European food relief after the war. When Hoover became secretary of commerce, Kellogg went to the National Research Council, organized during the war to coordinate the physical sciences. Now he was also helping to organize the Social Science Research Council, soon to achieve great influence owing to support from the Rockefeller Foundation, of which he was a trustee. Closely associated with Hoover's ideas for a managerial society, Kellogg was the perfect audience for Mayo's idea that the corporation could create social harmony.

Mayo offered up a vision of industrial psychology as a way of preventing strikes by curing workers of their unreasonable resentments. Kellogg instantly saw funding possibilities. In public health, the Rockefeller family had favored applications over pure research, largely eradicating hookworm, for example, just by making existing treatments widely available. Social scientists needed to promise similarly quick and tangible results to win Rockefeller largesse. Mayo's plan to cure workers' mental illness and, not incidentally, make them more tractable perfectly fit the bill.

He further impressed Kellogg with a letter from the prime minister of Australia, stating falsely that Mayo was a "Professor of Psychology and Physiology." In fact, his appointment was in philosophy. Mayo had probably written the deceptive letter, with its implication of scientific credentials, and had gotten one of his influential relatives to arrange for the prime minister's signature.

During this lunch with Kellogg, Mayo also seems to have begun his lifelong pretense that he was a physician, not a medical school dropout. Once the lie was established, the discreet Mayo lent it little support, just letting it pass uncorrected. Much later, after he was a well-established eminence at the Harvard Business School, he told the truth to a select few colleagues, maybe using his feat in scaling the Harvard heights without advanced degrees as a basis for inverted academic snobbery.

Kellogg bought Mayo's act and invited him to Washington. When the Australian pled thin finances, Kellogg sympathetically replied, "perhaps we'll send for you." A month later, down to his last few dollars and thinking he would have to take work as a laborer to earn his fare back to Australia, Mayo got his invitation. The National Research Council would cover his expenses in the East.

For several whirlwind months, Mayo made the round of conferences and met leading lights—J. B. Watson in behaviorism, A. A. Brill in psychoanalysis, John Dewey in social psychology. Pushing his ideas hard but nonthreateningly, Mayo charmed even those who held depth psychology in contempt. "It's a great method yours," Watson congratulated Mayo when, instead of reading a paper, he spoke extemporaneously.

He also cultivated relationships with holders of purse strings, most notably the psychologist Beardsley Ruml, the newly named, twenty-eight-year-old director of the Laura Spelman Rockefeller Foundation, whose capital he was preparing to steer away from Baptist charities and toward social science. Ruml had demonstrated psychology's practical value by developing aptitude tests for the army during World War I. After the war, he sold his tests to employers. With his "rambunctious inventiveness" and "strong sense of economic practicality underneath," Ruml projected, as one writer put it, "a sense of . . . safe and jolly revolution" that perfectly qualified him, as far as the Rockefellers were concerned, to organize American social science.

Ruml aimed to give the social sciences—still in their infancy—a politically safe middle-of-the-road approach that would enable them to join the establishment and help run the country. Sensing Mayo's fit with this goal, Ruml got him two weeks of work at the Wharton School at the University of Pennsylvania. Wharton students warmed to Mayo's charm, as did Philadelphia businessmen to whom he spoke at civic clubs.

With the support of Ruml and the Wharton dean, Mayo applied to the Laura Spelman Rockefeller Foundation to fund a research position for him at the Wharton School. When the foundation turned Mayo down, Ruml went straight to John D. Rockefeller, Jr., who personally guaranteed the Australian's support. Mayo jubilantly told his wife to come to America: "We are 'placed next' (as they say here) to the richest man in the world, religious, interested in social and industrial investigations."

Wharton officials arranged for Mayo to do research at a Philadelphia textile mill. The plant's enervating clatter supported Mayo's idea, formed in his early psychoanalytic practice during World War I, that factory conditions led to the same symptoms as shell shock. Approaching the plant as if it were a hospital for nerve-wracked survivors of Gallipoli, Mayo sat and waited for patients. To his alarm, only a few came to him. Fortunately, the factory's owner took offense at his counseling a woman employee about sex and insisted that he leave, allowing Mayo to say he had not had time to succeed. Obviously, he had to find another method to practice industrial psychology.

Moving on to another Philadelphia textile plant, Mayo found a departmental nervous breakdown. The spinning department suffered annual labor turnover of 250 percent, while the rest of the plant lost a handful of workers a year. Adopting an anthropological approach, Mayo took a lunch box to the factory and used the noon break to listen to employees' conversation, which revealed pessimistic reveries. He took blood pressures and found differences in workers' upper and lower bodies that he attributed to bending and stretching over the machines.

A local physician who had evidently served abroad during the war advised Mayo that the French army used rest periods to equalize blood pressure on long marches. So instead of individual talk cure, Mayo prescribed rest en masse. The company introduced work breaks and supplied sacking for employees to lie on while doing relaxation exercises favored by the French infantry. Voilà! Turnover in the spinning room dropped to that of the rest of the mill. Better still, output rose 20 percent.

The production increase showed, Mayo said, that workers' mental health improved by removing "the fatigue and the irrationality which manifest themselves in the phenomena of social unrest." Aware to some degree of the moral pit into which he was falling, he denied placing output ahead of his responsibility as a therapist. But he did not explain how he had established that "production . . . offers an interesting, and so far accurate, measure of the general effect of the more humane organization of work upon the men."

Mayo's discovery of a correlation between workers' productivity and mental health established him both intellectually and financially. Ruml informed Rockefeller of Mayo's findings, and the philanthropist agreed to pay his Wharton salary for three years.

Safely ensconced, Mayo began espousing his skepticism of democracy. To Charles Merriam, an ally of Ruml's and a go-getting political scientist at the University of Chicago, Mayo wrote that politics could "never establish a stable society." Revolutions, social unrest, and labor disputes proved it. It was senseless to carry the divisive methods of politics, especially democratic methods, into the factory and expect them to create peace.

But therapy, as opposed to politics, had a record of success in creating social order—for example, in the textile mill where Mayo had used rest periods to equalize blood pressure and reduce labor turnover. Mayo told Merriam that revolutions happened only in countries where a large part of the population had high blood pressure. Because Mayo believed that fatigue caused high blood pressure, the key to political stability was to reduce industrial fatigue. Here was a whole new method for political science—therapy aimed at lowering systolic and diastolic counts.

Mayo wrote up his idea of substituting therapy for democracy in a paper, "A New Way of Statecraft." Ruml, with his pockets full of Rockefeller money, circulated Mayo's paper, letting the anointed know that the Australian was on his way up.

Mayo found it tougher to sell Philadelphia businessmen on his idea of replacing democracy with therapy. After he explained to a progressively minded audience how he used rest periods to reduce labor turnover, they asked if that meant he rejected fair play, profit sharing, and generally democratic methods as a way of raising morale in factories. Mayo, falling back on depth psychology, explained to the businessmen that such methods presumed that workers knew what they wanted. But workers, driven by unconscious forces, did not know what they wanted. Therefore, psychological therapy, not fair play, was the path to higher morale. The businessmen would not buy it. Mayo finally admitted that perhaps it was at least a little useful to listen to workers' opinions on wage and working conditions. He further defused the tension by admitting that he might be biased by what he saw as the failure of industrial democracy in Australia.

From such exchanges Mayo learned to tone down, at least for business audiences, his skepticism of democracy. A vision of corporate community salable to Americans would have to have an at least partially bottom-up appearance. But his message remained the same. With employees ignorant of the causes of their discontent, management was a matter of therapy, not justice.

Mayo was of course right to doubt the usefulness of democracy in management. He saw as well as Mary Parker Follett that democracy's traditional acceptance and celebration of division had limitations as a source of wholeness. But Follett tried to reform democracy. Mayo would prove far less honest. He would aim to give a feeling of bottom-up community to what was really indirect and manipulative top-down power. Mayo's methods are popular today—and sometimes backfire in the hands of managers without his therapeutic gifts—because he achieved a prominent position at the Harvard Business School, which gave him the institutional power to develop and sell his ideas.

The Harvard Business School, Savior of Civilization

Wallace Donham, dean of the Harvard Business School, warmed to Mayo when he met him at academic conferences in the mid-1920s. In Mayo's therapeutic social vision, Donham saw a way to lift his school out of its then low status as a trainer of money-grubbers into a high-prestige educator of socially conscientious administrators.

Donham had infectious energy and the sort of entrepreneurial personality to which Mayo related well. The son of a country dentist, Donham had attended Harvard College and Law School. His youthful success as an investment banker led his close friend, Abbott Lawrence Lowell, president of Harvard, to tap him as the Business School's second dean.

When Mayo arrived at Harvard in 1926, Donham had been dean for seven years and had laid the groundwork for the Business School's rise to preeminence. The year after Mayo came, the school moved to its present location across the Charles River from the rest of Harvard. Donham had gotten the investment banker George Baker to donate the new buildings. Previously, the Business School had operated in cramped offices and classrooms scattered around Harvard Yard. With the new campus, Donham aimed to develop a positive identity for business students, who, alienated from the undergraduates, sat together at football games and cheered for Harvard's opponents.

Donham wanted business students to aspire to the same professional status as lawyers and doctors, so he turned the Harvard curriculum away from specific industries like oil and steel. Just as medical and law students did not specialize in neurology or criminal law until after taking their degrees, business students would wait to choose an industry until they had learned generic principles in accounting, finance, and marketing.

Law and medical students studied cases. Donham therefore pushed his initially reluctant faculty to teach business cases, then used the case method as a marketing ploy, asserting that Harvard alone taught business as a profession.

A profession's claim to high social status rests on its dedication to human service. That was where Mayo came in, with his idea that the manager's mission was to promote social harmony. Donham, like many conservatives after World War I, regarded Oswald Spengler's *Decline of the West* as a touchstone text and feared that social unrest and Bolshevism would do in civilization. Mayo's therapeutic ideas for relieving worker discontent would ease Donham's fears while giving the Business School social respectability in its new mission of fending off chaos and old night.

But getting President Lowell to hire so unknown a quantity as Mayo proved no easy chore for Donham. Mayo aided his own cause by creating the misimpression among Harvard Anglophiles that he was a prominent citizen of the British Empire. To complement his cultivated accent and good taste in dress, Mayo transformed his youthful three months of clerking for a West African mining company into experience in colonial administration. He recast his 1904 teaching at the Workers' Education Association in London as scientific research among the English working class. Again, Mayo pressed into service the letter from the Australian prime minister falsely identifying him as a professor of psychology and physiology. And he kept Donham under the false impression that he possessed medical credentials from England.

Meanwhile, Mayo used his negotiations with Harvard to good effect at the Rockefeller Foundation, and vice versa. He eased President Lowell's concern by bringing with him to Harvard an initial Rockefeller grant of $12,000, the first deposit in a mountain of swag that Mayo eventually extracted from the foundation. The next year the Rockefeller Foundation gave Harvard $155,000 to launch a program in industrial psychology, followed by annual grants of as much as $125,000, with Mayo's individual share at $68,000, an amount so large that he often did not spend it all. By 1940, the foundation had given Harvard $1.5 million to support Mayo's program.

The influence that the Rockefeller lucre gave Mayo at the Business School can be gauged by the salary then of beginning instructors— $1,500 a year. Mayo hired gifted young people who became collectively famous as the "Harvard human relations group." He supplied the group with an inspiring vision of therapeutic management while they did the dog's work of research and writing that immensely raised the reputation of the Harvard Business School.

His first recruit, Fritz Roethlisberger, would become the most important of them by perpetuating human relations after Mayo's death. A troubled young man who had lost his father in early childhood, probably to alcoholism, Roethlisberger had studied engineering, then enrolled at Harvard to study philosophy in a frustrated search for truth. He chose Descartes's notoriously difficult metaphysics for his doctoral dissertation, then gave up and was left with an aching sense of failure. Someone suggested he see Mayo, who promptly hired the youthful failure, perhaps because he saw in him the same struggles with self-doubt that he had endured two decades earlier.

Mayo's friend Malinowski supplied another important member of the Harvard human relations group, W. Lloyd Warner, who had met the Polish anthropologist while doing graduate work at Berkeley. Hired by the Harvard anthropology department, Warner won Mayo's interest with his idea of applying anthropological methods to modern society. Mayo's Rockefeller money funded Warner's research for his once famous *Yankee City* series, a study of an industrial town, Newburyport, Massachusetts.

T. N. Whitehead, son of Harvard's leading philosopher, Alfred North Whitehead, went to work for Mayo as a statistical consultant. His *Industrial Worker* (1938) supplied quantitative analysis of sociological data as underpinning for Mayo's imaginative ideas. Whitehead also wrote *Leadership in a Free Society* (1936), arguing, as Mayo did more tactfully, that the survival of "democracy" depended on developing an administrative elite trained in human relations to guide the ignorant masses.

During the 1930s, these and other members of the Harvard human relations group provided Mayo with the most congenial company of his life. A lover of fine food and wine, he occasionally hosted a restaurant dinner for his youthful colleagues. Over coffee and liqueur, Mayo played the curmudgeon for them, calling the rise of fascism the logical result of democracy and warning that communism was a sweetened version of the same poison. True democracy consisted of workplace cooperation, which Mayo tried to model in his "group" by maintaining harmonious human relations among them.

Protecting the flank of the human relations group against any charge of scientific softness was the Business School's Fatigue Laboratory. Despite its origins in Mayo's dubious claim that fatigue, high blood pressure, psychosis, and revolution are interrelated, the laboratory did excellent research with important finds. Directed by the biochemist Lawrence Henderson, the Fatigue Laboratory discovered that the human body can store little sodium, leading to simple salt tablets that saved sweating steel workers and summer athletes from cramps, strokes, and sudden death. From experiments with puffing joggers on treadmills in the Business School's Morgan Hall and from test sites in the Andes came high-altitude equipment that gave American pilots a saving edge in World War II.

Earlier, as a member of the Harvard College faculty, Henderson had done work on blood plasma that saved the lives of countless wounded soldiers and automobile crash victims. Even with Rockefeller money, it probably took all of Mayo's charm to induce so prominent a scientist to cross the Charles River to the then low-status Business School. But Henderson needed social understanding, and the empathetic Mayo provided it. Socially isolated by a mentally ill wife, Henderson also suffered from a brusque personality, social ineptness, and obsessive intellectual rigor. His "manner in conversation," an acquaintance observed, "was feebly imitated by a pile-driver."

Henderson, an arch political conservative, took the lead in creating a Harvard cult following the ideas of the Italian sociologist Vilfredo Pareto. During the Great Depression and its noisily radical politics, Pareto's ideas on how elites preserve social order appealed to Henderson. Despite having no credentials in sociology, Henderson taught a seminar on Pareto that soon became one of Harvard's best known and most influential courses, drawing interest from faculty and students in many disciplines.

Pareto held that elites maintain social order with idealized "derivations" of "residues"—inescapable drives such as sociability and self-preservation. Most ethical discussion, according to Pareto, is a derivation—window dressing for propping up the established order. It usually succeeds, especially if the elite has the stomach to back its moral assertions with force.

But Mayo revised Pareto, saying that modern society changed so rapidly that rationalized social ideals could not keep pace. Not Pareto's derivations and residues but psychological knowledge and therapeutic skill were the tools by which the modern elite would preserve social order. It all came together in the 1930s cry of conservative Harvard faculty for a therapeutic elite for American business. As Donham put it, "either we must succeed in providing a rational coordination of impulses and thoughts, or . . . see the collapse of the upward striving of our race."

Mayo established his therapeutic bona fides by becoming Harvard's unofficial shrink, often transforming the lives of troubled students referred to him by other faculty. The burden quickly became too much, so Mayo trained associates and students in clinical psychology. The trainees, as one of them reported, came to look on Mayo "as a kind of sorcerer."

Under his guidance, a patient would quickly "begin to pierce the crust of his symptoms and approach what was bothering him underneath."

Finding a research project to justify the Rockefeller grant was Mayo's largest challenge. Donham got him into New England companies, but middle managers and foremen usually viewed Mayo as a threat and blocked access to workers.

Mayo wrote up some ideas for the burgeoning film industry. He argued that monopolistic domination of the movies awaited the first studio to give up the star system with its meretricious egoism. Hollywood did not call.

But Mayo's luck held. In October 1927, Donham had arranged for him to speak to a business group at the New York Harvard Club. Explaining how he had used rest periods to improve the health and raise the output of textile workers, he made an especially strong impression on T. K. Stevenson of the Western Electric Company, which was experimenting with rest periods at its Hawthorne Plant.

The Hawthorne Experiment

By the 1920s, a half-century of experience in mass production had taught American firms to look for profit in economies of scale. So Western Electric, the manufacturing subsidiary of AT&T, had concentrated production of telephone equipment in the giant Hawthorne works in Cicero, Illinois, not far from Al Capone's headquarters. With 40,000 workers in the plant, small gains in individual productivity could mean big savings, stirring management interest in what was then called "personnel research."

Hot questions among industrial engineers of the 1920s included whether employees worked better under natural light that came free from the sun or under costly electric light. Some, like Frank Gilbreth, favored windows and white walls. General Electric disagreed, claiming that electric light paid its cost ten times over in workers' increased output. Wanting the claim endorsed by a neutral party, GE persuaded the National Research Council to sponsor a study at Hawthorne.

But the experiment proved nothing. Productivity rose with more light and also with less. The human subjects, as the experimenters recognized almost from the beginning, differed from chemicals in a test tube. Knowing that they were being watched, they worked harder—the "Hawthorne effect" as it is still famously known.

The ambiguous results were especially disappointing to George Pennock, Hawthorne's technical superintendent. Stuck in low-prestige manufacturing, he saw personnel research as his best chance to distinguish himself within science-oriented AT&T. Thus, he began to test the effect of changes in working conditions other than light—rest breaks, shorter hours, and midmorning meals.

In April 1927, the well-lit space previously used for the illumination study became the eventually famous Relay Assembly Test Room. Five young women, mainly from Eastern European immigrant families, sat at a bench and assembled springs, armatures, and insulators into four-inch-long "relays"—electromagnetic switches. They dropped finished relays into chutes, tripping an electric gate that enabled a ticker tape machine to track each woman's production.

Pennock had chosen Adeline Bogatowicz and Irene Rybacki for their strong personalities, in the hope that observation would not bias their work. Letting them choose three more participants, he asked them to work "at a comfortable pace." Pennock was studying the effect of changed working conditions, not extra effort.

Yet Pennock immediately gave the women strong economic incentive for extra effort by making the Test Room into a pay group. Hawthorne calculated piece-rate wages on the basis of departmental rather than individual production. In the main Relay Assembly Department, with its 100-plus workers, an individual's over- or underperformance did not much affect her pay or that of others workers. But in the Test Room, more effort would raise a worker's pay along with that of her four comrades. The women, knowing that Pennock wanted to control variables and would not cut the piece rate, let their fingers fly. Production rose by roughly 10 percent by the end of 1927.

Further easing the workers' fear of authority was the absence of their foreman back in the main assembly room. The Test Room observer, a man named Homer Hibarger, was not their boss, as he made clear by

engaging them in banter. Soon, they greeted Hibarger with a playful
"Hi!" The women chatted while working, listened to the radio, and
held parties to celebrate their birthdays, all unthinkable in the main
department.

Inevitably came the clash. In late 1927, Rybacki's output fell a bit as
she discussed men, movies, and marriage with Bogatowicz. Hibarger
stepped out of his role as observer and told her to stop talking. She defied him with loud chants: "We do what we want, we work how we feel
and we say what we know." Reprimanded by Pennock, Rybacki pointed
out that he was violating the experiment's protocol: "For the love of Mike!
They tell you to work how you feel, and when you do it, it isn't good
enough . . . ."

Bogatowicz led the women in resisting Hibarger's gaze at a time when
hemlines were well above the knee. She asked for a screen to shield the
women's legs, a request on which he delayed action until she said they
could work faster if they weren't constantly tugging down their dresses.
Bogatowicz also got "antagonistic," as Hibarger noted, at monthly physical examinations when doctors asked about the timing of her menstrual
cycle. The final straw came when Hibarger overheard Bogatowicz and Rybacki discussing whether to work faster or hold back effort. Pennock replaced them with two of the fastest assemblers from the main department, ensuring new production records.

Meanwhile, Pennock could not figure out, as he told the women,
whether their increased output was "due to the small gang; the lunches;
the rest periods . . . or what?" He had no interest in the obvious explanation that the women raised production in return for higher wages. More
work for more pay would not advance Pennock's star in the company. He
wanted more work for the same pay.

Western Electric's personnel director, T. K. Stevenson, may have given
Pennock the idea of having "a man come out from one of the colleges and
see what he can tell us about what we've found out." Stevenson remembered the impressive talk he had heard Mayo give at the Harvard Club in
New York. He sent Mayo a preliminary report on the experiment and invited him to visit Hawthorne at the company's expense.

PHOTO 5.2 The Relay Assembly Test Room with Rybacki (second from right) and Bogatowicz (right) in the foreground.

Arriving in April 1928, Mayo could scarcely have helped seeing the AT&T experiment as confirmation of his Australian idea that corporate monopolies could recreate at work the communal harmony of preindustrial society. He quickly set about using the experiment's results to prove his preconceived ideas.

As his first contribution, Mayo explained Rybacki's recalcitrance as a result of neurosis. Her medical record showed a low red blood count, evidence of "pessimistic or paranoid preoccupations." Omitting and maybe not knowing that Pennock had transferred Rybacki out of the experiment, Mayo told senior management in New York, that she had been "permitted to withdraw because . . . she 'turned Bolshevik.'"

When he returned to Hawthorne in October 1928, Mayo helped explain other unwanted results. As an experimental control, Pennock had temporarily returned working conditions to their original state—no rest breaks, no snacks, no short hours. Expecting productivity to drop with a return to original conditions, Pennock was left befuddled when output kept rising. Mayo assured Pennock that confusion was "a sign of health" in scientific research. The experimenters had to "wait for a new illumination to reveal itself."

A shaft of new light directed by Mayo soon revealed that gentler supervision in the Test Room had allowed the workers to overcome industrial anomie, forming them into an organic social group that worked with a will. Here was the answer to Pennock's question about why production had not fallen with a return to original conditions. The group's spirit was so strong that "any theory that there was 'a return to original conditions' is nonsensical."

Mayo helped win acclaim for the experiment, explaining with his customary panache to Pennock's superiors that gentle supervision created better group dynamics. Both Mayo and Pennock reported on the experiment at a 1929 meeting of the Personnel Research Federation. Mayo, in his paper, began to distinguish himself from Taylor by criticizing what he later called the "blind spot in scientific management." He rejected Taylorist bullying on practical grounds: "[T]he supervisor is expected to yell and bawl and swear . . . . So he 'talks' and does not 'listen'; and he never learns what is really wrong."

Pennock, sold on Mayo by now, put him up at expensive hotels and had him squired around Chicago in a chauffeur-driven limousine. He offered Mayo a job at Hawthorne, wined and dined him in his home, and even had him counsel his son, who was having trouble at school. Soon the boy was doing better.

When Pennock came up with the idea of interviewing all employees to get their ideas for improving supervision, Mayo easily redirected him toward therapy. Mayo trained the interviewers in nondirective listening, and the workers seem to have spoken freely, making the experience useful as a steam valve. An internal company memo soon noted, "Until Doctor Mayo came along the most important uses for the interview seemed to be in Supervisory Training and Research work. As we know, he revealed what seems to be the greatest use of all—emotional release."

The interviews turned up plenty of grievances against management, but Mayo cautioned Pennock against his excessively democratic tendency to accept workers' ideas at face value: "[A]n attitude of hostility towards a 'boss' includes always something of falsification." Complaints, in Mayo's analysis, never reflected a supervisory problem but instead revealed a need for therapy for some problem in the worker's home, family, or love life.

The goal of interviewing every employee even once, let alone yearly as had been planned, turned out to be impossible with the staff allotted to the program. Would the company have to forgo employees' emotional release and the higher productivity that came with it?

Again, Mayo provided the solution—turn supervisors into therapists. The Test Room's rising productivity had come from workers' relaxed conversations with the experimenters, amounting to "continuous interviewing" that provided ongoing emotional release. To get the same productivity gains throughout the plant, every supervisor would have to be a therapist.

Mayo personally launched Hawthorne's program for teaching supervisors therapeutic skills. Speaking to an audience of 200 managers, he explained the evils of "bullyragging" and the benefit of understanding. The company's training materials soon urged that the supervisor, instead of blaming the worker, should "get the employee to analyze the case himself . . . . This can be done by questions and repetitions of statements already made by the employee. The supervisor should remember that free expression will go a long way toward relieving emotional pressure."

Like today's gurus, Mayo aimed to give management audiences a rush of inspiration and motivation, which requires energy and charisma on the part of the teacher. Mayo had buckets of charisma, but his energy always flagged quickly. After five visits to Hawthorne in 1929, he cut back to one or two visits a year, even though Western Electric paid him a handsome annual retainer. Sending younger Harvard colleagues such as the almost equally charismatic W. Lloyd Warner in his place, Mayo hoped, as he told his wife in 1931, that his "absence this year won't be noticed as much as last year."

Mayo's absence almost cost him control of the experiment. William Dickson, a Hawthorne manager influenced by Warner, decided to start a new test room that would combine observation with interviewing. In the "Bank Wiring Test Room," established early in 1931, fourteen men worked on the direct dial machinery that was beginning to replace switchboard operators. Observers watched the workers solder banks of wires across which mechanical selectors would move to connect calls. The observers also conducted interviews, aimed not at therapy but at learning about the workers' ideas.

Dickson's findings in the Bank Wiring Test Room contradicted almost everything Mayo said about the Relay Assembly Test Room. Where Mayo attributed the relay assemblers' group identity to therapeutic management, Dickson said that the bank wirers achieved social solidarity in opposition to management. Mayo called Rybacki's holding back of effort an exception due to paranoia, but Dickson found routine "restriction of output" and, in italics, attributed it to the workers' rational fears: *The function of restriction of output . . . is to protect the worker from management's schemes.*

Still worse for Mayo's interpretation, Dickson extrapolated from the Bank Wiring Test Room and concluded that better pay explained the relay assemblers' soaring production. To get similar plantwide productivity increases, Dickson implied, management only had to guarantee piece rates, an idea uncomfortably similar to the approach of Frederick Taylor, whom Mayo was supposedly leaving in the dust.

Mayo, making one of his rare visits to Hawthorne at the time, seems to have gotten Dickson under control, probably with his magic charm. Dickson came around to the idea, as he later put it, that the workers held back effort because of "social factors" within the group rather than hostility to management. With dissent quelled, Mayo kept on minimizing the obvious fact that higher pay was the reason the relay assemblers raised their output. He claimed it was originally Pennock's idea, not his, that although pay had "some small part" in the output surge, it was mostly "due to changes in mental attitude."

By minimizing pay as a motivator, Mayo met Pennock's need for the experiment to have some economic benefit to Western Electric. Assembly of telephones was not capital-intensive work. As opposed to Taylor's machine shop innovations, higher speed from higher wages would produce no offsetting savings in machinery costs. Only noneconomic motivators for high-speed work would improve Western Electric's bottom line.

Mayo succeeded in selling his unlikely vision because he genuinely believed it. There was nothing contrived about his dream of making corporations into the organic communities that he believed democracy had destroyed in the rest of society. The vein of charlatanism in Mayo owed some of its effectiveness to his generous intentions and passionate convictions, enabling him to make believers of others. His more honest underling at Harvard, Fritz Roethlisberger, detected no ambivalence in Mayo and enthusiastically joined in teaching his ideas. By creating "Organizational Behavior" as a basic course at the Harvard Business School, Roethlisberger built an institutional base that enabled human relations and therapeutic management to outlive Mayo.

The Birth of Organizational Behavior

In the early 1930s, Mayo talked up the Hawthorne findings, then used the resulting interest to persuade Clarence Stoll, the plant manager, that the world would welcome a book on the experiment. Stoll stipulated that author's credit go to Western Electric because it had run the experiment. Pennock, evidently wanting none of Mayo's grandiose speculation, added that the book had to be "an account of the actual happenings rather than a discussion of implications." Despite these provisos, *The Human Problems of an Industrial Civilization* appeared in 1933 with only Mayo's name on the spine. And the book contained plenty of the big ideas Pennock had sought to avoid.

Yet Mayo made it hard for Western Electric to complain. Acknowledging the company's sole sponsorship of the experiment, he shrewdly credited Pennock for what was really his own idea—a new social situation had caused Test Room production to soar. By attributing his big ideas about Hawthorne to Pennock, Mayo was able to present himself as a reporter of empirical facts.

With his objectivity established, Mayo excitedly depicted the Relay Assembly Test Room as a near utopia. Forgetting Rybacki and Bogatowicz, he claimed, "At no time in the five-year period did the girls feel that they were working under pressure." Therapeutic supervision had created a "new industrial milieu" that paradoxically raised production by subordinating the company's interest to that of workers, a "milieu in which their own self-determination and their social well-being ranked first and the work was incidental." Not wild fantasy this, but "mere description of an empirical kind."

To create such communities was the elevated mission of the "new administrator"—the vision of the manager as civilization's savior that had charmed Donham into hiring Mayo at Harvard. By restoring workers' "capacity for collaboration in work," managers would also quell unreasonable democratic conflict: "The political function cannot operate in a community from which this capacity has disappeared."

Had the Hawthorne experiment depended for its fame and influence on Mayo's somewhat feverish book, it might well have been forgotten. He devoted only forty pages to Hawthorne, the rest of the book ranging with Mayo's typical ease across a dozen topics such as his work with Philadelphia textile workers, Pareto, and the need for a new "administrative *elite.*"

But Mayo had chosen well in making the scrupulous Roethlisberger his right-hand man. Roethlisberger, not understanding that his patron sold himself by his grandeur, feared the consequences of Mayo's disdain for anything resembling a report of his activities to the Rockefeller Foundation. When the Hawthorne records came to Harvard in the mid-1930s, Roethlisberger decided to write a thorough account of the Hawthorne experiment to show that the human relations group had given value for money received.

To Harvard along with the Hawthorne records came William Dickson, his Western Electric job preserved during the depression by Mayo's Rockefeller grant. Having abandoned his earlier idea of a conflict between Hawthorne workers and bosses, Dickson was judged a safe pair of hands. He joined Roethlisberger in writing *Management and the Worker* (1939), a huge tome that helped give the Hawthorne experiment credibility as legitimate social science.

Grinding away for several years, Roethlisberger and Dickson produced one of the dullest books ever written. Offering little that was new except copious detail on the already well-known experiment, they had trouble finding a publisher until Mayo used Rockefeller money to subsidize publication by Harvard University Press. To the surprise of all involved, *Management and the Worker* went through multiple printings, its 600-page heft adding to its usefulness as a prop in the offices of personnel managers.

In *Management and the Worker*, Roethlisberger and Dickson loyally did their best to support Mayo's ideas. The relay assemblers had built "a new type of spontaneous social organization" because management allowed them "to develop their own values and objectives," giving "sustained meaning to their work." Not realizing that they were codifying for American management the patronizing denial of conflict that Mayo brought with him from Australia, Roethlisberger and Dickson said that the Hawthorne findings promised "profit" to employers and "satisfaction" to employees through "working together."

However, the honest Roethlisberger and Dickson squirmed as they tried to reconcile Mayo's interpretive fantasy with their thorough presentation of the Hawthorne data. They had to explain, for example, a second experiment with relay assemblers that Mayo had conveniently omitted. To assess the effect of increased earnings in the Test Room, Pennock had made five assemblers in the main department into a separate pay group for nine weeks. Their productivity shot up 15 percent, then fell below normal when they went back to the old pay scheme. With more time and security, they might have gone on to match the ultimate 25-percent-plus gain in the test room. Hibarger at the time drew the obvious conclusion that "pay has been an important item in increasing output in the test room," a finding useless to Pennock, who let the second test drop, just as Mayo left it unmentioned.

But Roethlisberger and Dickson, with their comprehensive description of the Hawthorne experiment, could not dodge the data as Mayo had, so they admitted that pay was "an important factor" in both the Test Room and the main department. That left them with the job of finding a social cause for increased productivity in the main department so they could uphold Mayo's emphasis on social factors in the Test Room. The best they could come up with was the claim of the Test Room workers that their counterparts in the main department had raised production out of a sense of rivalry. On the basis of this thin evidence, Roethlisberger and Dickson claimed that "[c]onclusions about the efficacy of a wage incentive . . . unrelated to the basic social situation, would have been entirely misleading."

Roethlisberger and Dickson also proved less adept than Mayo at putting a human face on the idea that workers' complaints were "irrelevant." They expressed more forthrightly than Mayo their indifference as to "the 'real' state of affairs with regard to smoke and fumes," about which some Hawthorne workers complained. Only subjective attitudes counted: "[H]opes and fears . . . existed. To decide which were justified and which were not, to correct the former and to ignore the latter, was to lose sight of the real problem"—the "emotional significance" of complaints.

Unwittingly revealing the moral superiority of Taylorist bullying to therapeutic tyranny, Roethlisberger and Dickson said that an in-depth interview that began with a worker's grumbling about foul air might end with discovery of his neurotic "fear of contracting pneumonia." The bullying boss would have told the worker to shut up about the fumes and left the man the compensation of his resentful thoughts. The therapeutic tyrant would require the worker not only to breathe foul air but to like it.

—◦—

The early 1940s were a hard time for Mayo at Harvard, where he had alienated many colleagues. Some management faculty objected to what they saw as Mayo's too-soft approach to management. And he had offended rather than charmed others with his ability to substitute intellectual dexterity for painstaking research. Slowing down in the late 1930s from even his previous languid pace, he worked notoriously short hours. Arriving at the office in midmorning, he whiled away time talking with faculty and students, then concluded his day with a late lunch and sherry at a Harvard Square restaurant. Some faculty members saw Mayo's regimen, or lack of one, as a childish taunt of their own stronger work ethic. Mayo, said one colleague, "had a bit of the juvenile delinquent in him."

In 1942, Donham gave up his dean's post, leaving Mayo exposed. The new dean, Donald David, challenged him on the gaping void between him and the rest of the faculty. Mayo replied with his customary truth stretching, claiming that his travels to Hawthorne had involved much time away from Harvard, separating him from his colleagues. In fact, he had spent little time at Hawthorne.

David clearly would have preferred that he leave, but Mayo had to tough out a few more years at Harvard, his life's savings having been consumed by the rescue of his younger daughter, who had been trapped behind enemy lines at the start of World War II. In 1939, she had married a Polish refugee in France and then was stranded there with a newborn baby during the German occupation. Her autobiography, recounting her expensive and harrowing escape, also tells how before the war, during a family holiday in Italy, a local lad had courted her. Mayo had raged impressively, thrown furniture at the boy, and driven him off. But when she arrived in the United States after fleeing the Nazis, she found her father's vigor declining. Afflicted by a mild case of glaucoma, Mayo had adopted a long cigarette holder to keep the fumes away from his eyes. Antagonistic Harvard colleagues saw the cigarette holder as an affectation, one more indication of his aloof superiority.

Mayo spent his last years at Harvard trying to broaden his focus from industry to society and politics. Warning that "democracy" will not "act as a magic talisman" in a "society internally divided by group hostilities," he feared that "sheer ignorance of administrative methods in the political and industrial leaders of the democracies may give rise to increasing disabilities of cooperation." The economic coordination that had won the war exemplified the ideal relationship between manager and employee— "logical and purposive control from above, spontaneous and cooperative control from below." Democracy was fine as long as the lower-downs willingly followed the higher-ups.

In 1947, he retired from Harvard and left immediately for England, completing the journey interrupted a quarter century earlier when dwindling funds had trapped him in the United States. He may have believed that he still had a historic role to play in Europe: "If our social skills had advanced step by step with our technical skills, there would not have been another European war." Grandiose as ever, Mayo still saw his idea of substituting therapy for democracy as the way to save civilization from social disorder.

But the English did not seem to want saving. Mayo, struggling once more with the grim job of starting a new life in a new land, finally ran out of luck. Negotiations for a job at Britain's National Institute for Industrial Psychology fell through when officials learned that he would not be bringing Rockefeller money with him.

With his small Harvard pension taxed twice, first in the United States and then even more severely in socialist England, Mayo had to take whatever work he could get. Only visiting lectures could be arranged, and the strain of travel to give them brought on a stroke. It took almost two more years for Mayo to reach the end of his adventurous road. He died on September 1, 1949.

The future of the human relations movement lay in the United States, especially at Harvard, where, absent Mayo and the personal animus he provoked in his colleagues, his ideas now had a chance to enter the curriculum. Only Fritz Roethlisberger remained to carry the torch. Henderson had died in 1941. Warner, never a subscriber to Mayo's narrow psychological focus, had gone to the University of Chicago. Whitehead had left to serve in the war.

Roethlisberger, though always personally loyal to Mayo, had eased himself out from under his unpopular mentor. Moving his office well away from Mayo's, Roethlisberger had built connections with the rest of the faculty. Unlike Mayo, he enjoyed teaching and worked to include human relations in the Administrative Practices course taught to first-year MBA students in the 1950s.

Roethlisberger's bridge-building to the Harvard faculty moved him toward amoral realism. Hard-nosed professors at the Business School had accused him of teaching the Golden Rule instead of business methods, so Roethlisberger opted for scientific over humanistic values. Creating a new area of study within the Business School's doctoral program, he named it Organizational Behavior to indicate his empirical, amoral concern with

"the way people did behave—and not should behave—in organizations."
As the Harvard OB program graduated doctoral students who became
professors elsewhere, tough-minded psychological realism became part
of the general business-school ethos.

Yet the coming of OB realism amounted to a rebalancing, not a dismissal of Mayo's fuzzy mix of therapy and management, healing and productivity. If anything, OB's ostensible tough-mindedness lent credibility
to Mayo's soft ideas, his underestimation of both the necessity and danger
of top-down power, his idea of the manager as therapist with the accompanying temptation of psychological manipulation, his hyper fear of conflict, and his utopian claim that the interests of employer and employee
can be merged in a workplace where the principal reward is not money
but organic community.

Mayo helped shape a managerial culture that could coexist with a democratic society. His idea of willing, bottom-up cooperation meshed well
with the consciences of American managers committed to democratic
values. Top-down power, not to mention tyranny, seemed superfluous in
organizations where people worked with social spirit and outproduced
those driven by mere coercion and incentive pay. The next logical step in
the development of management ideas was for Chester Barnard, a friend
and associate of both Mayo and the Harvard Business School, to explain
what kind of person it takes to lead a bottom-up organization.

6

The Leader: Chester Barnard

Managing a Riot

TRENTON, NEW JERSEY. TUESDAY, APRIL 23, 1935.

In the grim sixth year of the Great Depression, eighteen leaders of Trenton's unemployed citizens are meeting with Chester Barnard, director of New Jersey's Emergency Relief Administration. Outside, 2,000 relief recipients are demonstrating for better treatment. Inside, Barnard has eased the tension by shaking hands with each of his eighteen guests, who are obviously suffering from "worry, malnutrition, and desperation."

Suddenly, shouting erupts outside. Rushing to the window, Barnard looks down into a street full of mayhem. The police, nightsticks flying, are attacking the scattering crowd. Five are arrested, one of them beaten badly enough to need hospitalization.

Inside, the demonstrators' spokesmen lament the violence and urge Barnard to postpone the meeting. Setting the next Tuesday to reconvene, he suggests that eight representatives of the unemployed will be enough. Afterward, he learns from his chauffeur, who has been waiting for him in the street, that the trouble started with an accidental shove and a few harsh words, bringing a violent overreaction from the police.

This incident still influences corporate life today because of a 1938 Harvard lecture Barnard gave in the Pareto seminar run by his friend Professor Lawrence Henderson. In his lecture, Barnard used the riot to explain his now enormously influential idea that the manager does not

PHOTO 6.1   A newspaper photograph of police attacking demonstrators against the New Jersey relief program managed by Chester Barnard.

wield top-down power but leads by moral influence. He claimed to have used his human relations skills to handle "revolutionary conditions" while heading off further demonstrations by the unemployed.

A seeming exemplar of the sort of socially responsible manager Elton Mayo wanted to educate at the Harvard Business School, Barnard reported that he used the people-handling skills he had developed in corporate life to control the democratic excesses of the dangerous classes. As president of one of his state's most prominent corporations, New Jersey Bell Telephone Company, Barnard had been involved in relief work since early in the depression. At the behest of the governor, Barnard had taken charge of creating New Jersey's relief program for the unemployed, whose numbers had outrun the capacity of charities and churches. After eighteen months he resigned, only to have the program mismanaged by successors. The unemployed organized to protest. The governor, seeing the need for a strong hand, pressed Barnard back into service in 1935. The riot had come within days of his resuming command.

Fearing a public relations disaster, Barnard aimed to prevent further demonstrations. He wanted to protect the unemployed from themselves. Their militancy "threatened . . . the relief organization of the entire State." Many taxpayers resented relief, which by 1935 consumed half of the state's budget. If political support for relief were to evaporate, tens of thousands of families might be left to beg or go hungry. The "revolutionary conditions" would be intensified. Who knew what might happen?

Putting to work the cool civility he had learned in corporate life, Barnard tried to spare the protesters further indignity. The arrested demonstrators were to be tried just two days after the riot. Barnard requested, as he told his Harvard audience, "that the least possible punishment be given" to the men, his terseness indicating the unseemliness of what he likely did, working behind the scenes to influence a judge. At the trial, the unemployed jammed the courtroom and jeered when the police chief testified that only one cop had used his nightstick. Barnard may have gotten his chauffeur's story to the judge, who dismissed the charges, saying the police had "lost their heads."

Meanwhile, to forestall inflammatory newspaper articles, Barnard made a statement to the *Trenton Evening Times* that relief was merely "public decency." The paper's editor reassured needy citizens and the tax-loathing public: "Fortunately, Mr. Barnard, even while entertaining rational faith in the . . . rank and file unemployed, recognizes the continuing need for a maximum of vigilant economy."

Barnard had credibility as both a humanitarian and a cost cutter thanks to his no-layoff policy at New Jersey Bell. The company had lost 100,000 customers in the depression and had to reduce its labor costs. Holding as closely as he could to policies of the kind recommended by President Hoover and Lillian Gilbreth, Barnard had preserved jobs by cutting back all employees' hours instead of dismissing some of the employees. Because prices fell during the depression, lower pay from shorter hours did not necessarily leave employees much worse off than before.

New Jersey's needy could take comfort in Barnard's sincere desire to do his best for them.

Barnard resumed his meeting with the unemployed the next Tuesday. Just as he had requested, the relief recipients sent eight representatives, not the unmanageable eighteen from the first meeting. Barnard went alone so that the unemployed, outnumbering him eight to one, had less reason to fear his superior position—just the first of many skillful human relations ploys by which he claimed to control the situation.

Barnard patiently listened to "trivial" grievances in order to meet the relief recipients' need "for self-expression and recognition." They complained that the food allowance of 6 cents per meal per person was inadequate, especially when paid in vouchers usable only at approved stores, limiting recipients' ability to shop for the best price. Able-bodied men, if they accepted jobs on public works, got cash instead of vouchers, plus a 20-percent bonus. But supervisors treated them harshly, knowing they had to take the abuse or lose the bonus that fed their families.

After two hours of respectful listening, Barnard turned to his goal of quelling political demonstrations. Moving swiftly from a sympathetic to a confrontational stance, he vowed that he would "be God damned if I will do anything . . . because you organize mass meetings." Protests alienated "the very people upon whom you or I depend to get the money for relief, and I assure you there are many who object to giving it now." One of the men, red with anger, jumped to his feet to protest. Only the rich, he claimed, were so ignorant of hard times that they begrudged aid to the unemployed.

No, said Barnard. The rich objected to taxes, but the "people who are most opposed to you . . . are those nearest to you—those just one jump ahead of the bread line." To Barnard's surprise the most radical member of the group, a Socialist agitator, agreed: "He's dead right. That's the crowd we have to fear."

Tension dissipated. Barnard and the unemployed had found a common enemy—proletarians still working who resented giving aid. The men decided that "we better leave it in Mr. Barnard's hands. He is . . . out to do the best he can for us."

What a triumph of people handling! Barnard told Henderson's Pareto seminar that he had never before "made a purely personal accomplishment the equal of this." He attributed his success to his tact in shaking the men's hands and generally respecting their "Personal Integrity," one of Pareto's "residues." The small group situation, Barnard said, brought to the fore Pareto's "Instinct of Combinations," driving the Socialist agitator to identify with the AT&T executive.

Barnard easily outshone the other speakers in Henderson's Pareto seminar, mainly academics with experience less dramatic than subduing the *lumpenproletariat*. Henderson called the lecture the best sociological analysis he had heard, confirming Barnard's status at Harvard as not only a master manager but also a deep thinker.

The most intellectually gifted businessman of his generation, Barnard lived a double life as worldly manager and ascetic scholar, reading voraciously in several languages and staying up to date in the social sciences. For the Harvard group, he exemplified the elitist virtuosity in social theory by which the new administrator would not just make money but also defend civilization against the rabble.

Barnard had serendipitously fallen into the lap of the human relations group, which made him a sort of auxiliary member. A former Harvard student, he served on university visiting committees where he met Donham and Mayo. They must have been astonished to find a CEO who had read Pareto *before* encountering Henderson and his near manic advocacy of the Swiss-Italian sociologist at Harvard in the 1930s.

In Barnard's idea of the senior manager as a moral leader, not a top-down boss, the human relations group found a way to extend its ideas on gentle supervision from the shop floor into the executive suite. Advocacy by Harvard-trained professors at the raft of midcentury business schools elsewhere turned moral leadership into a pervasive tenet of today's management culture, influencing the self-image and actions of managers around the world, even if they have never heard of Chester Barnard.

Yet Barnard's riot lecture—in which he most effectively expressed his idea of moral leadership—omitted some key facts and got others wrong. Reading Barnard's lecture today, it is natural to suspect him of overdramatizing the "revolutionary conditions." After all, the demonstrators had been peaceful until the police attacked. And their leaders inside did not get "hostile or bellicose" in the face of violence. It might seem that Barnard overemphasized their activism to impress his Harvard audience.

But in fact he did just the opposite. Barnard greatly understated the activism of the Trenton unemployed. Aside from mentioning that they had "organized" themselves, he omitted the fact that the riot climaxed a two-week-old strike of 1,600 unemployed men who refused to report for public work. The strike deprived the taxpayers of any return on their relief money and put state projects involving, according to a newspaper estimate, 6,000 other workers "virtually at a standstill."

Why did he omit evidence from his riot lecture of the strength and importance of the social movement he subdued? Barnard was a man of considerable integrity, much more so, certainly, than Mayo. But Barnard faced the same moral challenges of managerial power, including the intellectually and ethically dangerous opportunity to grind whatever theoretical ax he chose to explain the behavior of those beneath him. And he was aware that the Harvard human relations group had a large ax to grind—the downplaying of money in favor of organic community and social recognition as motives for work, as had supposedly been demonstrated in the Hawthorne experiment.

Devaluing economics in favor of psychological factors, Barnard said the unemployed were driven not by material want but by their "starving to be recognized," a hunger for respect that was "literally more important to these personalities than more or less food for themselves or their families." So why did they demand a higher food allowance? The well-fed Barnard admitted the food allowance was "insufficient" but denied it drove the protest, claiming "little was made of it."

Not true. A Trenton newspaper reported that the strikers wanted the "amount allowed for food relief to be increased 35 percent." One paper quoted Barnard himself that the protesters wanted "a very large increase in food allowance." And newspaper accounts show that, contrary to what Barnard told his Harvard audience, he ended the protests not merely by skillful people-handling but by promising to ask the relief council for more money. The unemployed made much, not "little," of money and food.

Barnard's understatement of the relief recipients' activism becomes understandable in the face of their emphasis on food and money. Had he emphasized their demand for a higher food allowance and his promise to try to get them more money, his lecture would not have supported so well the Harvard Business School doctrine that organic community and social recognition were powerful management tools. In the actual situation, Barnard had reacted with decency. But in the superoxygenated atmosphere of Henderson's seminar, he analyzed the riot by using the psychologically manipulative framework of the Harvard human relations group.

Barnard's idea of the manager as moral leader would create a deeper elitism than the bossism it replaced. He would claim that power is bottom-up and that managers lead by "influence," plus (if fortunate enough to have passed through the Harvard Business School) a rare understanding of human relations. This idea of the leader's moral superiority and arcane psychological knowledge, serving organizational alchemy beyond the ken of simple folk, gave management an element of priest craft, implying a vast distance between leader and follower. Employees today still struggle in the moral confusion that Barnard created. His mélange of off-putting elitism and tempting bottom-up community reflected his ambivalence about the working class from which he had risen.

The Scholar as Manager

Many of Barnard's subordinates found him a chilling person with a "semi-aristocratic demeanor." He probably owed the emotional wall separating him from others to his partially orphaned childhood. But his underlings, with no idea of his origins, never got used to his passing them in the street without even a nod, his failing to acknowledge them socially when they happened to eat in the same restaurant.

Barnard eventually surmounted his isolation intellectually, if not emotionally, and came to see all human achievement as social. But in youth he was a naïve individualist: "I looked upon the family, the social groups of which I was a part, the schools and universities, the railroads, the organizations of industry, the government, as things made available to me by nature."

Barnard's youthful belief that he lived on his own made sense, given how little parental support he had while growing up in Malden, Massachusetts. His father, listed in town directories as a "nickel plater," probably worked in one of several Malden plants that built electric motors. But after Barnard's mother died in childbirth in 1891, when he was five years old, the boy went to live with his maternal grandfather.

Later, maybe wishfully, Barnard described his father as a teacher of character: "[H]e taught me the wisdom of choice: To try and fail is at least to learn." But elsewhere, he described his father as "too tender-hearted" and lacking "the natural ability to be a real manager of anything." Maybe in reaction to his father's example, Barnard never slipped into softness. His reputation as a management humanist mixes with quiet suggestions of personal ruthlessness.

The brilliant Barnard surely shone as a student, but at fifteen he had evidently claimed all support available from his grandfather and left school for a job in a piano factory. He was already a fine pianist, thanks to his grandfather's musically inclined family. Now, working at a piano factory, he learned to tune the instruments. He had found a trade that could be practiced in off-hours, making it possible to earn a living while resuming his education, secular and religious.

Owing to his "conversion to the Lord Jesus Christ," Barnard wrote in his 1904 application to Mount Hermon School, he sought education "to be used of Him." Barnard had met a Congregational minister who brought the boy to God and steered him back to school at Mount Hermon. In adulthood, Barnard described himself as a "heathen," but religion may have appealed for a time to his strong character. Anyway, Mount Hermon met his worldly needs. Founded by the revivalist Dwight Moody, the Northfield, Massachusetts, school owned fields, orchards, and workshops where boys of humble origin worked off their tuition fees.

Barnard may have experienced crippling fear at stepping out of his family's well-trod working-class path. Suffering from "nervous fever," he took no classes during his first term but only worked in Mount Hermon's fields. Pitching hay and steering a horse-drawn plow—a typical regimen at the time for a nervous breakdown—the lanky Barnard recovered from the only collapse in his otherwise confident life.

In his Christian school, Barnard encountered the "great loyalty and deep faith" that later made human organization seem like a Gnostic deliverance to him. In adulthood he claimed that corporations embody the ethic of his school's evangelical founder: "Said D. L. Moody, 'The reward of service is more service,' which expresses the economy of organization efficiency at its highest level."

Planning to be a lawyer, Barnard studied modern languages and the classics while giving short shrift to science and mathematics. In 1906, after just two industrious years at Mount Hermon, he won admission to Harvard with "conditions" on account of his weakness in chemistry and plane geometry.

Barnard raced through Harvard in three years while supporting himself by typing other students' papers, playing in a dance orchestra, and tuning pianos. He left Harvard in 1909 with enough credits to graduate, provided he removed his entrance deficiencies in math and science. Soon too busy climbing the corporate ladder to bother with geometry, Barnard never got his Harvard degree.

His planned career at the bar had fallen by the way when an uncle working at AT&T put him in touch with Walter Gifford, chief statistician of the company. About the same age as Barnard and destined for the presidency of AT&T, Gifford had figured out that the quickest way to the top was to start there, as a staff member for senior management. He hired Barnard as a clerk and helped build his shining career.

When Barnard started at AT&T, Theodore Vail, the company's visionary president, had begun the acquisition binge that created a national telephone monopoly. By welcoming regulation to protect consumers, Vail countered the arguments of Progressives and Socialists who saw the telephone as an essential communication service, like the mail, that should be owned and run by the government. Vail's monopolistic handiwork lasted until the 1980s, ending with a court-ordered breakup of AT&T.

Barnard, who had studied languages at Harvard, fit neatly into Vail's campaign to fend off nationalization of AT&T. European countries had pioneered the "PT&T" model—government-owned postal, telegraph, and telephone service. Barnard, who read German, French, and Italian, set to work collecting data on European rates and costs to show that AT&T provided better and cheaper service than the PT&Ts.

Also successful in his personal life, at least outwardly, Barnard married up, to a childhood friend of his AT&T mentor, Walter Gifford. Vague suggestions of incompatibility are impossible to substantiate. If the marriage was not happy, Barnard characteristically made the best of it. With a presentable wife and, soon, a charming daughter, he had the respectable family life requisite for AT&T's higher echelons.

The Bell System often lent executives to good causes to establish the monopoly's bona fides as a corporate citizen. Thus, when America entered World War I in 1917, AT&T loaned Gifford and Barnard to the Council of National Defense. Barnard worked on setting phone rates at the optimum level for national economic efficiency.

Gifford and, probably, Barnard ran afoul of Bernard Baruch at the War Industries Board. Where Henry Gantt despised Baruch's ignorance of production, Gifford took issue with his failure to build a systematic organization to run war production: Baruch preferred to work through personal contact with his business cronies.

Baruch's style gave business opportunists easy wartime profits. But after the war, Gifford covered for Baruch to head off anticorporate feelings. Testifying to Congress, Gifford defended wartime economic coordination that never existed, helping to create the myth of an American industrial state that had efficiently organized itself to win the war.

After the war, Gifford scored points at AT&T with an ingenious idea for raising capital. Getting employees to sell stock to friends and relatives, he bypassed public offerings and the expensive services of investment bankers. The scheme also created an enormous public relations asset in AT&T's widely held stock. In those days, few ordinary citizens owned shares and those who did might own just AT&T, soon to become the bluest of blue chips during the depression by never missing a dividend.

Meanwhile, Barnard, thanks to his excellent staff work for top management, vaulted over the drudges working their way up from the bottom and became vice president of Pennsylvania Bell. Next came a CEO job. In 1927 Gifford, who had gotten the presidency of "Telephone" two years earlier, created a new AT&T subsidiary—New Jersey Bell—and made Barnard its president.

For his corporate headquarters, Barnard commissioned a twenty-story skyscraper of exquisite beauty. Situated on Newark's main street, across from what was then a lovely urban park, the building has an enormous facade cut in Greco-Roman and Art Deco motifs. The same mix of antiquity and modernity is pursued inside, for example, in the lobby's splendid eight-foot brass floor lamps, tapering at the neck and then flaring brilliantly outward, perfectly expressing Barnard's combination of classical heart and modern intellect. In his top-floor office paneled with black walnut and warmed by a fireplace of Rosato marble, he was well shut of his childhood poverty.

For modern corporate denizens, it is probably hard to believe that there were ever jobs with as much free time as Barnard enjoyed at New Jersey Bell, with years off at full pay for public service and, when on the job, long hours of self-absorbed reflection and study. With a vice president to handle daily operations, Barnard achieved a level of scholarly productivity that would be envied by many professors today. At New Jersey Bell, he wrote his still influential *The Functions of the Executive.* Two other books have been assembled out of his essays, and he wrote dozens of other articles never since reprinted.

Barnard made himself into the leading sociologist of the corporation in his generation by pondering questions related to the mystery of his own rise. He was neither an entrepreneur nor an engineer but a student of languages and music who had forfeited his Harvard degree by his deficiencies in high school science and mathematics. Yet he had achieved a high position in the world's most technologically advanced corporation and managed thousands of technically oriented employees.

He propounded the idea, increasingly prevalent in his time and ever since, that management is a technique unto itself, as important as technical competence. Chagrined at protests against management of engineers "by those not engineers," Barnard tried to correct Americans' ignorance of their organizational economy. Prosperity "which is usually ascribed exclusively to mechanical invention . . . is as much due to . . . the invention of corporations" and their "operating arts"—that is, management.

Yet Barnard's experience as president of a monopoly left him naive about economic pressures. AT&T headquarters went through the motions of judging the performance of its operating companies against one another, pitting New Jersey Bell's management against Pennsylvania Bell's, and so on. Although Barnard insisted it was a competitive system, he had little experience with market discipline.

Therefore, Barnard was ripe for conversion to the Harvard group's deemphasis of money. In a mid-1930s speech in which he said Mayo had proven the primary importance of "atmosphere" in personnel relations, Barnard added that employers, too, are not motivated by money. Profit, he said another time, was an "over-in-the-corner sort of thing." Asked by students to explain the place of economic considerations in management decisions, Barnard replied that the question "relates to a kind of world of which I have no experience—an economic world." His was an organizational world.

A cautious manager, Barnard husbanded capital. In the 1930s and 1940s, he only slowly adopted direct-dial equipment. Calculating that the new machinery only paid for itself in high-volume metropolitan areas, he apparently disagreed with managers of other Bell operating companies who installed direct dial in rural areas to stimulate calls and raise revenue. By 1947, New Jersey's telephone service was far behind the rest of the country, with 60 percent of the Garden State's phones still requiring operator assistance, while the national average was only 34 percent.

Other Bell managers' earlier conversion to direct dial left them less susceptible than Barnard to wage pressures from switchboard operators. In 1947, New Jersey Bell endured a costly operator strike, leading to the worst financial results of Barnard's tenure as CEO. He soon left for the presidency of the Rockefeller Foundation, a job he got partly because of strong support by Gifford, a foundation trustee, who may have been eager to replace Barnard with a more effective manager at New Jersey Bell.

If Barnard was a cautious manager, he was just the opposite as a scholar, offering a bold interpretation of the large corporations that had come to dominate the economy and whose workings remained an obscure mystery to most Americans. He found insufficient the conventional, resentful explanation of big corporations' success—mountains of capital along with operations on a scale dwarfing the little people and small businesses around them. The corporation owed its triumph, Barnard thought, less to material than spiritual power. From his perch at the top of a monopoly, it seemed to him that corporate employees worked together in a spirit of harmony that made them sing.

Leadership and Democracy

Barnard more than anyone else formulated today's often unrealistic ideal of the manager as a moral leader of others' cooperative efforts, an ideal he derived from self-reflection. As a young staff man at AT&T headquarters, the able Barnard had a lofty view of the company and saw clearly what needed doing. But bureaucratic rigidity and human stupidity often stood in the way. Only his steadiness—an asset as useful as his brilliance—enabled him to endure the frustration of working with others when his own ideas made the best companions.

Chastened by corporate experience, he gradually underwent a change of heart, taking a 180-degree turn toward a conviction that individual talent accomplishes nothing compared to the power of human beings working together. Barnard witnessed employee commitment that expressed a social instinct. Thunderstorms and downed wires brought employees rushing unbidden to work on Sunday. Switchboard operators soon to be replaced with direct-dial machinery nevertheless stayed to the end at their switchboards, so dilapidated and quirky that no one else could operate them.

Barnard's seems to have been an extreme case of the passage sometimes made by idealistic young managers from rugged individualist to
corporate communitarian. Now he had a passive idea of his individual
unimportance: "I was in danger . . . of treating myself as a slightly conscious and unimportant cog in a gigantic machine." But he could not dis-
solve his identity into the company: "I could not eliminate myself from
myself—since my supervisors continued to regard me as an individual."

Here was a discouraging impasse. Just as radical individualism had
earlier proven a false ideal, now absolute community did the same.
Barnard lapsed into "lethargy."

Eventually, he discovered a middle path. He would find both community and personal "self-expression" by "directing my individual efforts not
only in conformance with, but in furtherance of the objectives of the organization." Not "in the philosophies or the theologies" but in the humdrum life of the phone company Barnard found the answer to the "most
vital of all problems of human life," the "universal" problem of the individual and society. He would achieve both individual creativity and social
belonging by working cooperatively to move the company forward.

Out of such pensiveness, Barnard developed the Lowell Institute Lectures that Abbott Lawrence Lowell, Harvard's president, prodded by Henderson, invited him to give in Boston in 1937. Twice weekly for a month
in late autumn, in the Rogers Building on Boylston Street, Barnard spoke
to a small audience composed mainly of the human relations group. Published the following year as *The Functions of the Executive*, Barnard's lectures explained that human organization is an achievement of the spirit
in which a leader influences followers to cooperate and accomplish together what they cannot do alone.

The experience of listening to Barnard's lectures must have been only
moderately less painful than water torture. With his ear for music,
Barnard could write sentences of lovely rhythms, but he freighted them
with abstract diction that requires heroic effort to puzzle out. Yet *The
Functions of the Executive* has been in print for more than sixty years and
is often featured on lists of management must-reads. Its turbid prose
seems to meet some felt need within the management movement for a ca-

balistic book of bottomless meaning: "Legions of leadership trainers, or-ganizational consultants, and business school professors are still teasing out the implications of these words." But despite the atrocious prose, Barnard's main ideas are fathomable.

Barnard's book announced that authority is a "fiction" and that power flows from the bottom up because subordinates can consent, or not consent, to follow "orders." On a visit to the Soviet Union, Barnard had seen the man in the street flout Stalin's rules. Religious edicts, he pointed out, are often honored in the breach. As a manager, he had often been dis-obeyed. Authority, he concluded, is so delicate a flower it cannot "be sup-ported to a great extent merely by coercion." Managers have to be lead-ers, not bosses, who use moral influence to win employees' cooperation.

Barnard's idea that employees can consent or not consent to an order seems to fly in the face of experience. We have all seen servile employees jump with fright to obey the boss's orders. But Barnard, with his socio-logical sophistication, saw an order as a ritual with an occult meaning. An order appears to be an assertion of power by the boss but is really an es-cape from responsibility by the employee. An order is "the process by which the individual delegates upward . . . responsibility." By giving an order, the manager accepts responsibility for an action the employee had the power but not the courage to take on his own.

If the lowly have power, why do they feel powerless? Barnard an-swered that people at the bottom choose to feel powerless in order to dis-guise their moral weakness, their refusal to accept the burden of respon-sibility shouldered by managers. Low-level employees create the "fiction of superior authority" in order to cover up their "reluctance to take re-sponsibility for their own actions in organization."

Barnard's "consent" theory, as it is sometimes called, appeals to the dem-ocratic conscience of management theorists. Ignoring Barnard's insulting implication of moral cowardice in the rank and file, management teach-ers eagerly embrace his claim that managers lack power. "The elevator operator has more power than the CEO," a business school professor once rejoined when I questioned the idea that power is bottom-up. (Slow at repartee, I failed to ask my interlocutor the consequences should the elevator operator exercise his superior power by refusing to take the CEO up to his office.)

Even murderous tyranny, according to Barnard, is an example of bottom-up power: "Many men have destroyed all authority as to themselves by dying rather than yield." The merely verbal nature of this argument becomes apparent by reversing the point of view. There is a sound of bottom-up choice in Patrick Henry's demand: "[G]ive me liberty or give me death." But the same idea does not sound so nice from the mouth of a Hitler: "Do what I say or I will kill you." The oppressed may not think the hereafter a satisfactory place to exercise their bottom-up power.

There is, of course, some truth in Barnard's idea of bottom-up power. As political theorists have long noted, the oppressed often have some reciprocal power. Employees do sometimes thwart managers by withholding cooperation. Barnard spoke aloud the successful manager's secret rule of not overreaching: "There is no principle of executive conduct better established in good organizations than that orders will not be issued that cannot or will not be obeyed. . . to do so destroys authority, discipline, and morale."

Organizations do profit by the cooperation that Barnard said it was the leader's job to foster. But like today's gurus, some of whom unwittingly draw their ideas from him, Barnard understated the importance of top-down power in obtaining cooperation.

Barnard admitted that a great deal of managers' supposedly moral leadership is disingenuous posturing. But such dishonest managers, according to Barnard, inevitably fail. Workers, sensing "nothing more quickly than insincerity," lose "desire for adherence" to corrupt leadership. Therefore, "low morality will not sustain leadership long, its influence quickly vanishes."

Barnard's faith that immorality cannot sustain leadership is refuted by experience. (Or rather, by my experience. Because Barnard made his assertions mainly on the basis of his organizational experience, his readers may counter with theirs.) Immoral leaders do not always forfeit employees' cooperation. People often cooperate out of fear of top-down power. Immoral bosses find natural allies in opportunistic employees. And honest workers may cooperate in order to uphold values their corrupt managers violate.

Contrary to Barnard, there is no self-regulating moral mechanism whereby immoral managers automatically lose in the long run. The corporation is no less morally ambiguous than the rest of life, where bad guys have been known to finish first. Immoral managers can and often do succeed, not just momentarily but over a lifetime.

But experience counts for little against Barnard's appeal to managers' vanity. By exemplary courage in shouldering the existential "burden" of responsibility without power, the leader binds "the wills of men to the accomplishment of purposes . . . beyond their times . . . . Out of the void comes the spirit that shapes the ends of men." A better formula for promoting managers' moral arrogance could scarcely be devised.

Like other top-down moralizers in the corporate world, Barnard was so accustomed to getting his own way under the guise of "cooperation" from his subordinates that he did not realize how much he relied on power. He struck some over whom he had no authority as having "a difficult personality problem." When he served as a director of the Rockefeller Foundation in the early 1940s, some of his colleagues found him "overly ready to pick up his marbles and go home."

Barnard was not alone in pushing arrogant leadership theories in the 1930s, when national and international crises challenged democracy's idea that morality is bottom-up, not top-down. His claims for the moral superiority of the leader were mild compared to those of Der Führer in Germany and Il Duce in Italy. But the most likely influences on Barnard's theory of leadership were probably President Franklin Roosevelt and the political scientist Charles Merriam.

Merriam had worked with Elton Mayo on the Social Science Research Council in the 1920s. The Harvard group would therefore have followed developments closely in 1936 when FDR appointed Merriam to chair the Committee on Administrative Management. Merriam came up with the idea of the White House Office of Management and Budget (OMB), which exercised centralized financial control over the executive branch. The OMB reduced the influence that Congress, with its power of appro-

priation, had used to subvert the president's control over his departments. Merriam's waxing eloquent on leadership as an intangible thing,
different from organization charts, provided a cloak for FDR's expanded
top-down power.

The new ideas on leadership probably circulated around a now un-
traceable network that included the University of Chicago (Merriam's
base), the Harvard Business School, the Social Science Research Council,
and the Rockefeller Foundation. Princeton got in on the act in 1939 by
inviting Barnard to present a lecture, "The Dilemmas of Leadership in a
Democracy." Preparing for the lecture, Barnard wrote to Henderson that
he wanted speak truthfully about a subject usually treated sentimentally.

Speaking forthrightly, Barnard told his Princeton audience that democracy threatens social order by undermining cooperation. By giving citizens a sense of participation and responsibility, democracy causes them
to overinvest emotionally in the political process, leaving them unwilling
to cooperate with decisions they dislike. But in authoritarian systems,
Barnard asserted, people delegate responsibility to leaders and are therefore willing to cooperate. Democracy, inherently fractious, needs skilled
leaders in greater numbers than society is likely to produce.

The rise of management, Barnard thought, might save democracy from
itself. Due to the increase in appointed administrators "not only in government but . . . in corporations," the United States elected a smaller percentage of its leaders than in the past, making it "quite possible that adequate leadership is available" in the "limited degree" needed by
democratic political institutions.

Barnard judged democracy not by Jeffersonian standards of freedom but
by the managerial standard of effective decisionmaking: "Does the democratic process adequately determine what ought to be done?" He doubted it.
In his 1938 *The Functions of the Executive*, Barnard had realistically diagnosed the weakness that arises from democracy's focus on process. Democratic processes create "artificial questions of more or less logical character,
in place of the real questions, which are matters of feeling."

As fighting erupted in Europe in the late 1930s, Barnard did not ask
how to defend democracy but whether democracy could prevent world

chaos. He wasn't sure. In the summer of 1940, when England stood alone against Germany, Barnard wrote to Henderson that the real danger was advanced weaponry that made it vital that some country dominate the world and impose peace. He thought that if the English won, they might have to become as totalitarian as the Nazis in order to do just that.

Barnard's skepticism of democracy's ability to preserve order may have been right or wrong, but it came with his corporate territory, where effectiveness, not freedom, is the primary value. As the corporation becomes increasingly recognized as one of the modern world's most successful institutions, it becomes more important to think clearly about the undemocratic nature of management. Unfortunately, the tendency has been in the opposite direction, with managerial ideas carried unquestioningly into the general culture and public life, as if they amounted to an advance in democratic technique. Here, too, Barnard was a pioneer.

The USO: A Higher Stage of Americanism

By the late 1930s, Barnard had qualified for a nationally prominent role. As a leading management theorist, as president of a profitable depression-era company, and as a pioneer of relief for the unemployed, Barnard was occasionally suggested for a position in the Roosevelt administration. The coming of World War II inevitably brought him a bigger job than running New Jersey Bell. A few months after Pearl Harbor, Barnard became president of the United Service Organizations, soon to be the country's most important volunteer organization supporting the war effort.

An alliance of the YMCA, YWCA, National Jewish Welfare Board, National Catholic Community Service, and the Salvation Army, the USO was a cooperative effort by Protestants, Catholics, and Jews to meet the wartime responsibilities of all three faiths. Blessed by the Roosevelt administration as the country's principal morale-building agency, the USO had attracted the support of John D. Rockefeller, Jr. He recruited Barnard.

As head of the USO, Barnard would help model the cultural consensus of mid-twentieth-century America around the cooperative ethos he had used to reconcile individual freedom and corporate life. World War II and then the Cold War aided the management movement by formulating the problem of democracy and management in a political rather than a merely corporate context. How could the United States preserve individualistic values while developing the centralized military, governmental, and economic structures needed to defeat fascism and then wear down communism? Barnard, with his idea of cooperation as the method of balancing individuality and community, helped Americans convince themselves of their steadfast adherence to democratic mores while marching bravely into a new organizational world.

One element of continuity between older, individualist values and the newer corporate ethos is the American propensity for philanthropy and volunteerism in quantities not remotely approached in most of the rest of the world. Whether or not, as some say, this tradition grew out of pioneer barn raisings and frontier mutual aid, corporations now carefully tend and preserve generosity as a national character trait. Managers almost instinctively provide opportunities for employees to contribute money to the United Way, tutor schoolchildren, pick up roadside trash, build houses for the homeless, and do a thousand other good deeds. All this service, good in itself and useful as a public relations tool, preserves the spirit of voluntary cooperation useful in a corporate economy. No one has better articulated the cultural function of generosity in a managerial society than Barnard did during his wartime leadership of the USO.

The USO ran hundreds of clubs where soldiers and sailors found entertainment as well as spiritual guidance supplied by tens of thousands of volunteer workers and clergy. At USO canteens in railroad stations, soldiers between trains could get a coffee and a chocolate bar, stationery to write a letter home, or a bunk for a nap. To officers and men in distant and boring posts, Barnard's organization distributed over 10 million "victory books." Most famously of all, the USO staged more than 250,000 overseas "camp shows" with marquee-quality entertainers and film stars, enabling the troops, in Barnard's words, to "feel that they were in touch with the civilization back home."

Although the USO eventually succeeded brilliantly, Barnard found chaos in the spring of 1942 when he set up his headquarters in donated space in the Empire State Building. Northern and Southern churches seemed more interested in perpetuating schisms dating to the Civil War than in getting operations running at military bases. No one had taken the trouble to win over the army and navy brass, who looked at USO volunteers as interfering do-gooders more likely to weaken morale than boost it.

Worst of all was the fractious infighting over organizational purpose and philosophy. Was the USO strictly dedicated to service, or did it also have specifically religious goals? If the latter, how could the different faiths possibly work together?

In Barnard's corporate ideal of cooperation he had a ready-made solution to the problem of interfaith relations. Protestants, Catholics, and Jews would fulfill the highest potential of their distinct faiths neither by giving in to sectarian differences nor by ignoring them. They must accept their differences while working together. Barnard's cooperative strategy for balancing rather than escaping the tension between employee and corporation would become the model for sect and society in America.

At the outset Barnard contradicted his cooperative ideal by establishing his top-down control of the USO. At least partly because of Rockefeller's support, he managed to take control of fund-raising and spending, the real determinants of USO policy. Strong measures made enemies. An anonymous source at the Rockefeller Foundation later alluded vaguely to a failure of Barnard's cooperative ideal, "a big fight at the USO, a fight to the last ditch, his was not a tranquil and happy administration."

Yet a large amount of USO authority genuinely did lie at the bottom, in its various religious organizations. At the USO, Barnard had to lead much more by moral influence than he had done in the AT&T hierarchy. His claim that he ran the USO on cooperative principles is documented by a ten-page pamphlet on management that he wrote early in the war for inexperienced USO regional directors. He advised USO managers that "*your responsibilities are very much greater than your authority*," the typical existential burden of the leader as he had described it in *The Functions of the Executive*. Only by cooperating with those above and below them in the organization, as well as those outside it, such as the armed services—

in effect, their customers—would USO managers acquire "influence with all your associates and at headquarters."

To ensure that USO managers used influence rather than authority, Barnard insisted on cooperative resolution of conflicts between faiths. When a USO club managed by the YMCA clashed with one run by the Jewish Welfare Board, they had to settle the problem cooperatively rather than turn to a superior. "Where one agency must yield in the interest of all or in fairness to others," Barnard decreed, "it shall be by persuasion and agreement, not by instruction."

By practicing cooperation, the USO modeled the principle of freedom, at least in Barnard's mind, for which the war was being fought, the right not to escape society's chains but to help determine one's entanglement. Under a more centralized, top-down administration, he would have given "two years only before the USO would degenerate into a merely secular operation." Cooperation was the method for joining in a common enterprise while preserving individual identity, including religious identity.

Barnard judged the USO a success in preserving the cooperative spirit of the American people at large, thanks to huge fund-raising efforts. By war's end, the USO had raised more than $200 million. Critics questioned the usefulness of volunteers working long hours at fund-raising when the USO's budget would have been a pittance for the government to cover with its enormous wartime spending. Barnard answered that war requires so much regimentation that it "is desirable for us, as a people, so far as we can, to conduct our society on a basis of voluntary cooperation" in order to maintain the individualistic "spirit of American civilization."

USO cooperation came to embody a spirit of religious and racial tolerance of which Barnard, for much of his career, had not been a zealous advocate. Before the war, he practiced the white Protestant businessman's ordinary sacrifice of religious tolerance and racial justice to a felt need for corporate harmony. "Personal aversions based upon racial, national, color, and class differences often seem distinctly pernicious," he admitted in *The Functions of the Executive,* "but on the whole they are, in the immediate sense, I believe, based upon a sound feeling of organizational ne-

PHOTO 6.2   Barnard (third from right) at a USO meeting.

cessities." Cooperation and communication in formal and especially informal channels required "compatibility."

Barnard had personal experience with the difficulty of working with an incompatible person of a different faith—in the person of Henry Morgenthau, the secretary of the treasury and a Jew. A few months before Pearl Harbor, Barnard had accepted an invitation to join in the Roosevelt administration's preparation for war. Moving to Washington to work on the Treasury Department's plans for financing war if it came, Barnard had quickly grown dissatisfied and left the job after just nine weeks. Thin records leave the incident in the shadows, but Barnard developed an aversion to Morgenthau, to whom he attributed shrewdness "ordinarily associated with the Hebrew mind."

Yet Barnard developed a personal commitment to religious inclusion as a result of his USO presidency. Where he had once accepted the corporate need for "compatibility," he now proudly called for cooperation among "three great faiths." Contrary to his theory of leadership, morality flowed up, not down at the USO. He learned from the USO, not vice versa, that an inclusive spirit was "the very antithesis of Hitlerism."

The USO helped pioneer the idea that religious and racial inclusion could be a source of national strength and unity. This ideal of unity through diversity, widely used in the middle and late twentieth century by those who thought the civil rights movement needed pragmatic justification, has become America's quasi-official ethos in the early twenty-first century. It originated at least partly in Barnard's uniting of the USO's religious organizations behind his corporate banner of cooperation. He proudly recounted how Protestant volunteers steered Catholic GIs to mass as proof that the USO was pioneering "something new in the world."

In race relations, however, the USO made little progress. Barnard celebrated the USO's inclusion of "many races," but that hardly implied integration. USO clubhouses operated like the Jim Crow army, with segregated facilities for blacks and whites. Still, the USO was the largest nongovernmental organization up to that time to articulate an ideal of interracial cooperation, with white and black volunteers sometimes supporting each other's efforts.

In religion, the USO anticipated and to some degree helped cause a shift away from democracy's traditional emphasis on religion as a private matter and toward the idea of the American nation as a community of believers, albeit in different faiths. The USO acted out the post–World War II mainstream ethos, in which the solid citizen was a believer, whether Protestant, Catholic, or Jew.

Barnard believed that by contributing the method of corporate cooperation to the USO, he also contributed it to America. The USO, as "the most constructive attempt yet made on a large scale to find the way in which . . . cooperation and independence . . . may be simultaneously achieved," served during the war as "one of the most important integrating forces maintaining both American society and the American way of life." The USO, Barnard proudly proclaimed, "is one stage higher in Americanism."

Yet Barnard's USO work suggests a danger for our era as management values and the general culture increasingly converge. At the USO,

Barnard implemented an ideal of inclusion that earlier, as a corporate executive, he would have resisted as a threat to workforce "compatibility" and cooperation. Corporations have repeated that pattern many times in the past half century, often initially resisting, then effectively implementing policies for a more just society. As management ideas become, more and more, the national ethos, corporate values may replace democratic values instead of alternately resisting and implementing them.

The limitations of management methods as a tool of democracy show up most clearly in government and democratic politics. As opposed to his wartime success with the USO, Barnard failed in his most notable postwar use of his theory of cooperation, his attempt to help the United States avoid a nuclear arms race with the Soviet Union.

The A-Bomb and the American Trucking Boys

"This is the end of our democracy," Barnard exclaimed in August 1945 when he heard that the United States had dropped an atomic bomb on Hiroshima. In the anti-Communist witch-hunts of the next decade, his remark gained currency on the left as a prophetic vision of endangered liberty. But originally, Barnard probably intended a quite different emphasis, a realistic recognition of the necessity, as he sometimes saw it, of "totalitarian government" in a nuclear age. He thought that the United States, in self-defense, would have to take stronger measures than democracy would permit, such as forced dispersion of the population.

Barnard's underestimation of democracy's ability to handle the nuclear threat played a brief role in American foreign policy. In January 1946, Dean Acheson, under secretary of state, telephoned Barnard and asked him to come to Washington to help the Truman administration develop a plan to prevent a nuclear arms race. Many ordinary Americans and even some usually cynical bureaucrats believed that control of atomic energy by the new United Nations organization offered the best chance at national security and human survival. The State Department, needing a specific proposal for the UN, asked a select few, including Barnard, to prepare it.

PHOTO 6.3 Barnard at about the time the
State Department asked him to work on
prevention of a nuclear arms race.

Acheson already had a committee to plan for international control.
Some of its members had worked on the A-bomb. General Leslie Groves
had run the Manhattan Project that built it. Vannevar Bush of the
Carnegie Foundation and James Conant, president of Harvard, had
headed government science offices during the war. But Acheson's committee could not meet regularly. Harvard wanted Conant back full-time,
and Acheson was bogged down in the State Department.

So Acheson gave his committee a Board of Consultants and charged
them to work full-time on a plan for international control. Barnard
rushed to Washington to join his four fellow consultants—the charismatic physicist J. Robert Oppenheimer, who had managed the Los
Alamos lab that designed and assembled the bomb; Charles Thomas, a
plutonium expert and Monsanto Corporation vice president; Harry
Winne, a General Electric vice president who had worked on the Man-

hattan Project; and the group's chairman, David Lilienthal, head of the Tennessee Valley Authority (TVA), which had provided huge quantities of electricity to refine uranium.

Barnard and the others set to work in barren space the State Department had found for them on the top floor of the American Trucking Association Building at 16th and P Streets. Brushing aside cobwebs, the "American Trucking Boys," as the consultants would call themselves, sat on straight-backed chairs and for the first couple of days took a crash course in nuclear physics from Oppenheimer. A masterful teacher, the physicist held them spellbound as he explained top secrets like detonation by implosion and the possibility of building an H-bomb many times more powerful than the A-bomb.

Oppenheimer's personal magnetism helped draw the American Trucking Boys into a close-knit group. Driving through the New Mexico desert on a field trip to Los Alamos, "Oppie" learned that it was the birthday of one of the others, stopped the car in a remote village, and found a bottle of whiskey for a celebration. Barnard soon considered Oppenheimer the most masterful people handler he had ever met.

Barnard and the others shared a managerial, human-relations mindset. Even Oppenheimer had worked more as a manager than as a scientist at Los Alamos. From late January to late March 1946, these five organization men, trying to safeguard humanity against extinction, held the mother of all management retreats. Retreats have the well-known advantage of focusing exclusively on the big question. They also run the risk of moving in isolation toward idealistic solutions. In a corporate context of top-down power, it does not necessarily do much harm to purchase some energy and enthusiasm by endorsing an unrealistic idea at a seaside resort. The boss can straighten things out later. But Barnard and his managerial colleagues would learn it is another thing entirely to subject a big idea to the democratic political process.

Closeted together for weeks, the American Trucking Boys let themselves be guided less by political and security considerations than by their managerial, people-handling orientation. Groves and others on the Acheson committee considered international inspection essential for A-bomb control. But Barnard and the consultants decided that "human factors" made inspection unworkable. As a negative activity, inspection would not draw creative scientists but rather "the kind of man who was attracted to prohibition squads in years past." Enlightened managers all, the American Trucking Boys wanted to offer attractive, personally rewarding work to atomic scientists.

After weeks of wheel-spinning, the Monsanto vice president, Charles Thomas, expressed the frustrated managerial mindset of them all by saying they had to stop "thinking negatively." As a positive alternative to inspection, Thomas suggested a supranational corporation, chartered by the United Nations, to control the world's uranium and put it to peaceful uses. The idea instantly attracted the others by its human relations potential. Instead of policemen manqué, the new organization would draw constructive corporate types: "Atomic energy then becomes a new and creative field in which men may take pride as participants . . . . They are in 'on the ground floor' of a growing enterprise."

The UN agency, as the consultants conceived it, would have a monopoly of the world's uranium mines, would denature the ore to a grade useless for weapons, and would then sell it for peaceful use to corporations and universities. The consultants eventually called their brainchild an "authority" like the TVA instead of a "corporation" like AT&T. But it had the monopolistic, common-carrier look of the phone company, producing all of the world's uranium and selling it to all comers.

Reflecting Barnard's influence, the group decided that "cooperation," not inspection, was humanity's way forward. The key moment had come in late February, when, according to Lilienthal's diary, "everyone instantly accepted . . . a new set of words to describe what we were after—security through cooperative development—as a substitute for the term 'control.'" By abandoning "control"—the goal of Taylor's scientific management and the dirty word of the human relations movement—the UN authority might not only bring nuclear sanity but also contribute "new patterns of cooperative effort . . . among the peoples of the world."

In mid-March, at Georgetown's posh Dumbarton Oaks mansion, Barnard and his colleagues presented their plan for cooperative development of atomic energy rather than inspection and control to Acheson's committee. Security concerns immediately intruded. General Groves argued that a UN uranium monopoly would make inspection more, not less, important. The Soviets, if not subject to inspection, could withhold uranium deposits from the UN monopoly with no one the wiser. Bush and Conant supported Groves. Barnard and the other consultants glumly returned to their dusty aerie at American Trucking to spend a week revising their report and adding a section calling for inspection without suggesting a practical plan for implementing it.

Back at Dumbarton Oaks the next weekend, the American Trucking Boys succeeded—in their view because of their superior human relations skills—in bringing around the troglodytic Groves, Bush, and Conant. Later, in telling Harvard human relations classes about it, Barnard attributed success to a secretary's good sense in bringing in coffee for a break, just as the plan seemed to be unraveling. The human touch prevailed, as it usually does in human relations classes.

But such gratifying moments in small-group relations do not translate in the democratic political process. Harry Truman took the first step back. Warily refusing to endorse the report, the president simply released it for public discussion, which was mixed. *Time* magazine gave the plan a two-page spread, praising Barnard and the others for raising hope "that the 20th Century's most impelling quest was not necessarily doomed to failure." But Dorothy Thompson, in her widely read column, dismissed the plan as an "Elysian daydream."

Meanwhile, Barnard and some of the other consultants made the rounds of the capitol to try to sell their plan. Meeting with a Senate committee on atomic energy, Barnard was appalled by the senators' chauvinism. Unlovely as their xenophobia may have been, they had the good sense to distrust the Soviets.

Truman further undercut Barnard, Oppenheimer, and the others by naming Bernard Baruch, the management movement's World War I bête noire, as the U.S. representative to the UN's Atomic Energy Commission. Barnard and the other consultants watched with dismay as Baruch, refusing to be a "messenger boy" for their plan, added a new provision. To ensure punishment of violators, the Great Powers' UN veto should be suspended as it related to atomic energy. At a Blair House meeting in Washington, Barnard and Lilienthal warned Baruch that his focus on the veto would create a pointless procedural issue—a "blind alley" Barnard called it—in which the Russians could "dance up and down indefinitely," stalling for time while building their own bomb.

The Soviets did stall, though less over the veto than over the U.S. refusal to say when it would stop making bombs, let alone surrender its stockpile, the latter idea not even broached in the American plan. Painting the United States as an opponent of disarmament, the Russians justified developing their own A-bomb as a defensive measure. Baruch resigned in January 1947, with the plan dead in the water.

For several years, the American Trucking Boys held annual reunions. They took hope from Truman's 1947 appointment of Lilienthal to head the U.S. Atomic Energy Commission. But their get-togethers had the flavor of old soldiers recalling the lost cause and enjoying, as Lilienthal said, "how well we get along together. I don't know when I have felt a better sense of comradeship." Managers all, they had built a team. But the team had failed in its job because of its managerial ideology of cooperation, which stood in the way of a realistic approach to preventing an arms race.

McGeorge Bundy, looking back on the episode forty years later, argued that the government as a whole, not just the American Trucking Boys, suffered "a failure of . . . political imagination" in trying to deny Russia nuclear weapons. The only real chance to prevent an arms race, Bundy concluded, would have been to agree on some level of parity that put Russia as well as the United States in possession of the bomb.

Still, the American Trucking Boys' human-relations mindset had done the country no good at the start of the Cold War. They had devised a plan that not just Russia but also the United States refused to endorse. Barnard and the others had not faced the fact that only an airtight plan of inspection could have won American political support. They never overcame their human relations prejudice against inspection as a negative, Taylor-like system of control. Baruch's failure to secure Russian agreement may well have been fortunate for the United States, given the American Trucking Boys' refusal to come up with a workable system of inspection.

Barnard stayed loyal to Acheson, Lilienthal, and Oppenheimer when Red-baiters later targeted them. He testified at the 1947 Senate hearings on Lilienthal's confirmation as head of the Atomic Energy Commission, made controversial partly by the American Trucking Boys' plan that some misrepresented as a proposal to give the A-bomb to the Russians. After Acheson became secretary of state, Barnard condemned congressional witch-hunting in the State Department. And he held to his high opinion of Oppenheimer when the physicist was later branded a security risk. Barnard maintained his best personal qualities—loyalty, integrity, and good judgment of people—which had helped convince him that the manager leads by moral influence.

Barnard died in 1961 with the arms race running full tilt toward 100-megaton bombs. Neither cooperation nor moral influence but balance of power prevented nuclear war. Contrary to Barnard's prediction, the United States was not forced to opt for totalitarianism as a defensive measure but carried on about as normally as possible. It was not manipulative human relations but America's tacitly mixed system of political freedom and managerial power that outperformed communism economically and, decades after Barnard's death, won the Cold War.

PART 3

---◄O►---

SOCIAL PHILOSOPHY
Management as Everybody's Business

FOR THIRTY YEARS AFTER WORLD WAR II, THE UNITED STATES enjoyed such clear economic superiority over the rest of the world that American management gurus could rest on their laurels. Intellectual activity in business schools and consulting firms lacked the adventurous sense of exploring a new world that had given zest to the gurus from Taylor to Barnard. Professors such as Frederick Herzberg, Abraham Maslow, Douglas McGregor, and Herbert Simon came up with new theories of motivation and organization, systems analysis and bounded rationality. But the audience that enthusiastically received their ideas had been prepared for them by Mayo and Barnard, Taylor and Gantt. The broad outlines of management as a discipline seemed to have been laid out for good, all before the war.

As late as 1970 it would have been a bold seer who predicted that by the 1980s, America's attention would be riveted on improving corporate efficiency. Neither would anyone have believed in 1970 that management ideas would later enjoy immense prestige as a central part of American culture and be accepted not simply as recipes for business profit but as a new kind of social philosophy offering guidance to the nonprofit and public sectors.

This sea change in opinion came mainly from the rise of international competition, especially from the Japanese in the 1970s and 1980s. As

American automobile, electronics, and steel companies lost market share, the threat to those industries' high-wage jobs and to the prosperity of other industries down the food chain powerfully concentrated people's attention on management. Challenged by Japanese "quality management," Americans took comfort in the fact that one of its main creators, W. Edwards Deming, was a compatriot whose teachings had been ignored by American industry. Surely, we could outdo the Japanese by using a management technique we had invented.

Quality management had the merit of both being an American invention and emphasizing employee participation, which lent consistency to the democratic facade that the management movement had erected over the previous half century. The quality movement seemed consistent with the faith in teamwork and small groups that had come out of the American human relations movement. Few realized the degree to which Japanese worker involvement took place right alongside top-down power exercised by Japan's rigid and powerful management hierarchy—inspired in part by American scientific management.

During the 1980s, the American gurus' new push for quality production through employee participation seemed perfectly in tune with the broad direction of American culture and politics. While the Reagan administration attempted to downsize government and strengthen private initiative and volunteerism in American society, Deming used his often naive ideas about human psychology and bottom-up power to call for changes in education and government, an example of the gurus' new confidence not only in tackling management problems but also in serving as social philosophers for American society.

Peter Drucker, Deming's colleague in the 1950s and 1960s at the Stern School of Business at New York University, was the most admirable social philosopher among the gurus. Facing the threat of fascist barbarism in the 1930s, Drucker decided that the corporation was the central institution of modern society on which the future of civilization depended. He came to the United States and tried with little success to teach managers that they had broader moral and social responsibilities than just making a profit. But his moral concern contributed to making Drucker a brilliant success as a practicing management consultant and teacher. His influential idea of "management by objectives," for example, was in part a protest against what he saw as the immoral, manipulative techniques of the human relations school.

In the 1980s, Drucker found a new source of hope for a morally legitimate management. The United States was becoming not just a corporate society but an organizational society, with managers running universities, hospitals, charities, and so forth. Drucker hoped that nonprofit managers, with their larger social concern, would pioneer morally superior methods of management. But the absence of the profit motive does not remove and may even heighten opportunities for managers to abuse their power over employees. Profit is a more objective standard of performance and discipline than do-good ideas, which are easily used to rationalize wrongdoing. Jefferson's admonition that no human being is fit to hold power over another, not Drucker's hopes to legitimize management, remains the best moral touchstone for management power in a democratic society.

7

The Statistician:
W. Edwards Deming

Wyoming's Willing Worker in Einstein's Universe

CHEYENNE, WYOMING. SEPTEMBER 1917.

W. Edwards Deming—bespectacled, six feet tall, and sixteen years old—keeps careful sight of the railroad station for fear of not finding it again. The callow but brave youth is between trains on his way to Laramie to matriculate at the University of Wyoming. It is the unlikely start of a life's pilgrimage that will revolutionize the business world.

Ed Deming went on to become a pioneer of statistical quality control (SQC), a production method he taught on a large scale to weapons manufacturers during World War II, though it had little immediate effect on civilian production in the United States. After the war, he found an audience in Japan, where manufacturers used SQC to launch an economic rebirth of their country's industry, ruined by American bombing. In no small part because of Deming's teaching, Japan eventually swamped the United States with high-quality, low-cost goods. American corporations themselves had to adopt "quality management" (a phrase Deming disliked). American managers, responding to international competition of unprecedented intensity, were forced to create lean operations that raised productivity and wealth while sometimes making work harder and harsher.

PHOTO 7.1   Deming (top) in Tokyo in 1950, giving his famous lectures on quality and (bottom) making a dinner speech to Japanese managers.

In maturity, Deming offered a win-win philosophy for corporate life that reflected his frontier origins. Emphasizing the pioneer virtues of co-operation and willing work, he deemphasized, as did frontier culture, a substratum of competition and conflict.

W. Edwards Deming was born in 1900 in Sioux City, Iowa, situated on a bluff above the Missouri River, along which Lewis and Clark had passed a century earlier on their way west. The pioneer families that had followed in the path of the explorers were often selected in a cruel struggle for family continuity. The successful in each generation accumulated enough land for their offspring to stay put, while the losers' children went west. Ed Deming's father, William, was one of the landless latter.

In 1891, William Deming had showed up at the school in Correc-tionville, Iowa, dusty and tired after a twenty-mile walk from his family's remote farm. The penniless, barely literate teenager craved education. In just three years, he obtained a teacher's certificate and married up a notch to a local girl with musical training. Later, he moved to Sioux City to study law. In 1906, William decided to try his hand at homesteading and filed on forty acres in Wyoming. But his cactus-covered claim held no prospect of supporting his family until the U.S. Reclamation Service pro-vided irrigation. Taking a job as a law clerk, William moved his family into a rented house in Cody, Wyoming.

The Wild West impresario Buffalo Bill Cody had founded the town and lived there, promoting government irrigation projects aimed at mak-ing the Big Horn Basin bloom. Although the showman's vision was bright, the reality in Cody was sordid and bleak. Ed's mother escorted the boy through saloon-lined streets peopled with homeless drunks.

Ed's father eventually moved the family into a tar-paper shack on his claim, twenty miles from Cody. Luckily, his barren land fell within the boundaries of the soon-to-rise town of Powell, home to builders and op-erators of the Buffalo Bill Dam going up on the nearby Shoshone River. But the sale of a few house lots from his claim did not relieve William from the debt he had accumulated. A legal career had not worked out, so he eked out a living as a traveling land salesman, while his family at home anxiously feared notice that their property had been seized for back taxes.

They survived on the mother's fifty-cent piano lessons, sometimes paid in stringy meat. (In later life, when Deming ate well, his diary dwelled on his good food.) Photographs show the family clinging to upward aspirations, the mother sitting gowned at her piano, daughter in bows, father and two sons in three-piece suits.

Ed Deming learned to work with a will. Mornings, before school, he fired a boiler in a boardinghouse, using his weekly earnings of $1.25 to treat his family to Sunday dinner in the same establishment. At fourteen, he got $10 a month from the town to shinny up poles and light the village's five street lamps.

His parents believed that the path out of poverty led through the schoolhouse door. The boy skipped a couple of grades, graduated with ten other students in Powell's high school class of 1917, and then headed for the University of Wyoming to study circuits and switches. In the era of Edison, electrical engineering promised prosperity even if, or more likely because, Deming had grown up in a house without electricity.

Working his way through college by cutting wood, mopping floors, and doing a dozen other odd jobs, he emerged seeming to be one of the white-shirted, close-cropped, horn-rimmed engineers who governed American production in the twentieth century. But he also had a thirst for big ideas that belied the stereotype. He later criticized his undergraduate curriculum, which had made him more an electrician than an engineer, for teaching mostly "chipping, filing, hacking, sawing, gluing."

Following his 1921 graduation, Deming stayed on for a year as an instructor at Wyoming. The next year found him at the Colorado School of Mines, followed by two more at the University of Colorado as an assistant professor of physics. While teaching, he earned a master's degree in physics and repaired his deficient undergraduate education with correspondence courses in probability and the theory of errors. A Colorado dean recognized his bent for theory and urged him to study for a Ph.D. in physics at Yale.

Few traces remain of Deming's Yale years except for a suggestion in old age that he had feared failure: "Some people go to Yale but do not get their degrees." But he got his doctorate in two years for a dissertation arguing that the structure of the helium atom could be better explained by the "idea of equipotential electrons" than by the standard postulate of "negative mutual mass of electrons and protons."

Deming's Yale thesis, filled with equations inferring subatomic nature, showed the importance of statistics in the new physics. Relativity and, later, quantum theory brought to the fore what a few generations earlier would have been the blasphemous doctrine that nothing is exact, that everything is fringed rather than firm at the edges. The clockwork universe and machinelike exactitude of Newtonian physics came to seem an illusion. The iffy title of Deming's thesis on the helium atom, "A Possible Explanation of Packing," bore witness to the tentative, probabilistic nature of knowledge. As Deming said in his maturity, "There is no true value of anything."

But he did not let the impossibility of absolute truth discourage him from believing in the possibility of objective knowledge. He resembled Einstein, who, learning of quantum theory, protested that God does not play dice with the universe. Deming reinforced his faith through statistics. If variable experience is analyzed with a statistically sound, "ideal method of counting," it will result in "values that people can use with confidence."

By improbable chance, Deming had already worked briefly at one of the first companies to realize the industrial significance of post-Newtonian physics. In the summer of 1925, en route to his graduate studies at Yale, he had stopped in Cicero, Illinois, to work for Western Electric. At the Hawthorne plant, whose experiments on worker productivity Elton Mayo would soon use as the basis for the human relations movement, Deming worked on improving mica transmitters. There he first heard of statistical quality control, though he seems to have made little of it in 1925.

Invited back to Hawthorne for a second summer, he got hints of a possible permanent job offer at $5,000 per year. That salary, high for the time, would be only a down payment, one of his coworkers told him, on the prospect that he might develop "into a man worth $50,000 per year."

What a contrast with the situation of Hawthorne's assembly workers! Their pay was good and their conditions scarcely Dreiserian. But they had no prospect of a better future, and assembly work offered nothing to their imaginations. Whether or not they lapsed into reverie and neurosis, as in Mayo's theory, they lived their real lives on the other side of the time clock. One of Deming's coworkers cautioned him not to "get caught on the stairway" when the plant whistle released the workers from their daily limbo: "Those women would trample you to death."

In his later career, Deming made assembly jobs less boring by giving workers responsibility for monitoring quality. And by using statistics to reveal how managers mistakenly blame systemic problems on workers who have no ability to fix them, he eliminated some irrational tyranny. Deming would distinguish himself morally from many other gurus by trying to improve work's satisfaction not by manipulating employees' psyches but by trying to improve objective working conditions.

It would be a quarter century, however, before Deming became a sort of social philosopher propounding the idea that statistical quality control can be a force for workplace justice. Before he could consider the significance of a relativistic universe for the factory's social order, he first had to learn to use SQC to improve the factory's products.

Quality Widgets for an Inexact World

Long after physicists discarded Newton's machinelike universe and its clocklike precision, factories kept on manufacturing products—clocks, for example—to specified tolerances, as if meeting specs constituted precision rather than falling willy-nilly within the limits of a minimally acceptable range. The concept of "tolerance"—implying permissible deviation from an absolute standard—helped maintain orthodox faith in exactitude while tacitly admitting that no product can be manufactured perfectly and that quality is a matter of "good enough."

But how good is good enough? By explicitly holding to exact standards while tacitly tolerating imperfection, mechanical engineers risked blinding themselves to the possibility of improvement. Walter Shewhart, a Bell Labs scientist, averted that danger. By inventing statistical quality control, he aligned the industrial world with relativistic physics. Denying any chance of perfection, he called for an infinite process of improvement.

Deming, with his combined love of big ideas and practical work, could only be attracted to Shewhart's vision of an intimate relation between the

new physics and mass production. His forty-year friendship with Shewhart began in 1927, after the Wyoming youth had gone to work for
Uncle Sam. Deming's boss in Washington knew Shewhart, and seeing
that the two men had common interests, introduced them. Deming frequently visited the Bell Labs scientist in his New Jersey home and assiduously "tried to understand his thoughts."

The "breakdown of the orthodox scientific theory," according to Shewhart, had implications for "industrial development." Industry should
abandon its false standards of perfection in favor of continuous improvement. Nineteenth-century mass production, Shewhart said, drew on "the
concept of the exactness of science," but statistical quality control "was
born of a probable science."

Photographs show Shewhart looking mild and reasonable, an easy
man for a young Westerner to like. Deming later described his mentor as
"never ruffled, never off his dignity." From Shewhart, he learned or at
least was reassured that steady personalities like theirs had a good shot at
success in big organizations.

Shewhart found intellectual support for statistical quality control in
some of the most advanced philosophy of his era, such as C. W. Morris's
Foundations of the Theory of Signs (1938) and C. I. Lewis's *Mind and the
World Order* (1929). Deming read the latter seven times without profit,
only to have Shewhart urge him to keep trying, with the remark that it
took him fourteen readings "before it began to mean anything."

Morris and Lewis were prominent philosophers at, respectively, the
University of Chicago and Harvard. They followed the great but still little-
known thinker Charles Sanders Peirce (1843–1914), the creator of "prag-
matism." Peirce's philosophy fit well with what Deming described as Shewhart's "operational . . . criteria of meaning." Peirce rejected Descartes'
notion of mind and matter as unknowable metaphysical substances underlying and upholding phenomena. Phenomena and their interrelations
were reality.

Shewhart realized that such seemingly esoteric philosophy contained
practical lessons for production managers. Giving up on metaphysical
figments like exactitude and perfection that no one had ever witnessed in

the real world, Shewhart focused on variation in quality, which was an observable phenomenon.

Minute variations in telephone parts could leave one customer satisfied and another with a piercing earache. But Shewhart's answer to the problem—narrowing rather than eliminating variation—was lost on AT&T's marketers, who advertised that the expression "alike as two peas" might just as reasonably be "alike as two telephones."

The production manager, Shewhart said, should "accept as axiomatic that a controlled quality . . . must be a *variable* quality." Production managers wrongly attributed variation to "chance," an excuse that Shewhart called "just about as good" as our ancestors' device of attributing "lack of success to the . . . gods." Like his primitive ancestor, the modern manager hides his ignorance with cloudy words like *luck* and *divinity*. The first step toward wisdom is to recognize one's ignorance.

According to Shewhart, recognizing one's ignorance does not necessarily mean one should try to learn. The smart manager invests effort in learning only when there is an odds-on chance of attaining knowledge. That was where statistics—the science of probability—became useful. Shewhart helped production managers figure out the odds as to whether the cause of an error could be found and fixed.

In everyday life, we all use probabilistic thinking to decide whether it is worth trying to learn. When a football team loses the pregame toss to see who chooses to kick or receive, it wastes no time trying to figure out why the coin came up tails. Sorting out all the causes—from wind velocity to a nick from the coin's recent passage through a vending machine—would be impossible. But if the team lost the toss every game, season after season, this statistically improbable series of events might make it worthwhile to look for some special cause, such as crooked referees.

Ditto in manufacturing. Extreme variations are the most improbable and therefore are most likely to be, in Shewhart's terms, "assignable" to some "special" cause such as flawed raw materials, a malfunctioning machine, or a careless worker. Managers should obviously try to find and fix such problems.

But managers should not waste time looking for the cause of variations that fall within a normal range. Shewhart's strategy was not to eliminate all variation—an impossible feat in an inexact world—but to focus on those variations whose causes could probably be found and fixed.

Testing a new electrical insulation at Bell Labs, Shewhart found that it varied from 3,600 to 5,200 megohms (electrical resistance). Using a standard deviation "derived from past experience," he concluded that the range would be 4,000 to 5,000 megohms if the manufacturing process were "in control"—that is, subject only to common variation inherent in the production system. That meant that on the following figure, the eight variations outside the 4,000–5,000 range were probably assignable to "special causes."

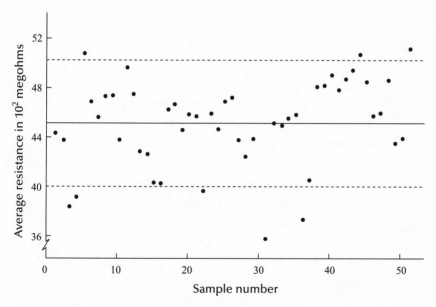

FIGURE 7.1   Quality Control Chart.

Shewhart demonstrated the usefulness of his analysis by finding and fixing the problems, though he did not identify them when he wrote about the incident. Quality improved dramatically; eliminating the causes of assignable errors also removed some unassignable errors and narrowed

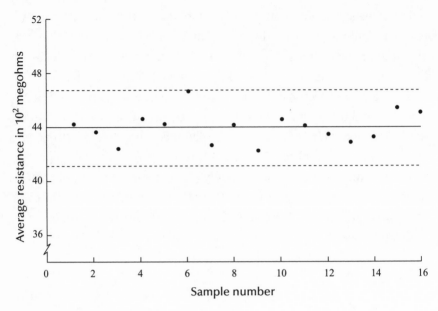

FIGURE 7.2   Quality Control Chart.

the control limits. Now the system produced insulation in the range of 4,300 to 4,700 megohms, as shown on the figure above.

Now that the process was "in control" it was "not feasible . . . to go much further in eliminating causes of variability." That idea could be wrong, of course, since it was based on probability analysis, and the improbable does sometimes occur. But in an inexact universe, the production manager, like everyone else, is a gambler who should not try for unlikely wins: "It is too much to expect that the criteria will be infallible. We are amply rewarded if they appear to be working in the majority of cases."

Once manufacturing is in control, then, the best bet is not to look for more special causes of error but to improve the production system with new materials, new machinery, better design of the product, and so forth. Workers may sometimes make small improvements in the process, but they lack authority to make big changes. Deming believed management must do that job.

Deming would become a fierce critic of American management's focus on human performance—the legacy of both Taylor and Mayo. "Unaided by statistical techniques, man's natural reaction to trouble of any kind," he said, "is to blame a specific operator or machine. Anything bad that happens, it might seem, is somebody's fault." However, the trouble may be due to some "common cause" inherent in the production system and correctable only by top managers.

In time, Deming and his followers would emphasize the seeming potential for workplace justice in the distinction between assignable errors and common variation. They hoped that managers, understanding that most variation resulted from common causes, would focus on improving the system instead of harassing willing workers.

A great deal of late-twentieth-century optimism about the possibility of workplace goodness depended on the idea that quality production broke down the boundaries between management power and worker subjection. Because workers were closest to the process, it made sense for them to monitor quality, plot their findings on charts, and correct assignable errors before they caused major trouble. Workers were supposedly "empowered" by this new responsibility.

Some of these changes did help workers do a better job, vastly improving quality. Although computers have long since replaced graph paper, it is true that, as Deming said, "the world lives better" because of Shewhart's charts. In the best-managed plants, employees' suggestions for small improvements get quick attention from workers on the next shift reading the notes left by their predecessors.

But the worker authorized to post a note to help the next shift can still fall into the hands of a bad boss or get laid off for reasons unrelated to performance. Maybe that's unavoidable in a vital corporate economy, but it's good reason to think straight about "empowerment," which has certainly not liberated employees from arbitrary power.

Mr. Deming Goes to Washington

Deming got his Ph.D. in 1927 and took a $2,400 a year Civil Service job in Washington, D.C., in the U.S. Department of Agriculture (USDA), which would give him immense opportunities for professional and intellectual development. The Department of Agriculture was one of the most important and creative parts of the government, serving the 40 percent of the nation that still lived on farms in the 1920s and 1930s. Roosevelt in the 1930s would give the Agriculture Department a charismatic leader in Henry Wallace, who vastly expanded its programs and its employees, from 40,000 to 146,000. Deming, unlike most Americans during the depression, worked for a thriving organization.

Government-sponsored science to increase yield was the American recipe for agricultural success. This tradition continued in the 1930s, despite the ruinous overproduction of food that had collapsed prices and brought farmers to despair.

Deming, in the Ohio Building that the Agriculture Department rented from American University, studied reduction of nitrogen from an atmospheric gas to a solid component of fertilizers. Behavior of gases at the molecular level, impossible to observe directly, could only be statistically inferred from larger-scale measurements. Deming was soon writing prolifically on the properties of compressed gases, the ignition of explosives, and other statistical applications in chemistry and bacteriology. He reported to his Yale professor that he could see no end to the interesting work ahead. Judged "excellent" on the Taylorist "efficiency ratings" used by the Civil Service, Deming grew prosperous with annual raises of a few percentage points while most wages and prices fell during the depression.

In the process, he also found an intellectual community. His supervisor not only introduced him to Shewhart but to other experts on quality control such as Colonel Leslie Simon at the Aberdeen Proving Grounds and Harold Dodge, an important Bell Labs statistician. Dodge pithily summarized the philosophy of SQC for Deming. Quality has to be "built-in" rather than "inspected out."

He continued his statistical education with customary diligence, studying the nineteenth-century writings of C. F. Gauss, corresponding with Professor R. T. Birge of the Berkeley Physics Department, and in 1936 visiting University College, London, where the eminent philosopher and statistician Karl Pearson had taught. The visit to London amounted to acknowledgment of Deming's fitness to mix with leading mathematicians like Pearson's son, Egon, who published one of the earliest books on industrial quality control. Back in the United States, Deming coauthored a book with Birge, titled *On the Statistical Theory of Errors*.

From 1930 on, Deming taught mathematical physics to Bureau of Standards employees. His energy, simplicity, and directness made him a superb teacher, especially effective with adult students. In the Civil Service, Deming found the good aspects of academia—intellectual freedom, research opportunities, stimulating students—without the downside of know-it-all adolescents, faculty phonies, and self-serving administrators.

In 1933, he began teaching statistics in the Graduate School of the Agriculture Department. This large but little-known school still operates today as in Deming's time, instructing tens of thousands of government employees. Deming quickly turned the statistics program into one of the best in the world.

Inviting leading statisticians for guest lectures, Deming crowned the list in 1938 with four lectures by Shewhart on quality control. More than 400 USDA Graduate School students attended, even though Shewhart turned out to be a poor speaker. Before one lecture, as Shewhart enthusiastically explained his ideas, Deming suggested that he speak to the students in the same informal style. No, said Shewhart, his lectures had to be "foolproof." They were, Deming replied, "so damned fool-proof that no one could understand them."

The incident captured the difference between Shewhart, the lofty theorist, and the more practical Deming. Shewhart's message of statistical quality control might have gone nowhere without Deming to serve as his Saint Paul, building the church and spreading the word. It took Deming a year to edit Shewhart's lectures, trying to clarify their meaning, before he published them under the USDA Graduate School imprint. The well-spent year editing Shewhart made Deming an expert in the most advanced theory of mass production, despite no practical experience in manufacturing.

During these years, Deming must have felt joyful self-fulfillment, pouring himself into important work that he loved. Some of his later optimism about organizational life can only have arisen from his rewarding quarter century as a civil servant.

Personal tragedy scarcely slowed him. His first wife died of a brain tumor in 1930, leaving him with a three-year-old adopted daughter, for whom he faithfully cared. Soon, he married again. His second wife, Lola Shupe, a mathematical assistant in the Agriculture Department, interrupted her career for motherhood but, as opposed to the usual pattern at the time, eventually resumed her career. Deming, with two more daughters and a stable family life, had a secure base from which to move outward.

In 1939, he worked temporarily at the Census Bureau, a momentous event because it stimulated him to develop some of his "quality" management techniques. Contrary to those who think government bureaucracy can only be stultifying, some of the methods on which the corporate world now vaunts itself began in the U.S. Civil Service.

An energetic spirit of innovation prevailed at the Census Bureau, where Morris Hansen, a civil servant almost as gifted as Deming, led an effort to improve the quality of census data. In those pre-computer days, tens of thousands of census workers went door-to-door, asking questions and recording the answers on file cards that they mailed to Washington. There, in the massive Commerce Department Building that Hoover had built in the 1920s, hundreds of clerks compiled the data by hand, resulting in slow, costly, and sometimes unreliable information.

Deming developed sampling techniques that enabled the government to respond quickly to shifts in unemployment, housing, and population. His methods for analyzing the death certificates that poured in to the Division of Vital Statistics made it possible for Washington bureaucrats to spot potential epidemics before local health officials did.

Many gaps in census information could be filled statistically. For example, some people, especially in rural areas, did not know the date or even the year of their birth. Deming worked out correlations between a person's age and the age of his or her children, making it possible to assign probable ages for many people with unknown birth dates. The probable ages were not always accurate, but on average they improved the overall accuracy of census data on the age of the population.

He kept down calculating costs with a special cart, a sort of pre-electronic computer, which held volumes of data and a program of branching instructions. Clerks could push the cart to their desks and use high school algebra to solve the complex problem of assigning a person's probable age.

These seemingly small innovations later had world-shaking consequences when Deming used what he had learned as a civil servant to bless the Japanese quality movement. His age-assigning cart showed that mathematically unsophisticated workers could use statistics. His sampling techniques for the census would work well in consumer research. The Census Bureau's achievement of more reliable but less expensive information showed that quality could be a resource rather than a cost. The dedication of senior civil servants showed the importance of top management's involvement with operations. It all came together in Deming's teaching in Japan following World War II.

But first the United States had to enter and win the war. In December 1940, a year before the Japanese attack on Pearl Harbor, Deming moved to the War Department to bring statistical quality control to arms producers. Once the United States was in the war, Shewhart suggested that a committee of Deming, Leslie Simon, and Harold Dodge create the *American War Standards on Quality Control* to guide weapons manufacturers and military ordnance inspectors. Manufacturers bought more than 18,000 copies of these "Z-1 guides," as the three thin but important pamphlets were known in industry.

For nearly twenty years, statistical quality control had improved telephone equipment but otherwise had little effect on American industry. Now there was an opportunity to spread the word. Deming proposed a crash course for production managers in the war industries.

At Stanford University in July 1942, Deming ran a ten-day course for thirty managers, mainly from metal producers and aircraft manufacturers such as Northrop and Hughes. Focusing on control charts and the distinction between assignable errors and normal variation, Deming scored a hit with the participants.

While at Stanford, he rushed into San Francisco to speak at the annual meeting of the American Statistical Association, urging the assembled academics to leave the ivory tower for wartime factories. They did not have to know how to make weapons; they could serve the cause by just figuring out whether variation in weapons came from special or common causes.

Deming's July success at Stanford led to another crash course in September at UCLA for Southern California aircraft manufacturers such as Douglas and Lockheed. Soon Deming was a road show. By war's end, he had taught his SQC course, reduced to eight days, to hundreds of production managers in a dozen industrial cities.

With his experience as a civil servant, Deming was probably not surprised to find that government personnel in general and soldiers in particular were enthusiastic innovators. Just as armories had eagerly embraced the ideas of Taylor and Gantt in World War I and earlier, now they enthusiastically went in for SQC. Soldiers eagerly adopted bold production ideas because they bore no risk of financial loss.

But senior corporate managers showed no wartime interest in SQC. Production managers embraced Deming's teachings, but top executives forfeited the opportunity to make quality a unifying, companywide concern, an oversight that later gave a huge competitive advantage to the Japanese.

Deming tried but failed to get his message to the top floor. Giving his course in Detroit in December 1943, he added a one-day session for executives. Promising to avoid technical discussion, he hoped that a general explanation of SQC would win over the brass. But Ford, General Motors, and Chrysler did not send a single senior manager.

As the morality tale is usually told, the leaders of American industry benightedly ignored Deming and paid dearly for their hubris by losing market share later to Japanese manufacturers. Nonetheless, during World War II there were good reasons for executives of the automobile manufacturers to pay little heed to Deming. Pouring forth jeeps, tanks, and planes while forced by the government and public opinion to limit wartime profits, they planned for a postwar return to the American recipe for profit in mass production—high volume, low costs, and aggressive marketing. SQC might be good for government armories or a phone monopoly like AT&T, but the big three auto producers were locked in oligopolistic competition for market share. Already making the best cars in the world's largest market, they could see little competitive advantage in further improving quality. Instead, they would try to increase sales with tail fins and garish colors while increasing profits by cutting costs, often with lower quality. In view of their quarter century of phenomenal success after the war, they can hardly be called shortsighted.

SQC also seemed irrelevant to civilian production, because during the war, managers often used SQC not to raise quality but to lower it. For example, by setting timed fuses for antiaircraft shells at two-tenths of a second instead of one-tenth, factories could manufacture four times as many shells. Lowering the quality of the fuses by 50 percent yielded four times as much firepower (assuming the guns could also be quadrupled). Quality half as good killed twice as well (4 divided by 2 equals 2).

In other words, the war put statistical control to the service of neither cost nor quality but of maximum effective firepower, giving SQC the appearance of irrelevance to the civilian, market economy. Deming would only slowly learn that he had to pitch SQC to American corporations on their terms, not his, as a way of lowering costs.

But it would be no more appropriate to blame Deming than the auto executives for the failure of SQC to take hold in the United States. The war and the twisted purposes to which it put SQC meant that Deming and the American auto executives alike were caught in the wrong moment in time to understand each other.

If Detroit did not see Deming's value, Uncle Sam had long since recognized him as one of America's most valuable civil servants. As the Cold War got underway, he grew uncomfortably familiar with the canvas bucket seats strung between the freight and the fuselage of army C-54s as they ferried him to hot spots where American foreign policy could profit from a statistician's skills.

The State Department used him in 1946 to monitor the election in Greece where the Communists' defeat marked the limit of postwar Soviet expansion in Europe. Deming spent several months in the contested country, validating the election results by sampling population density in key areas, disproving the Russians' claim that the Americans had padded the rolls with nonexistent voters.

Then in 1947 and 1950, when General Douglas MacArthur's headquarters in occupied Japan needed statistical surveys of the country's economy and population, Deming got the call.

Rebuilding Japan

Japanese industry suffered broken morale from losing the war. The Japanese public blamed defeat on the inhuman A-bomb. But their engineers knew, as one said, that they had also been beaten in their factories, which had built airplanes so deficient that some could not "keep aloft long enough to meet any enemy," dooming "many promising youths . . . to die in the Pacific Ocean."

After the war, Japan endured a two-year purgatory under American reparations. Factories not reduced to rubble sat idle while crowds of unemployed workers lived in the streets of Japan's bombed-out cities. Then, in 1947, the Truman administration decided to replace economic punishment of Japan with an economic recovery. The "American U-Turn," as the Japanese called it, aimed to make Japan a capitalist bulwark against communism in the incipient Cold War.

General Douglas MacArthur, head of the occupation, aimed to create a hybrid culture in Japan, grafting a shoot of democracy onto the native stalk of hierarchy. A master of symbolic politics, the "Supreme Commander" got great press from his defeated subjects. Once, when he strode onto an elevator, a Japanese worker tried to sidle off as he would have done for Admiral Tojo. MacArthur insisted the man ride along. Japanese democrats publicized the story, making it a metaphor for America's creation of social order without aristocratic haughtiness.

Even before the 1947 decision to rebuild Japan, MacArthur's men were trying to improve the country's unreliable telephone system, which hampered the American occupiers as much as it did Japanese industry. By February 1946, occupation headquarters had a Civil Communications Section (CCS) that included two AT&T engineers named Charles Protzman and Homer Sarasohn, who were familiar with Shewhart's methods.

Protzman and Sarasohn believed that the Japanese needed basic management techniques before they could use SQC. Japanese factories were even dirtier and more disorderly than those of pre-Taylor America. At Tokyo Telecommunications, in a shack with a leaky roof, Sarasohn found managers working during a rainstorm with umbrellas over their desks. He "got up from a meeting with them and walked out without even saying good-bye." The insult worked its intended effect on the company, today named SONY.

In late 1949 and early 1950, Protzman and Sarasohn taught scientific management in a couple of four-month seminars for electronics executives from Toshiba, NEC, Sanyo, Sharp, and Hitachi (or their ancestor companies). The CCS course emphasized standard procedures, clear lines of authority, and, according to the most thorough account of the seminar, scientific management's legacy of "the pyramid of management . . . as a complex functioning structure that had to be nurtured, organized, trained, and motivated."

The CCS seminar ran for many years afterward and contributed to the blend of Taylorism and indigenous culture that became "Japanese style management." Taylor's emphasis on order and system as methods of cost control contributed to Japanese innovations such as just-in-time production. But the Japanese found other American methods such as detailed job descriptions unsuitable for their culture, so they mellowed Taylorist rationality with what they called "art of management."

Yet even some of the Japanese "art of management" grew out of the scientific management tradition. Protzman, who had worked at Hawthorne in Mayo's time, held the famous experiment in low regard and said it was "the way not to go." Rejecting psychological manipulation, Protzman and Sarasohn taught leadership as the modeling of behavior to which ordinary employees could aspire. In the Taylorist "pyramid" of power that an English writer on the CCS seminar called "modern America's greatest invention," a manager could lead with mere know-how rather than therapeutic skill.

Sarasohn and Protzman, in their CCS seminar, gave more attention to quality than any other subject. But they disapproved of early Japanese attempts at statistical quality control as "too theoretical" and recommended Deming's mix of theory and practice.

Defeat in the war had necessarily turned Japanese attention toward quality. Poor in raw materials such as coal, iron, or oil, Japan had tried to take them by conquest. Having lost the war, Japan would now have to pay for raw materials with cash earned from exports. Yet who would buy the country's products when "Made in Japan" meant cheap and shoddy?

Quality became the mission of the Japanese Union of Scientists and Engineers (JUSE), which had grown out of a wartime association of public-spirited production managers. During the war, they met to discuss Japan's woes over sake bartered from peasants in return for scarce manufactured goods like light bulbs. After the war, with militarists and capitalists humiliated by defeat, the scientists and engineers of JUSE achieved a leadership role in industry, partly because they embraced SQC.

Under the influence of MacArthur's economics advisers, JUSE's leaders had acquired the *American War Standards* and learned of Deming. They had missed him in 1947 when he visited Japan to help with an economic survey. But JUSE's director, Kenichi Koyanagi, heard that Deming would return in 1950 to help plan a Japanese census. Koyanagi eagerly wrote to Deming, inviting him to lecture during his visit.

July 10, 1950, therefore found Deming in a stifling Tokyo auditorium, lecturing to 230 Japanese managers and engineers. For four hours that morning and on the next seven days, he stood dripping with sweat, despite an electric fan blowing on him from a few feet away. Speaking slowly between long pauses for translation, he gave the Japanese a quality control course adapted to their needs but based on the eight-day seminars he had taught to U.S. weapons manufacturers during the war.

Deming opened his first lecture dramatically: "We are in a new industrial age, created largely by statistical principles and techniques." Playing to his audience's desperation for export success, he said that statistics had revolutionized "requirements of international trade" such as quality, price, standardization, and communication.

His audience members had each paid ¥15,000 ($40) to attend, not a small sum in their ruined country, but nevertheless the tuition bargain of the century. Deming expounded to them the most sophisticated concept of mass production ever, laying out a vision of Japan as one big, integrated, manufacturing system.

Later in Japan, after economic recovery and triumph, it became fashionable for cognoscenti to discount Deming's 1950 lectures as overly technical, needing the addition of a broader view later by other American gurus such as Joseph Juran and, above all, by communitarian elements in Japanese culture. In the heady prosperity of the 1970s and 1980s, Japanese patriots claimed SQC was made in Japan.

Now that American companies have long since domesticated quality, some commentators on this side of the water also dismiss Deming's work in Japan and its supposed influence, later, in the United States. Because Deming did not teach important ingredients of today's quality model, such as time to market, it is claimed that American companies found their own way to quality rather than being inspired by Deming and the Japanese. Ignoring predecessors is "a necessary part of the adoption process in the context of American organizational culture." Some of this may be true, but it runs the risk of missing the importance of the broad social context outside the organization.

Deming's influence in Japan and eventually in the United States lay not just in statistics but in social philosophy. With a strong sense of his audience's needs, Deming taught SQC not merely as a production technique but as a principle of social order around which Japan's badly divided people could unite. He gave SQC an aura of communitarian moral authority, helping Japanese management regain their lost control of workers.

MacArthur, to weaken Japan's industrial and military elite, had initially supported workers' enthusiastic organization of labor unions. But with the onset of the Cold War and the decision to support Japanese economic revival, he tilted back toward the industrialists, leaving the newly established unions frightened and bitter.

Deming helped supply what MacArthur could not—social unity via corporate loyalty. Deming's notion of quality was not just a statistical technique but an inclusive vision of managers joining hands with workers, suppliers, and consumers. Partly, this was a logical consequence of a focus on quality, which could be no better than raw materials permitted and customers demanded. But Deming also had an intuitive sense of Japan's postwar morale problem and aimed to help supply a unifying vision. Whether the resulting Japanese unity constituted, as Marxists said, oppressive capitalist hegemony or, in the fond description of management enthusiasts, an idyll of trusting social relations, Deming helped create it.

Recent studies—by historians, scholars with genuine knowledge of the culture—suggest a balance of power in the Japanese quality model. Job security and higher wages purchased worker quiescence while management's recovery of top-down control was masked by deferential, "cooperative" mores in Japanese culture.

Yet Deming's unifying social model also contributed because it suggested genuine improvements in the Japanese business system, such as closer relations between manufacturers and their customers. Most manufacturers, whether Japanese or American, thought in terms of a three-step process:

1. design the product
2. make it
3. put it on the market

Deming added a fourth step—consumer research—which both began and ended the process, linking the other three steps in a spiraling cycle of improved quality:

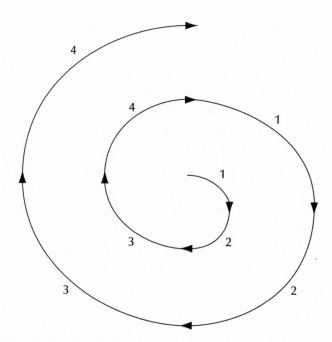

FIGURE 7.3   The Deming Cycle.

1. do consumer research
2. design the product
3. make it
4. put it on the market

1. do consumer research
2. *redesign* the product

In 1951, on the first of many return visits, he taught Japanese managers survey techniques he had used for the U.S. Census, then sent them into the streets to canvass consumers about their need for sewing machines, bicycles, and pharmaceuticals.

Deming did a kind of consumer research of his own, learning all he could about Japanese culture. Traveling around Tokyo by subway instead of taxi, he attended Noh plays, ate in Japanese restaurants, and acquired a taste for sake.

Deming's attention to Japanese culture distinguished him from most Americans during the occupation. MacArthur, to avoid friction, had set up a separate infrastructure for Americans. They watched Hollywood movies, ate in American-style steak houses, and drank Jack Daniels. What they learned of Japan came from taxi drivers and bar girls.

The "servile spirit" of defeat in Japan led many Americans to adopt an "air of importance" as JUSE's founder, Kenichi Koyanagi, resentfully put it. But in Deming's frontier-bred humility, courtesy, and work ethic, the Japanese perceived values akin to theirs. Instead of lording it over them, he told his hosts that their superior education in mathematics let him address them on a higher level than their American counterparts.

Deming's graciousness got him several private meetings with Ichiro Ishikawa, a powerful businessman who chaired Keidanren, the country's largest trade association, which exerted great influence in the postwar political vacuum. Ishikawa also served as figurehead president of JUSE, relieving it of any charge of radicalism or irrelevance. Koyanagi probably felt that in delivering Deming and his socially unifying vision of SQC, he had justified Ishikawa's blessing of JUSE. Ishikawa invited the American to speak to twenty-one Keidanren executives from major companies.

After dinner at Tokyo's prestigious Industry Club, where Ishikawa graciously repaid his guest's interest in Japanese food with a lavish American-style meal, Deming spoke for an hour to the lords of Japanese business. What a contrast with the United States, where even during the war he had been unable to get the attention of the auto executives! Deming seized the opportunity to win a high-level following in Japan. Explaining SQC in only the most general terms, he expressed confidence in his hosts, asserting that Japan could achieve a competitive level of quality in five years and a dominant position in ten.

In Japan later, a formulaic myth evolved that the Keidanren executives had grave doubts but nevertheless embraced Deming as their only hope. The reality was probably an initial tilt by the executives toward Deming as Ishikawa's man and then a necessarily unspoken agreement that the American offered the possibility of moral and social advantage. The executives agreed to hear more and later reconvened at a resort on

Mount Hakone, a few hours' train ride from Tokyo, where Deming struck the right note by teaching them, in his words, "the theory of a system, cooperation."

Earlier, in his Tokyo lectures, Deming had stressed customer relations. Now, on Mount Hakone, he emphasized "an enduring fruitful relationship" with suppliers. In Japanese factories, he had seen huge variations in raw materials, which in turn made for huge variations in product quality. His solution: Manufacturers should teach SQC to their suppliers, an educative relationship most easily fostered with a single supplier.

Even competitors had to be made part of the system. Firms that shipped shoddy goods would lower the reputation of all Japanese companies, so the strong had to help the weak. Quality, Deming explained, "must be a prairie fire; all Japanese on fire. Everybody will win." The Japanese had never seen the prairie, but they got the idea.

Taking advantage of his access to Japan's top managers, Deming told them that everything depended on their personal commitment to SQC. Only top managers could authorize the constant upgrading of the production system that would bring continuous improvement in quality. SQC challenged managers as well as workers by turning "the spotlight on . . . various levels and positions."

Deming offered a strategy in which Japan would offset its lack of raw materials with its "vast pool of . . . engineers, mathematicians, and statisticians, to improve quality." With such an advantage in human resources, manufacturing for export was the path to prosperity. The disadvantage of purchasing raw materials from abroad would be offset by the advantage Japan's well-educated population would have in implementing SQC: "Any saving of . . . scarce materials through the use of statistical methods . . . was the equivalent of going out and finding deposits of coal, iron ore, copper, oil, etc."

Did his Japanese audience ponder Deming's neglect of the danger of dependence on foreign power? The truth is that if your prosperity depends on coal, buying it is not nearly as good a thing as owning a mine. But their hope of conquering natural resources having been lost with the war, the Japanese had no choice but to try for prosperity through trade.

Fortunately for them, Deming's 1950 visit coincided with a miniboom touched off by the start of the Korean War and the procurement needs of the U.S. military. This running start helped Japanese companies adopt the new quality focus.

Deming signed the royalties from his printed lectures over to JUSE, which used the money to fund the "Deming Prize" for quality. Now the world's most prestigious industrial award, the medallion bears his profile and his words: "The Right Quality & Uniformity Are Foundations of Commerce, Prosperity & Peace."

Medals and prizes—potent symbols of approval in undemocratic hierarchies—abound in Japan. In 1960, Deming got the Second Order Medal of the Sacred Treasure, Japan's highest honor for a foreigner. A few years later came an invitation to meet the emperor. So acculturated was Deming by now that he knew he gave no offense to Hirohito by stepping back to snap his photo.

During visits to Japan for Deming Prize ceremonies in the 1960s, he observed "circles" of workers doing what he had thought was management's job—improving processes to eliminate common causes rather than just using charts to catch assignable errors. Meeting on employees' own time, often in their homes, Quality Control Circles sped up assembly by redesigning components, lowered banking costs by inventing automatic payroll deposits, and improved thousands of other work systems. The QC Circles further improved Japan's already looming productivity and quality.

Deming saw the QC Circles as bottom-up, but the main Japanese authority over them—Professor Kaoru Ishikawa, son of the JUSE president who introduced Deming to top Japanese managers in 1950—suggested that they were an ambiguous mix of bottom-up and top-down power. Top management, said Ishikawa, had to be "promoting QC activities" while allowing workers to be "active of their own accord and at their own initiative."

Deming left unexamined the ugly underside of social harmony, neglecting to ask to what degree cooperation in Japanese corporate society rested on power and fear. He saw Japanese economic success as a simple fulfillment of his vision of a vast cooperative community where there would be no losers, only winners, most of all the consumer, who would get "a better product, better suited to his needs, and cheaper. *Democracy in industry*, one might say." Deming's democratic social vision made quality management an easy sell in the United States once it had proved its economic value in Japan.

Reorganizing America

ANY ONE OF 14,000,000 AMERICAN HOUSEHOLDS. 8:00 P.M., June 24, 1980.

The psychologically bruised viewers tuning in to NBC's documentary "If Japan Can . . . Why Can't We?" probably expected yet one more jeremiad on the U.S. loss of industrial supremacy. Only the comatose remained ignorant of Japan's export blitz, flooding the U.S. market with consumer electronics and—the ultimate insult to Americans—automobiles of a quality and price unmatchable by Detroit.

How did the United States dissipate its post–World War II economic superiority so quickly? That year's soon to be nominated Republican presidential candidate believed the nation had lost its core values of freedom and self-reliance in a half century of big government. Reducing taxes, Ronald Reagan promised, would stir Americans to create wealth through work while shrinking government and creating a new birth of freedom.

But Reagan's America had long ceased to be Thomas Jefferson's. Many citizens lived under the government not just of the United States but of corporate management. A smaller federal government might bring economic growth, but would it bring freedom and justice? Few foresaw the coming two-tier society, with frontline employees getting level pay for more work and less job security while more than a few managers vastly multiplied their salaries and drained off company equity with off-the-books stock options.

The late-twentieth-century surge in management power borrowed a democratic disguise from Japanese quality management. The television viewer learned from "If Japan Can . . . Why Can't We?" that the land of the rising sun owed its industrial prowess to power sharing by managers, implying that the United States should similarly empower its workers. The idea was made all the sweeter by the NBC documentary's announcement that Japanese workers' empowerment was the brainchild of an unheralded American, W. Edwards Deming.

By teaching managers to share power with subordinates, Deming had supposedly brought sweetness and light to Japanese factories. According to NBC, Japanese workers' "larger role in the management of the factories and production lines" meant that "acquisition of advanced machinery and robotics has taken place with the . . . support of line workers . . . [who] . . . moved to more mentally stimulating jobs, while the machines were left with the more tedious jobs."

With its comforting message that Japan's seemingly democratic, cooperative style of management had been invented in the United States, "If Japan Can . . . Why Can't We?" stirred great interest. Distributed as a film, it sold 30,000 copies in the next few years. Deming, a few months shy of eighty, became a celebrity.

During the quarter century since his retirement from the U.S. Civil Service, Deming had thrived as a consultant while commuting from Washington to teach at NYU's Stern School of Business. Finding little interest in the United States for his idea of quality as a social philosophy, he had focused on the statistical aspects of SQC. Now he suddenly had an American audience for his broader ideas about quality management, including his idea that human society should be one big production system.

Donald Petersen, president of Ford, first heard of Deming through the NBC broadcast. Attempting to recoup huge losses from Ford's reputation for low quality, he hired Deming to improve the company's cars.

Deming, a fierce curmudgeon by now, consulted monthly with Ford top managers and openly blamed them for the company's problems. The eighty-year-old served, in the words of one Ford executive, as "a burr under our saddle," warning that the company's bitter history meant that employees would need years to learn trust and teamwork.

By the late 1980s, thanks to a sleek, tightly built new model, the Taurus, Ford surpassed GM in profitability for the first time in half a century.

The victorious Petersen authored the obligatory book of CEO wisdom on how to combine the "vitality . . . of American individualism with the power of teamwork." He quoted Deming that the Ford experience could "have a major impact on this country."

Yet power and participation remained confusingly entangled at Ford. Petersen, later remembered by some employees as a merciless tyrant, said he had learned "trust" that allowed elimination of "many elements of control and structure." But many lower-level Ford executives probably agreed with managers throughout American industry who saw employee participation and the like as "carrots" to be mixed with "sticks." For Ford workers, management's threat of plant closings and job losses in the face of Japanese competition probably contributed as much as trust and teamwork to focusing their attention on quality.

Meanwhile, many other American companies raced to embrace recipes for Japanese-style management. William Ouichi, a management professor at UCLA, wrote a book called *Theory Z* (1981) that won twenty-two weeks on the best-seller lists by proposing a mix of Japanese and American methods. Ouichi offered the encouraging news that many American companies already operated in a spirit not too far distant from Japanese "collectivism." Not much to wonder at, really, given that management mavens had been fighting American individualism ever since Elton Mayo first called for workplace community.

American human relations gurus eagerly adopted "Japanese-style management" as if it were just the latest variation of the Hawthorne experiment. What was a "Quality Circle" if not a "small group," the core concept long emphasized by Mayo's intellectual heirs? Ignoring the strong Taylorist influence in Japanese management as well as Japan's history of bitter labor relations, American gurus called for Nipponese-style "cooperation" in behalf of which they could just as easily have invoked the name of Chester Barnard. A tweak or two to the old human relations techniques, and the United States would be on the right track.

Many U.S. managers, ignoring Japan's painstaking attention to statistics, customers, and suppliers, confidently "slotted in" QC Circles as if quality was just the latest feel-good idea for pepping up the workforce.

Expensive "quality trainers"—often, human relations retreads—taught workers to grab their magic markers and crowd around acetate boards, scrawling pithy ideas in self-conscious "brainstorming" sessions. As employees warily "cooperated"—sometimes a little like political prisoners in a reeducation camp—covertly authoritarian managers demanded ever more effort in the sanctimonious "spirit of continuous improvement."

Deming deplored the phoniness: "Many QC-Circles are, I fear, management's hope for a lazy way out." He loathed the slogan "total quality management," which had originally meant a sensible organization-wide focus on improvement. But it came to stand, along with the mad motto of "zero defects," for the ridiculous goal of perfect products, a fundamental contradiction of Shewhart's principles that variation is inevitable and improvement never-ending. Deming rushed a book into print, *Out of the Crisis* (1982), that damned American management for taking "refuge" in quality and turning it into a "dud." But Deming's book, just one of a flood of quality texts, failed to stem the rising tide of nonsense.

Once American companies figured out that quality meant more than sitting in circles and touching fingertips, they improved production via customer focus, leaner inventories, integrated processes, and top management involvement. Given the profitable results, some now say the faddish rush to quality provided useful entry into a new kind of management where the wheat could later be separated from the chaff.

Deming, in the thick of the fight, took no such long view but tried to counter quality fads with what he called "profound knowledge," which contained some dubious propositions of his own. All through the 1980s and into the early 1990s, he gave, every year, dozens of four-day "seminars" on quality management to audiences in the hundreds. All told, maybe 100,000 people heard him speak. To this enormous audience he taught his old idea of quality as a social philosophy plus a new psychological emphasis to justify getting rid of performance reviews, merit pay, and prizes for excellence.

The namesake of the Deming Prize urged the abolition of prizes! Maybe he knew that the Deming competition had developed a negative side, taking thousands of hours of preparation time and diverting Japanese managers' attention from their jobs. In 1989, an American company, Florida Power and Light, won a Deming Prize after years of work, then had to tone down formal quality methods to refocus on business challenges.

How much worse would inevitably be the Baldrige Award, the Reagan Commerce Department's copycat prize for quality, managed by a private foundation but still a government initiative! Deming probably bristled at congressional stupidity in not foreseeing the inevitable confusion of standards as interested parties strove to get their particular recipe included in the quality cookbook. Even those who thought the Baldrige criteria helped to cull useful information from the fad-ridden marketplace warned that the award risked losing "its core emphasis on processes and customers."

Far weaker was Deming's criticism of performance reviews and merit pay because they frightened willing workers into withholding cooperation. Delighting his naive seminar audiences, he urged them with unwitting irony: "Drive out fear." Apparently no one ever retorted, "Yeah, scare the hell out of it."

In his seminar Deming illustrated irrational, fear-producing management by "hiring" a half dozen audience members. Giving them each an indented wooden paddle, he told them to scoop as many white beads as possible from a box containing 80 percent whites and 20 percent "defective" reds. Acting the part of the frightening, tyrannical boss, Deming "fired" the poor performers for scooping up too many red beads, only to have the high performers disappoint him in a succeeding round when common variation dictated that they too dip out a higher-than-average number of reds. Then he drove home the moral: "[T]he ranking of people . . . is wrong and demoralizing, as it is actually merely ranking the effect of the process on people."

This "red bead" exercise, which Deming had used forty years earlier in Japan to illustrate common variation in production processes, served him poorly as a management philosopher. Surely some of the audience saw his weak thinking, even if they kept quiet out of courtesy for the older man. Scooping red beads is one thing; real-life jobs are another. Whether sweeping a floor or managing a company, the individual's ability and spirit, not just the process in which he or she participates, helps determine the individual's performance.

Evaluation, ranking, and merit pay do frighten employees. But there are other soul killers besides fear, such as the hurt felt by high achievers when their earned rewards go to the undeserving. Elimination of merit pay will show fear the door, but achievement may leave with it. Getting rid of evaluation is not a way of improving management but rather of abolishing it.

Because power is a necessary part of effective organizations, sensible reactions to it, such as fear, are inevitable. Good managers minimize fear by accurately rewarding performance and achievement. But some amount of fear is a rational response to even the best managers who, being imperfect human beings, inevitably use their power unjustly some of the time. The goal of driving out fear is a recipe for a doubly fearful "culture" where employees will be afraid to appear afraid.

Some of Deming's lack of realism about corporate life probably stemmed from his having known little fear as a civil servant. Later, as a professor, he easily drove fear out of his classes at NYU. Dispensing with grades because they demoralized the C and D students, he gave a simple "Pass" to all comers, including those who had not completed their course work. Their papers might come in a year late, he reported, but they were always worth reading. No doubt they were, given the small enrollments in his courses, his supportive teaching, and the fact that his students were adults whom he asked to choose projects related to their jobs.

Even personal experience as rich as Deming's made a thin basis for generalizing about human society, as he did in his last book, *The New Economics for Industry, Government, Education*. Published in 1993, the year of his death, the book chastised lots of American institutions, schools above all, for their use of fear. Grades, he warned, damage self-esteem and destroy children's love of learning. But public schools deal with a range of variation far wider than anything a production worker ever noted on a control chart, making grades vital to discipline. Still, today's emphasis on testing and "accountability" in schools may easily overshoot the mark, giving new relevance to Deming's warning that use of fear as a motivator can destroy love of learning.

With extraordinary energy and dedication, Deming worked up until within a few weeks of his death from kidney failure at the age of ninety-three, giving one of his famous seminars to a large audience while tethered to an oxygen bottle. In the hospital, near the end, he suggested ideas for better care, then lamented the miserable management skills of his doctors, who used his suggestions to correct individual nurses instead of improving the system in which the nurses worked.

Like many other gurus, Deming underestimated the inevitability of top-down power and overestimated the possibility of democratizing management. Yet he can scarcely be blamed for the harsher working conditions that sometimes accompanied the increased competitiveness and lean organizations he helped make possible. He towers over most other gurus in the real good that he did, raising quality and lowering costs as well as using the distinction between common and special causes to reveal how managers mistakenly blame systemic problems on employees.

8

The Moralist: Peter Drucker

From the Hapsburg Empire to the Third Reich

VIENNA, CAPITAL OF THE HAPSBURG EMPIRE. LATE SUMMER 1914.

With his ear to a heating duct, four-year-old Peter Drucker eavesdrops on his father's study. Adolph Drucker and his friends are lamenting the end of civilization. Events have spun out of control in the Balkans, bringing the start of World War I. The Hapsburg Empire, in which Adolph is a senior civil servant, will perish in the conflict.

The ruinous war and its aftermath would eventually drive young Peter Drucker out of Austria, ultimately to America, where he adapted brilliantly to corporate life. Applying vestiges of Hapsburg liberalism to corporate life, he believed that people do not have to hold power for an organization to be legitimate but only have to be treated well by those who do. His realistic recognition of top-down power made it possible for him to exercise practical influence on so many companies that in effect, he helped shape American society. He missed nothing except the fact that top-down power cannot be made morally legitimate in a democratic society.

Drucker's lifelong belief in top-down generosity owed much to his father's success at improving the lot of many within the Hapsburg domains. As a senior civil servant in the Ministry of Economics, Adolph Drucker promoted free trade within the empire. Abolishing internal tariff barriers among Serbs, Croats, Slovaks, and a dozen other subject peoples, the

231

PHOTO 8.1   Peter Drucker.

Austrian liberals built a common market of 60 million people with increasing prosperity in the prewar years.

But that was a partial picture. Much misery persisted among the empire's landless agricultural workers. Moravians and Magyars departed for Pennsylvania steel mills, finding even in the pitiless likes of Frederick Taylor an improvement over the cruel landlords of central Europe.

The empire's rulers blinded themselves to misery in the countryside with the splendor of their capital. Vienna, architecturally dazzling, was a magnificent center of cultural and intellectual life. The city produced in Sigmund Freud one of the formative geniuses of the century; in economics, Joseph Schumpeter, Ludwig von Mises, and Friedrich Hayek; in music, Gustav Mahler, Richard Strauss, and Arnold Schoenberg; in art, Gustav Klimt and the Secession. Among the provincials drawn into the city's cultural ferment, young Adolf Hitler tried his luck as a painter, failed, and lived homeless for a time, until the war filled his life with a new meaning and mission.

Adding to the optimism of the liberal civil service was its considerable power. Parliament and politicians held little sway. Neither did barons or bishops. The crown had imposed order from the center via its able administrators such as Adolph Drucker. Working to create a cosmopolitan regime in Central Europe, the civil service justly credited itself for much of the empire's material and cultural progress.

But the emperor aimed at stasis. In the latter half of his lengthy reign (1848–1916), Francis Joseph I escaped his hellish private life—his alienated empress living abroad and his only son a suicide—by spending long days at his desk poring over state papers, his only goal to preserve the status quo. Neither the conservative emperor nor his liberal administrators recognized how little they had in common.

To hobble his aristocratic opponents, the emperor promoted his administrators according to merit, with the result that the civil service included many Jews. Adolph Drucker, a Christian, may have been a convert from Judaism. Certainly, the Druckers had Jewish relatives. "There is no Austrian of my class," Peter Drucker has said, "who doesn't have Jewish relations."

In a few generations, Vienna's Jews, drawn by the lifting of repression in the capital, had soared in number from a handful to nearly 200,000. Their success in publishing, banking, medicine, and law offended anti-Semites. Newspapers and politicians ominously debated the "Jewish Question."

Imperial Vienna, with its mingled nationalities, was a hothouse of identity confusion, with "Jewish self-hatred" the most extreme case. Identifying with progressive elements in Austrian culture, some liberal Jews rationalized abandoning their heritage as a commitment to cosmopolitan humanism. Integration of Jews into Viennese society symbolized the Hapsburg Empire's promise of a transnational community in Central Europe. If the empire could assimilate its non-Christian subjects, surely it could also win the loyalty of its Czechs, Serbs, and other minorities.

Yet national spirit was rising, not falling, within the Hapsburg domains. The relatively powerful Hungarians, for example, had received autonomy at the start of Francis Joseph's reign. But when Thomas Masaryk proposed a similar arrangement for the Czechs, he got nowhere. Destined to be president of postwar Czechoslovakia, Masaryk was one of the men Peter

Drucker heard lamenting the end of civilization in his father's study at the outbreak of the war. Perhaps Adolph Drucker disagreed with his fellow civil servants, who, instead of supporting an unrealistic cosmopolitanism, would have done better to try to transform the empire into a multinational federation. As it was, the empire had no chance of winning the loyalty of its diverse peoples. After World War I, the Hapsburg holdings were divided into Czechoslovakia, Hungary, and Yugoslavia.

Loss of the empire left Vienna as capital of the tiny Austrian republic, a bit like a magnificent ship whose ocean has dried up beneath it. Formerly governing 60 million imperial subjects, the city now ruled only 6 million Austrians, many of them unemployed former paper pushers for the empire. The new national boundaries in Central Europe hindered free trade and impoverished Viennese businessmen.

As a child, Peter Drucker survived Vienna's starvation years of 1917–1920, partly because of Herbert Hoover's food relief program. Then as a teenager, he lived through bitter 1920s street fighting between Socialists and Catholic Conservatives.

Vienna remained a splendid school. Owing to his parents' prominence, Drucker even as a child knew many of the intelligentsia, including Freud, an acquaintance of his father's. As a teenager, Drucker published his high school thesis in a leading economics journal and frequented a salon with such high-caliber guests as Thomas Mann.

But Vienna offered an economically bleak future to a gifted young man like Peter Drucker. In 1927, at the age of eighteen, he escaped to Germany, working first for a Hamburg export firm and then a Frankfurt bank. When the 1929 Wall Street crash reached across the Atlantic and deprived him of his place at the bank, he moved on to a job as a reporter for the Frankfurt *General Anzeiger.* In his spare time, he enrolled at the University of Frankfurt and got a doctorate for a thesis on international law.

Traveling widely for his thinly staffed newspaper, Drucker witnessed Europe's political weakness and moral failures in the late 1920s and early 1930s. The League of Nations lacked resolve, the Soviet Union was a horrible tyranny, and Germany's Weimar Republic hung on not because there was popular support for democracy but only because authoritarianism needed time to recover from the discredit of losing the war. Hitler and the Nazis had begun the noisy, violent surge that would bring them to power in 1933.

Drucker attributed Europe's moral and spiritual crisis partly to the rise of managers. Free trade worked differently in Drucker's time than in Adam Smith's. In the eighteenth century, Britain and Portugal could increase their wealth by exchanging woolens and wine, in which they had respective natural advantages. But in modern industry, managers could offset natural advantages. A nation that today could not produce nails "except at a price five times as high as its neighbor" may be "the largest and cheapest nail producer twenty years hence. Production in the industrial system is *competitive* and not complementary." The new competition heightened individuals' economic insecurity.

Marxism was no better than free trade, according to Drucker. Marxists mistakenly saw capitalists, not managers, as the source of inequality. Managers were not the "expropriators" of Marxist bugaboo, but they "have a vested interest in the maintenance of unequal society." Drucker thought that Russian industrialization under communism led to the same managerial autocracy "which rose as a corollary to big business under capitalism."

Christianity, at least in institutional form, was also no help in a managerial society. The churches spoke only to individual conscience, leaving people to face alone "permanent unemployment, and 'too old at forty.'" Himself influenced by Søren Kierkegaard and Fyodor Dostoyevsky, Drucker called existentialism politically and socially useless: "The average individual cannot bear . . . blind, incalculable, senseless forces."

With liberal economics discredited, with neither Christians nor Communists able to provide realistic alternatives, with the ordinary person unable to face a meaningless, existential universe, Drucker felt he understood why Germany fell under the Nazis' spell. He heard Hitler speak at least once in person and often over the radio, scapegoating the Jews for their supposed manipulation of the financial system.

Drucker also saw the Nazis' evil more clearly than most. Social integration of Jews had symbolized his family's cosmopolitan ideal of the

Hapsburg Empire. In 1933, the year that the Nazis came to power, Drucker published his first book—*Friedrich Julius Stahl*—about a conservative Jewish philosopher who had converted to Christianity. But the Nazis disdained Christian ethics, glorified power, and dismissed concern for its moral danger as "a ridiculous relic of 'Jewish liberalism.'"

Once in power, the Nazis moved quickly to "coordinate" the press and the universities. Having begun to teach part-time, Drucker attended a University of Frankfurt faculty meeting where the university's new Nazi commissar dismissed the Jewish professors. The Nazi told the gentile faculty members, in language then uncommon in universities, that if they didn't like it they should "fuck" themselves.

That same day Drucker prepared to leave Germany by resigning from the Frankfurt *General Anzeiger*. The new Nazi press commissar, Reinhold Hensch—himself an editor at the paper—urged Drucker to reconsider and in the process revealed how stigmatized he felt by his working-class background. But now he gloried in having a Nazi "party membership card with a very low number and *I am going to be somebody!*" Hensch ended up one of the worst Nazi butchers, leading SS troops who systematically killed the mentally retarded.

This incident stuck with Drucker as a symbol of Nazism's spiritual appeal to workers' wounded dignity. Industrialism had failed to create a "free and equal society." Capitalism had fostered a managerial elite, creating spiritual injustice: "Ford . . . forgets that economic expansion and increase are not aims in themselves." The Nazis offered a communal vision that spoke to the lost dignity of workers in managerial society.

Drucker left for London to work for four years in banking and journalism. There he wrote a pamphlet, *Die Judenfrage in Deutschland* (The Jewish Question in Germany), published in Austria in 1936, arguing for religious tolerance. Later burned by the Nazis, the pamphlet survives in a single copy in the Austrian archives with a swastika stamped on it, probably preserved by a Nazi librarian for its historical value as an example of liberal decadence.

Then Drucker crossed the Atlantic, still hoping to create dignity in the managerial economy that had shortchanged the human spirit and brought Europe to the edge of night.

PHOTO 8.2   The cover of the only surviving copy of Drucker's pamphlet, *The Jewish Question in Germany*, one of the many reasons the Drucker family had to leave Austria one step ahead of the Nazis.

Management in America

Drucker arrived in the United States in April 1937, the year of the "Roosevelt Recession" when, after a brief improvement in 1936, the economy turned downward again. Settling in New York, he reported for British papers and advised European banks on their transatlantic investments. As he got to know the country, Drucker saw through the depression to America's vitality and found its democracy more stable than Europe's.

Pragmatic Americans focused more on the corporate economy and less on ideological abstractions like "capitalism" and "communism" than did Europeans. Adolf Berle and Gardner Means, the former a member of Roosevelt's "Brain Trust," had coauthored *The Modern Corporation and Private Property* (1932), arguing that managers, not owners, controlled corporations and implying that government regulation did not violate traditional property rights. Drucker would soon cite Berle and Means in support of his idea that managers' power over workers was morally illegitimate.

Drucker was impressed by the 1930s celebration of American history and democracy. Rockefeller money rebuilt Williamsburg, the eighteenth-century capital of Virginia, and fashionable suburbanites went in for "colonial" houses with the neoclassic lines that had been popular in the era of the American Revolution. Best-seller lists included Carl Sandburg's *Lincoln* and Carl Van Doren's *Benjamin Franklin*. Drucker, in his first book published in America, *The End of Economic Man* (1939), joined the chorus: "The earlier influences which the United States had upon the victory of capitalism and formal democracy in Europe . . . probably cannot be exaggerated."

In *The End of Economic Man,* Drucker explained to Americans that Nazism's appeal lay in its remedying the spiritual injustices of a managerial society. Hitler had created new noneconomic institutions such as the Nazi Party and auxiliary social organizations where a janitor might well have power and status over a factory manager. The Nazis had raised workers' dignity and met their spiritual needs. Hoping that America would save the world from Hitler, Drucker could not yet say why the managerial economy that led to fascism in Europe would not have the same effect in America.

The End of Economic Man made the right friends and enemies. Alienating American Communists by predicting, accurately, a Hitler-Stalin alliance, Drucker's book appealed to the conservative publisher Henry Luce, who offered him an editorship on *Time* magazine. Drucker declined, detesting the weekly news magazine's superficiality. But he accepted special assignments for Luce's *Fortune* as well as the *Wall Street Journal*, giving him a chance to visit rising companies like IBM and to meet movers and shakers like labor leader John L. Lewis and agriculture secretary Henry Wallace.

Then Drucker moved on to academia. First at Sarah Lawrence and then for much of the 1940s at Bennington College, he seized on the opportunity to educate himself by teaching American history and political thought. By 1942, when he published *The Future of Industrial Man*, he believed he had found in America's decentralized political and social structure a reason to believe fascism would fail in the United States.

The American founders, Drucker said, had provided checks and balances, not just within the government but within society at large, by pitting the propertied elite against the democratic masses. Government by majority rule checked the wealthy few, but just as important, elite economic power prevented tyranny by the masses. The founders had prevented both plutocrats and populists "from becoming *the* ruling class."

Propertied Americans did not share wealthy Germans' respect for authority. Even if the American masses were to turn to Nazism for spiritual solace, the plutocracy had enough self-confidence to resist totalitarianism. Nongovernmental organizations such as foundations, churches, and charities through which private citizens rather than the government exerted social power seemed to Drucker "the strongest antitotalitarian force extant in the world."

The balance between democracy and plutocracy had endured in the United States, Drucker said, because they each had an ethical foundation. Democratic political power had a moral basis in people's commitment to human rights. And the plutocratic social power rested on popular belief in property rights. The founders had balanced not just powers but principles.

But there was a new, unethical power loose in America. Managerial power "is derived from no one but from the managers themselves, controlled by nobody and nothing and responsible to no one. It is in the most literal sense unfounded, unjustified, uncontrolled and irresponsible power."

Drucker said that managerial power contradicted democratic rights. Jefferson's faith that the people would be safe as long as the government remained too small to bother them had been fine for his time. But in Drucker's time, corporations and managers, not just the government, ruled people's working lives.

Almost alone among the economic critics of the era, Drucker focused not merely on corporations' external political and economic power but on their internal power over employees. Managerial power was illegitimate because America as a society had never formally agreed to corporate life. Corporate power had come into being as a matter of economic development, not a conscious political decision, leaving citizens little voice in the process that placed them under managers with "more power over the lives and the livelihood of a greater number of people than most of the political authorities proper."

Drucker's *The Future of Industrial Man* got much less attention than a book he attacked—James Burnham's famous *Managerial Revolution* (1941). Burnham saw an unstoppable worldwide tyranny of managers behind different government facades—New Deal, Third Reich, and Soviet Union. But Drucker criticized Burnham's "denial of the reality of the moral issues." Morality, Drucker optimistically asserted, was a real force that could head off managerial tyranny and create a legitimate society.

Drucker found American managers guiltless for the evils of a managerial society. Impressed with American managers' integrity, Drucker abandoned the idea he had developed in Europe that managers were exploiters protecting their perks: "[T]here has never been a more efficient, a more honest, a more capable and conscientious group of rulers."

As a newcomer, Drucker may not have known that American democratic culture requires the powerful to pretend that they do not enjoy power. He took seriously managers' claims of "acute discomfort" in "their positions of uncontrolled and nonresponsible social power which they did not seek, but into which they have been pushed." He was beginning to believe that managers could be made legitimate rulers, governing for the good of their employees.

He proposed that American managers adopt Nazi methods for good goals. The Nazis addressed workers' status anxieties by creating noneconomic hierarchies in which the janitor might lord it over the plant manager. American managers, Drucker said, should similarly soothe the industrial worker's wounded dignity with noneconomic social organizations within the factory.

The difference, Drucker hoped, was that democracy rather than totalitarianism would characterize the social life of the American factory and make it a "self-governing community." Managers could legitimately make strategic decisions and run the company for economic gain as long as social status came from participation in the plant's social organizations. In his book, Drucker offered few specifics except for a suggestion that workers should run the cafeteria. Later, he hoped, the factory community would control work assignments, training, and even pay, within limits set by management.

Drucker was attempting to deal with an immense deficit in decency that, despite all our talk of "empowerment," still troubles many, probably most, large organizations. Anyone who has worked for a time in a managerial organization has seen the walking wounded suffering from the humiliating contradiction between their legal equality as citizens of a free country and their de facto subjection, not just at the bottom of the ladder but beneath it. Drucker wanted to do something about it.

But could what worked for the Nazis have worked in America? Noneconomic social hierarchies may have satisfied German workers, but they would have been feeble sources of dignity in America, where money and status greatly overlap. Electing the cafeteria board may ensure employees a decent meal at a fair price, but corporate control and its rewards, not the lunch menu, secures dignity in America.

As Drucker became better acquainted with both American culture and corporations, he would slowly abandon his idea of a democratic adaptation of the Nazis' noneconomic status systems where justice and dignity came free, with no effect on the bottom line. But he continued to hope that managers would govern legitimately for the benefit of employees, never resolving the contradiction with corporate profit.

Maybe the enormous moral difference between a corporate CEO and a fascist dictator blinded the immigrant Drucker to the impossibility of morally justifying management power in a democratic culture. Democratic legitimacy requires that rulers not only try to do right by the people but answer to them. Because managers do not answer to those they govern, the people's best safeguard is a realistic acceptance of undemocratic managerial power as part of the world's moral imperfection. We live in two realms because each has its benefits. Democracy keeps us politically free and top-down managerial power makes us rich. Instead of searching for a principle of legitimacy, Drucker would have done better to accept management power for what it is—morally illegitimate, but useful.

Detroit: Heart of Industrial Civilization

With American entry into World War II, Drucker found a job in Washington, at Vice President Henry Wallace's Board of Economic Warfare. But Drucker the organizational philosopher was always too independent for organization work. He lasted only briefly in Washington, probably relieving his supervisor's unhappiness as well as his own by giving up his place as "a cog in a bureaucratic machine." Returning to Bennington to teach, he would satisfy his desire to contribute to the war effort by consulting for Uncle Sam, though it is not clear on what.

Meanwhile, Drucker cast about for a way to continue studying the political and social effects of the American corporation. The war's deepest moral objective, as he saw it, lay not just in defeating the Nazis but in creating a legitimate industrial civilization. He tried library research, but at that time little existed in print on management. And executives turned him down when he proposed to study their companies.

Drucker's self-assurance, fierce intelligence, and European cultivation—all eventually useful to him as a consultant—may have stood in his way as a supplicant for corporate access. He was short and slender but had an imposing personality and a mane of thick dark hair over an impressive dome (later, he was almost entirely bald). Who knew what this brilliant but unmanageable young man would do if let loose inside a company? The chairman of Westinghouse called him a dangerous "subversive."

Then out of the blue, as Drucker tells the story, came a phone call from General Motors, asking him to meet Donaldson Brown, with whom Drucker's *Future of Industrial Man* had struck a chord. Little known outside GM, Brown had helped create administrative tools for managing not just the automaker but much of modern industry.

A quarter century earlier, Brown had worked closely with Pierre du Pont, who pioneered the structure of industrial corporations. Originally a gunpowder manufacturer, the Du Pont Company had gone into paint, chemicals, and cellulose, then found its centralized structure wrong for its diverse products. To have just one sales department made no sense; a customer for explosives was not going to buy paint for whatever he was about to blow up. Similar problems arose in making diverse products in one big manufacturing department; should the manager give priority to paint or dynamite?

For those reasons, Du Pont decentralized into product divisions. The paint and chemicals division amounted almost to a freestanding company

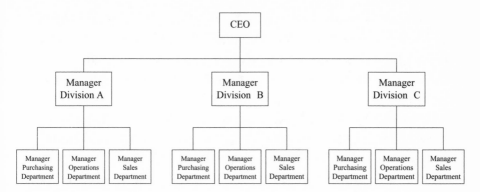

FIGURE 8.1   The M-form.

with a top manager overseeing purchasing, manufacturing, and marketing departments devoted exclusively to its products. The same applied to explosives and cellulose. This was the multidivisional corporation, famously known as the "M-form," because on an organization chart the different product divisions, with their functional departments under them, looked like a series of M's, cascading downward.

Division managers could be held responsible for results because they had complete control over making and selling their product line. But how should top management compare and evaluate division managers' performance? Their different products might require more or less capital investment, so return on investment (ROI) seemed the fairest comparative measure. Calculating ROI requires more artfulness than the layman might think, because the accountant is dealing not with a fixed investment but with a continuous process of depreciation and reinvestment. Brown, working in the Treasurer's Office, created the "DuPont formulas," as they are still known, for measuring corporate performance.

Secure in the Du Pont firmament, Brown went along in 1920 when Pierre du Pont came out of semi-retirement to reorganize General Motors. Du Pont had invested heavily in the new automobile company assembled by an energetic entrepreneur, William "Billy" Durant, only to see the firm almost go belly up.

Durant, originally a carriage manufacturer, had acquired a hodgepodge of car, truck, and parts manufacturers that he ran out of his hip pocket.

Entrepreneurially gifted but administratively challenged, Durant failed to coordinate his multifarious operations and missed the savings that rational integration would have brought. He overexpanded, piled up debt, and then, as sales fell in the post–World War I recession, could not meet his obligations. The company's creditors ousted Durant. In came Pierre du Pont and Donaldson Brown.

Brown and du Pont found ready-made at GM the organization plan they needed, drawn up by Alfred Sloan, former owner of Hyatt Roller Bearing, which he had sold to Durant. Sloan proposed an M-form, with separate divisions selling low- and high-priced cars to low- and high-income customers. Soon, GM would have five divisions—Chevrolet, Buick, Pontiac, Oldsmobile, and Cadillac—each with a top manager responsible for making and selling one and only one make. Pierre du Pont approved the plan and returned to semi-retirement. Brown stayed on at GM, with Sloan as president.

With its M-form and broad line of cars, GM surged past Ford, which stuck too long with its low-priced single product, the Model T, available as Henry Ford said in a self-defeating quip, in any color the customer wanted as long as he wanted black.

By 1943, when Drucker met Brown, GM was, had been, and would long remain the world's largest corporation. Brown held legendary status inside GM as the genius who designed the financial controls that saved the company from Durant's haphazard management. The resident intellectual in GM's hands-on culture, Brown was drawn to Drucker's emphasis in *The Future of Industrial Man* on the corporation as the modern world's "socially constitutive sphere" that had to be made morally legitimate.

Although Brown had a reputation for prolixity—the "brains of GM," a colleague said of him, but unable to speak "any known language"—he managed to explain his interest in Drucker's idea of the corporation as "constitutive" of modern society: "[M]y generation in General Motors has been aware, if only dimly, that we were doing pioneering work." But the oncoming generation of managers took GM's structure and operations for granted. A study of the corporation's internal and external social relations might open the minds of GM's next generation of managers.

Drucker delightedly accepted Brown's offer to match his Bennington salary for a two-year study of GM, an offer that would let him replace his sometimes lofty generalizations about industrialism with close-up knowledge. The new corporate society could be nowhere better studied than in Detroit, the center of the world's leading industry.

Detroit had attracted a workforce more varied than the peoples of the Hapsburg Empire—a dozen different nationalities from Europe, old-line Anglo-Saxon stock from the Midwest, French- and English-speaking Canadians, impoverished descendants of the Protestant Scotch-Irish from the upper South, and from the Deep South, blacks who found in motor city not equal opportunity on assembly lines but dirty and dangerous foundry jobs, casting engine blocks.

Detroit suffered what a local magazine called "subterranean race war," which sporadically erupted above ground, most recently in the summer of 1943 when a race riot had left thirty-four dead. Father Charles Coughlin's bigoted preaching, Henry Ford's anti-Semitism, a thriving Ku Klux Klan, and Detroit's pro-Nazi political groups showed that the city had not escaped the social ills that had yielded up fascism in Europe.

GM's labor relations festered with hostility left from the "sit-down" strike at Flint, Michigan, in the winter of 1937. Newly unionized workers had occupied two GM plants to prevent their reopening with scab replacements. The state's Democratic governor had refused to use force to eject the strikers, leaving management no option but surrender. Top GM managers, including Drucker's patron, Donaldson Brown, had made a humiliating 3 A.M. trip to the Detroit hotel room of labor leader John L. Lewis to admit defeat. Management believed a trespassing mob had cowed the government into failing to uphold GM's property rights, whereas workers saw GM's managers as tyrants who had to be forced to honor employees' legal right to unionize.

Despite the background of social tension, Drucker found GM's managers uninterested in his study of the company's place in society. They may have conceived of themselves, in Brown's word, as "pioneers," but only of new management techniques, not a new civilization, which could care for itself as far as they were concerned. Drucker shrewdly told Brown that though managers saw no internal use for a study of GM's social role, they would understand public interest in a book on the subject and would cooperate with such a project. The reasoning convinced Brown to give Drucker permission to publish his study.

But some remained skeptical of Drucker's project, including GM's president, Alfred Sloan. Nevertheless, Sloan cooperated fully and invited Drucker to sit in on top-level meetings. From late 1943 into the first half of 1945, Drucker shadowed Sloan as he shuttled by Pullman car between GM's New York and Detroit headquarters, the latter rivaling Vienna's Imperial Palace in size, with 2,000 offices and 6,000 employees.

Sloan worked as hard and lived as austerely as the Emperor Francis Joseph. On the road, the aged CEO stiffly climbed into Pullman upper berths or spent the night in a spartan sleeping cubicle in the Detroit GM building. But where the closed-minded monarch got the news he wanted to hear, Sloan, after top-level meetings, would take Drucker into his corner office on the fourteenth floor and ask for his opinion. Only a corporate outsider would tell him "whether I'm an Emperor without clothes."

Many GM managers, Drucker soon learned, had stories like his own of getting full support from Sloan for a project he disliked, stories that underlay Sloan's quiet cult of personality. With a hearing aid protruding from one ear, which exacerbated the asymmetry of his ruddy horse face topped by thinning white hair, he utterly lacked charisma. But his open-minded fairness won loyalty from subordinates.

Sloan's generosity was genuine, but his otherwise austere corporate persona was at least partly a contrivance, an intentional model of the kind of professionalism that he believed appropriate for modern management. More volatile than he usually allowed himself to appear, Sloan could be merry with family and angry with subordinates. In small work groups he sometimes lost his temper, breaking into tirades and loosing the street language of his Brooklyn youth. But unlike Henry Ford, whose tantrums gave his company the spiritual aura of a police state, Sloan used his outbursts as a paradoxical symbol of self-control. He let no more of his temper be seen than was useful in burnishing his image of performance-centered discipline directed at himself as well as others. Drucker encountered such a moment of theater when, trailing the company lawyer, he entered Sloan's office to find him screaming in fury about a GM manager. The lawyer suggested letting the man go, and Sloan calmed down instantly, "What an absurd idea; he *performs.*"

Sloan's disciplined persona became the idealized self-image of many managers ever since, an impassioned personality subject to still stronger self-control to allow for rational discussion and decisionmaking. In place of Durant's one-man show, Sloan had created management committees to discuss important decisions. He usually spoke last at meetings, hoping that consensus would be established by then. Sometimes accepting proposals with which he disagreed, he created an ambience of reasonable openness in which subordinates could work with dignity and self-respect. But no one doubted that Sloan was in charge. He could crush others' ideas when necessary.

More than anyone else, Sloan created the role of CEO, and Drucker's chance to observe the performance close up probably accounted for his later lack of sympathy for the human relations movement in general and Elton Mayo in particular. Where Mayo wanted to give organizations a somewhat disingenuous feeling of bottom-up democracy, Sloan accepted the fact that undemocratic government is part of the manager's job. GM was no Shangri-la under Sloan, who made no pretense of running the company without top-down power.

Yet there was also a profound difference between Sloan and Drucker concerning the manager's responsibility. Sloan focused on making money rather than on some easily abused ideal such as making his power morally legitimate. At some level, Sloan saw more clearly than Drucker that do-goodism, as a guide for management ethics, easily runs amok without the discipline of profit. Sloan's concern for the bottom line enabled him to build the "culture" and "develop" his people without mistaking those goals as ends in themselves. The self-control that held his temper and tyrannical urges in check, enabling him to focus honestly on employee performance, came from his focus on using his power to get the job done. Drucker, with his larger goal of making management power morally legitimate in order to fight Nazism, would inevitably produce in his study of General Motors a book that Sloan disliked.

From Social Critic to Management Guru

Drucker surely understood that Sloan's generous cooperation was aimed at influencing his study of GM, just as the CEO's openness with subordinates was a subtle method of control. Understandably, Drucker resisted, and his book on GM, *Concept of the Corporation,* suffered as a result. He missed Sloan's lesson that profit, not "legitimacy," is the best guide to corporate conduct.

Drucker noted that Sloan's subordinates wrongly credited their CEO's generosity for GM's success. This "'personality' explanation" missed the role of the M-form and the Du Pont formulas in giving managers creative autonomy and judging their performance objectively. The M-form and the Du Pont formulas made possible Sloan's collegial style, not the other way around. The company "could, if necessary, function without the personal qualities which Mr. Sloan has shown in his long administration."

Sloan had little vanity and probably agreed with Drucker that GM's success did not depend on his personality. Yet he disliked *Concept of the Corporation* and according to Drucker never allowed "it to be mentioned in his presence." "Engine" Charlie Wilson, Sloan's successor as CEO, later told Drucker that Sloan wrote *My Years with General Motors,* one of the best-selling business books of the 1960s, as a reply to Drucker, a point that has recently been disputed. Regardless of the source of Sloan's inspiration, parts of his book—such as the chapter "Concept of the Organization"—do present an opposing viewpoint to Drucker's *Concept of the Corporation.*

But Drucker somewhat mischaracterized their difference, claiming that he focused on corporate "social responsibility" and Sloan on managers' "professional" responsibility to the company. Drucker believed not that the corporation had a responsibility *to* society but that it *was* society or at least "our representative social institution."

According to Drucker, then, his study of GM raised universal moral questions about the legitimate use of power. On a second level, Drucker addressed "how the large corporation functions in America's free society." Only on his third, lowest level did he get down to customer and employee relations—that is, management as Sloan conceived it.

Drucker claimed that GM "alone of all American corporations—has for almost twenty-five years been consciously and deliberately working . . . on the conception of the modern corporation as a social institution." That was true only on the third and lowest level of his book—management technique. Sloan and most other GM managers had no interest in Drucker's notion of the corporation as the modern world's "socially constitutive sphere" on whose moral legitimacy the future of civilization depended.

Maybe Drucker thought his wish could father the fact—thought that he could move GM toward conceiving of itself as a social institution by claiming that it already did. In any case, by analyzing GM from this social perspective, Drucker sometimes lapsed into the airy moralism that Sloan had probably feared in the first place.

Drucker saw the M-form as an ideological compromise between socialism and laissez-faire, providing the benefit of both a "market check" and the scale economies of "state socialism." He claimed that GM managers saw "decentralization not as a technique of top management but as a basic economic principle of the industrial order."

One of decentralization's advantages lay in developing future leaders of the company. Under the M-form, each division needed its own manufacturing manager, sales manager, and so on, giving "four or five times as many men a chance" at "an independent command." Because of the huge size of the Chevrolet Division, some GM managers thought it should be broken up to create more opportunities for leaders to develop. Drucker gave implicit support to the idea of breaking up Chevrolet by comparing its centralized operations to the "units in a planned economy" such as "the Russian 'trusts.'"

Wherever Sloan stood on this issue, he could never have agreed with Drucker's idea that it did not matter that Chevrolet as it stood was immensely profitable. Drucker considered profitability a secondary question: "The issue between free enterprise and . . . collectivism, should not be decided on grounds of economic efficiency. It is first of all a question of the organization of a free society and secondly one of full employment." Drucker paid no attention to the fact that Chevrolet owed its huge size—equal to GM's other four automobile divisions combined—to operating in the largest, low-end part of the market. According to Drucker's idea of the M-form as a sort of public works program for creating management jobs, Chevrolet had to be broken up: "General Motors has not worked out fully the organization of the large corporation, as long as its largest divisions tend towards centralization."

Drucker also wrote about the contradiction between Christian respect for every human soul and the modern world's aligning of social status with money. But he kept to himself his idea that the Nazis had solved the problem by creating noneconomic social organizations where workers could recover their dignity. Sloan must therefore have been mystified at Drucker's idea that giving workers control of "the cafeterias, the health service, or, in places where women work, the day nurseries" would give employees "a meaningful life, with a status and function in their community."

As opposed to Drucker's idea that the corporation had to create a legitimate society, Sloan said that "[t]he primary object of the corporation . . . was to make money." In *My Years with General Motors*, he told how, during the war, he correctly predicted postwar growth in the car market and put $500 million into expansion. Drucker, by contrast, had mistakenly predicted in *Concept of the Corporation* that the car market would "become again predominantly a replacement market as it had been from 1930 to 1941." Fortunately, Sloan was the one in a position to act. Concern for profit, he might have summed it up, created the jobs on which workers' well-being depended.

Sloan also dismissed the supposedly democratic benefits of decentralization, which Drucker treated as *the* concept of the corporation. "An industrial corporation," Sloan said with sardonic understatement, "is not the mildest form of organization in society." He used the decentralized M-form to make money, not share power: "I never minimized the administrative power of the chief executive officer."

Ironically, Drucker's idea of the manager as a social leader may have had the most influence at GM's main competitor. His *Concept of the Corporation* became a must-read at Ford in the late 1940s, after Henry Ford II took over, just in time to save the company from being killed by his grandfather's quarter century of mismanagement. Ford brought in a new group of managers, the "Whiz Kids," who helped save the company by reorganizing it into an M-form, no doubt partly because of Drucker's book.

The Whiz Kids, a dozen prodigies including Robert McNamara, had run the U.S. Army's Statistical Control operation during the war and afterward sold their services to Ford. McNamara already had tendencies toward the idea of the manager as a social leader with larger responsibilities than making money. He would have found no discouragement in Drucker's book.

McNamara succeeded so well at Ford that in 1960, he became its CEO and then, a few months later, president-elect John F. Kennedy named him secretary of defense, a job in which he helped put the United States and Vietnam through a terrible ordeal. Just after the Vietnam War ended in the mid-1970s, the U.S. automobile industry began to decline because of superior quality in Japanese cars, while the Fords that did not explode on impact took only a little longer to rust.

McNamara's central role in America's two late-twentieth-century debacles—defeat in Vietnam and loss of industrial supremacy—made him the era's bogeyman, the too-smart-for-his-own-good MBA. He was accused of managing by the numbers and overruling the blood-and-sweat–stained wisdom of professional soldiers, just as he had done earlier to Ford's "car men." According to the new orthodoxy that made McNamara a symbol of managerial hubris, intuitive feeling for the product trumped quantitative analysis as a business tool. Strategy, not kill ratios, won wars.

However, McNamara, with some reason, conceived of himself not as a soulless quant but as a more generous spirit than Ford's "car men." He often employed his by-the-numbers style to further his concern for safety, economy, labor, and the environment. His broad social concerns put him at odds with Ford's ill-educated old guard, preoccupied with tail fins. They had never, McNamara later said, "taken a course in ethics, in philosophy or morals." With his saddle shoes and greased-down hair, McNamara looked the consummate square, but he came as close as any manager in his generation to the kind of socially responsible leader for which Drucker called.

McNamara's hubris can scarcely be entirely attributed to Drucker's *Concept of the Corporation*. McNamara's self-conception as a visionary leader also originated in his education at the Harvard Business School, where he studied and taught in the heyday of Elton Mayo. But McNamara's downfall supports Sloan's idea that asking managers not just to make money but build a civilization, as Drucker proposed, heightens the risk that they will lose sight of profit, which is why the corporation exists in the first place.

America eventually domesticated Drucker. The post–World War II era brought prosperity, not a new depression, relieving many of his fears. Slowly, he evolved a dual role for himself—a social critic for a corporate nation and a practical teacher of management, thanks to his fortunate eighteen months at Sloan's feet.

World War II had enlarged the market for management knowledge. Thousands of managers had gone to work for the government where they met like-minded others. Those who stayed with their companies had met their counterparts in other firms, a result of wartime economic coordination. As returning GIs entered business schools, as managers returned from government service with a new sense of group identity, they provided a market for *Concept of the Corporation*. It became recognized as the best book on management available—filled with insider information about General Motors, the world's most successful company. Hundreds of corporations structured themselves along the lines of the M-form that Drucker had celebrated in his book. He used the opportunity well and emerged as a powerful voice in the business world.

One of the best things Drucker did with his new celebrity was to question the validity of the human relations movement, though with unfortunately little effect. In *Concept of the Corporation*, Drucker had criticized Mayo's equation of workplace monotony and wartime shell shock, sensibly observing that factory humdrum differed from battlefield explosions. When Drucker, the newly ascending star, spoke kind words at the 1947 Harvard ceremony honoring Mayo on his retirement, the Australian was unappeased. He stood up and thumbed his nose at Drucker, pretending that he intended the rude gesture only as an example of workers' attitude toward top-down management.

Drucker, however, believed that Mayo's psychological manipulation was only a disguised form of top-down management. In *The Practice of Management* (1954), the major book of his career, Drucker attacked the human relations movement. Even a person reading this work alone will find it hard not to stand up and cheer Drucker's criticism of soul-meddling management fostered by a "new Freudian paternalism."

Drucker deplored the wasteful self-consciousness created by human relations' emphasis on "behavior and attitudes" instead of getting the job done. Unfortunately, workplace artificiality is probably worse now than when Drucker diagnosed the problem: "So help us, the old man has read a book; we used to know what he wanted of us, now we have to guess." Post-Mayo, workers needed to refocus on "what the job—rather than the boss—demands."

To liberate employees from the workplace's new psychological tyranny, Drucker proposed "Management by Objectives." By articulating goals based on "the objective requirements of the enterprise," managers enable subordinates to work with autonomy and "self-control" rather than as irrational neurotics manipulated from above. There is less risk of hurt and a better chance of good work when manager and employee focus on the objective needs of the business rather than each other's subjective psychology. Still influential today, "Management by Objectives" holds the longevity record for business buzz phrases because it has some genuine psychological and philosophical depth.

Hence, Drucker voiced his respect for Frederick Taylor's focus on workers' objective performance. He hyperbolically called Taylor's system of breaking work into constituent parts "the most lasting contribution America has made to Western thought since the Federalist Papers." Drucker was aware that Taylor had not solved the ethical problem of management and allowed that his ideas for handling people "have proved dubious."

Nor did Drucker solve the ethical problem of management power. He kept calling for managers to use "private virtue" in the service of "public good" as "the only legitimate basis for leadership." Keeping faith with the top-down generosity of his father's generation of Hapsburg civil servants, Drucker condemned capitalism's "cynical" streak, which based public good on private gain. But he would have labored more in the American political tradition if he had warned that no one, ever, is morally qualified to hold power over others, even if some must do so. Drucker's moral superiority to other gurus lies in his honest recognition of management's top-down power and his emphasis on its present illegitimacy, not his faith that management could be made legitimate in the future.

Over time, Drucker grew more realistic about the source of status and dignity in managerial society. He still called for worker control of the cafeteria, which he saw as an entering wedge in teaching employees the art of management so that they could gradually take more responsibility and power. But he no longer aimed to imitate the Nazis' use of noneconomic social organizations to salve souls wounded by subjection to management. Instead of an alternative to management, running the cafeteria would teach "the managerial vision," which was the only path to power and dignity within the corporation.

Managerial Idealism Defeated

Drucker became skilled at blending the role of social critic and management seer, making it hard to distinguish which of his voices had the upper hand. Even Alfred Sloan, who had thought *Concept of the Corporation* hopelessly idealistic, later believed Drucker to have become realistic enough for Sloan to try to recruit him as a professor when he endowed the Sloan School of Management at MIT. Drucker by then was at the Stern School of Business at New York University and turned Sloan down. Later, he moved to Claremont College in California.

Despite his increasing realism, there was still a disconnect between Drucker's concern for a legitimate society and his management teaching focused on profit. Managers who swallow all of Drucker's ideas may run the risk of becoming unwitting anti-corporatists. Recently, Drucker has asked, "Will the corporation survive?" and he has answered, "Yes, after a fashion." Maybe part of him wishes the answer were no.

Yet on management technique, a CEO could scarcely do better than to listen to Drucker. For more than fifty years, in dozens of choice consulting assignments, he taught managers what he had learned from Alfred Sloan, especially the benefits of decentralization and the art of mixing power with discretion. Using his inside seat to keep on learning and innovating, Drucker also contributed to new management techniques, some of which he may have hoped would weaken corporate power rather than expand it.

At General Electric, Drucker exercised great influence, beginning with his advice to Ralph Cordiner, GE's chief in the 1950s, on restructuring the company into an M-form. Successive GE leaders seem to have passed Drucker on to the next, until in 1981 he reached Jack Welch, whose fame and influence came to rival that of Alfred Sloan half a century earlier.

Drucker supplied Welch with a criterion for deciding whether to keep any particular line of business: "If you weren't already in the business, would you enter it today?" Deciding to exit any industry in which the company could not aspire to be the first- or second-largest producer, Welch multiplied GE's profitability many times over in the next two decades.

Drucker's other contribution to GE's success under Welch was the simple observation—no doubt made profound by Viennese gravitas—that "your back room is somebody else's front room." Drucker saw that the revolution in information technology lowered transaction costs and made outsourcing more profitable than previously, leading to corporate America's massive, late-twentieth-century divestitures.

In Alfred Sloan's time, it made sense for GM to serve as its own supplier of goods and services, even those for which the company had no special skill or advantage. Savings in transaction costs offset other inefficiencies. Sloan himself had come to GM through Durant's purchase of his company so as to "in-source" ball bearings.

But in Jack Welch's era, information technology lowered transaction costs, making it more profitable for GE to buy many services and parts from specialist suppliers with the expertise to do the job for less. Under Welch, GE led corporate America toward outsourcing, not just of support services but even of key manufacturing operations. It was a sort of general fulfillment of Drucker's support in the 1940s, at GM, for the idea of breaking up Chevrolet.

To the annoyance of Welch and no doubt many other CEOs, out-sourcing became a popular symbol of corporations' social irresponsibility and lack of creativity. As head count declined at major corporations, pun-dits and talking heads waxed eloquent about small entrepreneurs' success at creating new jobs. Welch resented the media's notion that small busi-nesses were more creative. According to him, the media missed the point that small business had benefited from corporate management's "con-scious transfer of work out of big business."

While Welch believed corporations were demonstrating great creativ-ity, Drucker grew ever more dissatisfied with them for their failure to use their power for the benefit of the employees they ruled. The extraordi-nary American prosperity of the mid-twentieth century had reduced his concern for corporations' legitimacy, but the harsher business climate of the century's closing decades gave Drucker's old moral concerns new rel-evance. He may have seen a larger social benefit to outsourcing than eco-nomic efficiency. Corporations shrank in size under outsourcing, a hope-ful step toward a smaller social role for illegitimate management power.

Drucker's increasing disenchantment with corporate life in the 1980s and 1990s also reflected his disgust with the era's paper profiteering and its disappointment of his 1960s and 1970s hope for "pension fund so-cialism." He had thought the rise of stock-owning pension plans meant that workers in retirement would receive the product of their labor, an event that would be a big step toward corporate legitimacy. But the pen-sion funds joined in the speculative binge, buying, selling, and dismem-bering companies for "*immediate* gain" at the cost of "long-range, wealth-producing capacity." Destructive speculation cost corporations whatever chance they had at social legitimacy and therefore seemed to Drucker "the most serious assault on management in its history."

Drucker also disagreed with the 1980s idea that Japanese corporatism marked a social advance. He had advised the Japanese on labor relations from 1953 on. After a bitter strike by Nissan workers that year, Drucker played a role in creating the system of lifetime employment by which the Japanese bought social peace. For a time he seems to have seen Japan's promise of job security as a partial fulfillment of his dream of a legitimate corporate society. But he eventually anticipated the hard lesson the Japanese learned in the 1990s—no corporation, at least in a market economy, can guarantee its employees' security.

Drucker finally gave up his nearly lifelong hope that the corporation's power could be made legitimate. Reluctantly, he admitted that "the industrial community cannot do what I hoped it would do fifty years ago," that is, build a civilization that would prevent the human wreckage, the spiritual and social havoc created by modern economic life.

Now he hoped for a "sapping" of "business as a distinct culture" and believed it was happening as America increasingly became not just a "corporate" but an "organizational" society, with nonprofit hospitals, universities, foundations, schools, churches, and charities taking over the job of legitimizing management power.

Since 1980, Drucker has increasingly devoted his consulting time, often for free, to nonprofits and has celebrated volunteerism in his writings, seemingly putting him in the spirit of the Reagan and two Bush administrations. But he had a bigger goal than did right-wing illuminati deploring dependency's harm to human character. Drucker valued volunteering and private charities not only as a way of reducing the welfare state but as a way of correcting the spiritual deficiencies of a corporate society. Volunteering benefits the volunteers, relieving the alienation created by modern business life.

Drucker said out loud what many gurus refused even to think: In the roiling global economy, the role of corporations as providers of spiritual kinship was over. But people could get "a sense of community" by contributing time and effort to nonprofits. Instead of trying for control of the cafeteria, people could carve out a sphere of fellowship in the American Cancer Society, the Heart Association, and so forth. Drucker hoped that nonprofits would give Americans the kind of alternative, noneconomic community pioneered by the Nazis, but of course for a very different, moral purpose.

What could come closer than nonprofit management to Drucker's top-down test of "legitimacy"—the exercise of power for the people's good? The nonprofit's "product is a *changed human being*"—the college's educated graduate, the hospital's healed patient, the church's healed soul. Better yet, a nonprofit "cannot command" its volunteers. So in "the non-profit agency, mediocrity in leadership shows up almost immediately." According to Drucker, in order to survive, nonprofits would have to be "management pioneers" for a morally legitimate postbusiness society.

Adding to Drucker's hope for the coming of legitimate management was the rise in numbers and importance of "knowledge workers." In the 1960s, he first called attention to the fact that "knowledge technologists" were rising alongside the traditional learned professions of law, medicine, and clergy. Paralegals and X-ray technicians often do not earn much more than assembly line workers, but their identity depends on their knowledge as well as their pay.

The new knowledge workers do not respond well to many traditional, paternalistic management techniques. Therefore, a whole new field of "knowledge management" has sprung up, with some of its attention devoted to how to instill organizational culture and spirit in knowledge workers. Drucker thought, probably hoped, that "such efforts will get nowhere."

Drucker evidently believed that knowledge workers had the power to resist management control. Possessing the new economy's key resource—knowledge—they "collectively own the means of production." Here in new form was Drucker's old, conservative hope that economic evolution would bring social justice. Instead of the corporation as the "master" and the employee as the "servant," the new knowledge worker would be "an equal—an associate or a partner."

Due to the difficulty of managing knowledge workers, the corporate sector, Drucker hoped, would have to imitate nonprofit pioneers of gentle management. Profit-oriented enterprises would have to handle their powerful knowledge workers "in the same way as volunteers who work for non-profit organizations." While other pundits lament the rise of part-time jobs and lack of corporate commitment to older employees, Drucker serenely notes that an increasing percentage of part-time, semi-retirees will be knowledge workers. Able to walk away from jobs they dislike, knowledge workers will require generous management.

Managers, in turn, will be able to be more generous because they are becoming more powerful vis-à-vis owners. In the increasingly complex corporate world, owners know too little to exercise power effectively. Companies, Drucker hopes, can only be run by "management control," insuring that "shareholder sovereignty is also bound to flounder" in favor of management.

As often before in Drucker's writings, a legitimate managerial society seems just over the horizon. With nonprofits gently managing their volunteers, with the profit sector gingerly handling its powerful knowledge workers, and with corporations too complex for control by shareholders, managers should be able to use their power for the benefit of those they manage. Drucker's vision of the near future is more attractive in many ways than today's harsh business world. Many would like to see such a society emerge.

But will it emerge? Drucker has extrapolated his vision from trends he has identified today. Has he omitted anything from the picture?

Much nonprofit work is handled by paid employees rather than benignly managed volunteers. Some of the well-paid movers and shakers who manage nonprofits ape the ruthless savvy and self-interested style of their worst corporate cousins. In the absence of bottom-line discipline, ineffective and tyrannical nonprofit managers can probably cover up their incompetence and abuse of power longer and more successfully than their corporate counterparts.

Yet Drucker believes that it is a sign of progress that "management" is no longer "a very bad word in non-profit organizations." He hopes that nonprofits will develop new management techniques and pass them on to corporations. Surely, the reality is the other way around, with nonprofits being run more and more like corporations, with museums living off their gift shops, hospitals profiting from their medical research, and universities turning their bookstores into retail chains. Drucker has not explored the possibility that management values may distract nonprofits from their goals.

Drucker has also not considered the possibility that a nonprofit, whose success is not measured in dollar signs, can use sophisticated marketing and management-speak more successfully than a corporation to cover up its failure to achieve its mission. Corporate values, with long experience at speaking the soft, seemingly generous language of human relations, mingle comfortably in nonprofits, often under cover of the managerial focus on building the "team" and creating a "new culture" that easily substitutes for, instead of assisting in, the nonprofit's mission in education, health, or science.

Drucker's blindness to the harsh reality of work life for at least some nonprofit employees suggests how inapt the moral standard is that he brought with him from Europe—exercise of power for the benefit of the powerless. His vision of America as a managerial society with little power for owners would amount to a vicarious victory for his father's generous social vision, a triumph of the ideals of the enlightened Hapsburg civil service over those of the benighted emperor. But as with any high ideal, imperfect human beings will often fall short of it, which is why Drucker's appeal for a legitimate managerial society is a poor substitute for Jefferson's democratic reminder that power is always suspect.

Yet as soon as Drucker climbed down from the question of moral legitimacy that had confounded him all his life, no one offered better practical advice on managing nonprofits with their dedicated staff for whom being "betrayed . . . hurts much more." Who more likely to betray the dedicated than those against whom he had always warned—the egotistic leader, the cocksure judge of people, the manager who loses sight of the organization's real goal, like the college president "so totally preoccupied with money-raising" that he betrays academic values in the name of booster success? What better guidelines could there be for handling dedicated nonprofit workers than Drucker's idea of managing by objectives and evaluating performance, not personalities?

As I write, Drucker carries bravely on, living in a modest ranch house in California, contributing advice to nonprofits, consulting for corporations, and still prophesying the coming of a legitimate society.

Conclusion

THE STORY OF THE PIONEER GURUS MATTERS TODAY BECAUSE they helped to create unrealistic hopes for democracy and moral legitimacy in the workplace that continue in our time. Today's gurus push far harder than Gantt and the Gilbreths the idea that reorganizing work to make it more efficient and profitable will also give employees more freedom, community, and satisfaction. In view of this conventional managerial wisdom, it can only be harder than ever for managers to strike the right balance between power and participation.

Attempts at manipulative control of purportedly bottom-up organizations, pioneered by Mayo, are now widespread, thanks to the idea of managing culture. More than Barnard could ever have imagined possible, today's leadership gurus teach that management is mainly a matter of moral authority. The moral ambiguity of corporate life—with which Deming and especially Drucker struggled bravely if unsuccessfully—is brushed aside with simpleminded assurances that the right thing to do is also the most profitable.

As in the past, today's gurus are mostly generous, well-intentioned people. Often, they seem like old-fashioned political liberals, combining bottom-up idealism with a taste for top-down benevolence. The idea of managing the life of Joe Six-Pack better than the poor sap could do for himself tarred late-twentieth-century heirs of the New Deal with a reputation for elitism. Aspiring social engineers these days find little opportunity to tinker in government. Flocking to the corporate workbench that Elton Mayo first built for them, they are all the more eager to sell their managerial visions in the language of democracy and idealism.

Even the brashest gurus, while claiming to be earthy realists, cannot help reaching for the sublime. Management consultant Tom Peters has said, "Profit is fine—a sign that the customer honors the value of what we do. But enterprise (a lovely word) is about heart. About beauty." It is, of course, exactly the other way around. Most customers have little interest in "honoring" anyone's work but want it for their own purposes, which is why they pay for it. Heart and beauty are "fine" if you can find them in business, and some do. But "enterprise" is first and foremost about profit, which is good because it is money in our pocket.

The gurus' false high notes often make it hard to take them seriously, but along with the hype, they offer some good ideas. Their advice, both good and bad, sells because those who live the corporate life need an interpretation of it. The gurus' market is demand driven. They overreach for freedom and heroic virtue in business, but that does not prove that "business" is no "way of remaking oneself, of achieving the elusive original relation to the universe." The gurus just have a hard time admitting the moral ambiguity of the real world. But they should. Doing so would not negate but rather would make clear the importance of the gurus' often sound and practical ideas for increasing our personal effectiveness at work, for avoiding organizational short circuits, and even for living an examined life.

Unfortunately, the glitter of the gurus' good ideas spills over onto the dross. Their useful insight and advice adds attractiveness and credibility to their pretensions to portentous significance, to their pandering flattery of their audience as moral leaders, and to their unrealistic denials of the importance and necessity of top-down power in corporate life.

The gurus' mixed bag of ideas understandably appeals to many real-life managers, who after all have a tough job. But some of the gurus' unrealistic ideas, especially on power, may only make managers' jobs tougher. Managers who underestimate their authority may not know how to use it when they most need it. And unrealistic preaching of bottom-up empowerment may promote wariness rather than enthusiasm in the ranks. Painful as it may be for managers to admit that their top-down power sometimes puts them at odds with the values of a democratic society, such realistic honesty has a better chance of winning employees' support and trust than denying the obvious. Still more important, managers may achieve some useful moral caution and humility by acknowledging that they possess dangerous power as a matter of necessity in an imperfect world, not because they are morally qualified for it. That is a far better safeguard against self-righteous arrogance than the popular notion of the manager as a moral leader, which appeals to vanity and runs the risk of promoting immoral hubris.

Sorting out good management ideas from bad may be managers' toughest job of all. Managers are alert to the danger of sweetened medicine, which is why every guru claims to be selling bitter pills. Even experienced executives sometimes fall for chimerical comforts marketed as tough-to-swallow tonic. The elixir is all the more enticing when it has some salubrious ingredients mixed with the snake oil. That's the case with much of the conventional wisdom that recent gurus have offered us about work, culture, leadership, and ethics.

Work

If there is one principle on which gurus agree, it is that work is getting better: "Life at work can be cool—and work that's cool isn't confined to Tiger Woods, Yo-Yo Ma, or Tom Hanks. It's available to all of us and any of us." That's a quote from Tom Peters. It comes from an article in which he claims as his discovery the idea that people and passion count—just a few paragraphs after he has modestly credited the idea to predecessors like Warren Bennis and Douglas McGregor. Peters does not mention that those humanist luminaries were in turn preceded by Mayo and Gantt. Does he know that about once a decade for the last century, it keeps being rediscovered that making work cool gets the most productivity out of people? When such a nice idea keeps getting forgotten and rediscovered, it may be only a partial truth.

The idea that work should be personally rewarding has certainly moved up the charts in recent years. Work is no longer God's retribution for the Adam in us but a "sacred" part of what gives life meaning. Mar-

keting surveys report that more than our forebears, we want, if not sanc-
tification, at least satisfaction from work.

Information technology is the new grail. Computer networks, we are
told, enable us to reengineer corporations, flatten hierarchies, tip vertical
structures on their sides, and design organizations themselves as learning
systems "where it is safe for people to create visions, where inquiry and
commitment to the truth are the norm, and where challenging the status
quo is expected." And it sometimes works. The gurus have now and then
not only improved our organizations' operating efficiency but have also
enlarged our jobs in satisfying ways.

Sure, reengineering was overdone, got confused with downsizing, and
became as ugly as its name. Only a bold and reckless manager would an-
nounce a "reengineering" project these days. However, only the name has
gone out of fashion. Reengineering's basic concept about integrating work
processes is alive and well.

Michael Hammer, one of reengineering's creators, now says the "big
idea" business book is one of the "sins for which I may one day be called
to account." Still, the 1993 book he coauthored with James Champy,
Reengineering the Corporation, contained a good idea. Using the computer
to break down department boundaries and organize work along the lines
of business processes helped a lot of companies fatten the bottom line.

Unfortunately, the reengineers claimed that spiritual rewards were a
central feature of their program and way oversold the idea. They
promised not only to make us more productive but also more human.
They argued that abandoning the task orientation of industrialism and
centering work on organic business processes would be more psychologically gratifying because workers do a "whole job—a process or a subprocess," giving them "a greater sense of completion, closure, and accomplishment." Focused on the "customer," the "process performer" has
the satisfaction of providing a service or product someone "cares about."

A moment of reflection suggests how dubious those promises are. Any
"whole job" is a subprocess of a larger job. Not larger responsibility, but
the imaginative and intellectual ability to see oneself in a bigger context
is the main ingredient that gives one a sense of wholeness. The reorgani-

zation of work will never relieve finite human beings of the difficulty of finding meaning in the fragmented and the mundane.

The reengineers called downstream workers "customers," but that did not guarantee that they would "care about" what came down the line. Hammer and Champy were surely right that doing work that others care about adds a lot of meaning to life. But figuring out what others really care about in an organization is no simple task. One of the loudest signals we get about whether others care about our work is what they are willing to pay for it. And the people who decide on the pay of most of us are managers, not customers or fellow employees down the line.

In regard to pay, reengineering's prophets offered a simplistic, near utopian vision of justice just around the corner. By putting the process first, by putting teams of workers in charge of the process, and by putting evaluation in the hands of teammates, the reengineers promised to make pay an objective matter of what the employee has earned. With compensation objectively determined by performance, employees would no longer be at the mercy of a tyrannical manager's subjective evaluation. And because process-centered organizations would create more value, "there is more income, therefore, to be shared with those who create that value." Employees would not be underpaid because reengineering requires high-caliber workers, giving companies "a real incentive to pay people what they are worth."

A caravan of eighteen-wheelers could drive through the gaps in that reasoning. Being evaluated by teammates is not the same thing as having them determine one's pay. Management still puts the dollar number beside the evaluation. And the way managers determine that number is not so different now than in Taylor's era. Like today's reengineers, Taylor reorganized work and increased the value of workers' contribution. But the relative power of management versus labor, both in the company and in the marketplace, determined who benefited from the extra value.

That doesn't mean that managers don't care about the quality of the work employees deliver. But it means that it may be impossible for them to signal their caring with higher pay for higher value. That's why so many gurus have focused on intangibles. That's all right, but only as long as the possibility of personal fulfillment is not substituted for material rewards. To turn spiritual rewards into an alternative to material compensation takes a rare talent for leadership in combination with a great cause. Few of us, whether managers or not, are capable of acting the part of Gandhi. And because the corporation's basic cause is material gain, it is dishonest to try.

At least the reengineers empowered workers, right? Sure they did, some of the time. But extended responsibility for work processes can also mean disempowerment, not just for factory hands but for knowledge workers and professionals. Next time your HMO doctor wearily spends a minute or two hunting and clicking with a mouse to punch your prescription into a computer—a job that once took a few seconds' scribbling on a pad—ask if he or she feels empowered. The computerized process may be an improvement because the prescription automatically gets e-mailed to the pharmacy as well as included in your medical record with less chance of error. But the doctor's new responsibility detracts from the interest of the job and has been imposed at a time when physicians are being disempowered, not empowered, by "managed care."

Like the pitchmen for many big management ideas, reengineers promised that the process-centered workplace "democratizes the traditional organization." Using work processes as an organizational principle gets rid of "feudal relics" like "a proletariat of frontline workers, a bourgeoisie of middle managers, and an aristocracy of senior executives." Value added, not position, supposedly determines status. Putting "customers and those who serve them at the top" negates "the very notion of top."

What those noble sentiments leave out is that with job descriptions no longer carved in stone, the folks who run the company (regardless of whether they are called by some New Age substitute for "management") have more, not less, arbitrary power and capacity to create injustice. In reengineered organizations, many people work not just smarter but much, much harder for pay envelopes that grow no fatter. Some of the harsh working conditions that reengineering created may have been unavoidable in an increasingly competitive global economy. But reengineering also provided cover for unnecessarily and unjustly sweating more productivity and profit out of many people's skins, helping to provoke the despair and resentment that has become a larger part of the work-place in the past two decades.

Reengineering, with its focus on reorganizing work to raise productiv-ity, is sometimes described as latter-day Taylorism. That's unfair to Taylor. Scientific management often made work harder and harsher, but at least it never promised to turn corporations into spiritual rose gardens. Nei-ther will any sensible manager.

What managers need to know about work is basic. By all means reor-ganize and restructure to do the job best. Make work as much fun as pos-sible, but not a bit more. Employees didn't sign up for nirvana and won't be disappointed if you don't offer it to them. If you do, the meaner spir-its will think you're a liar and the more generous will suspect you of kid-ding yourself.

Culture

If we can't manage work to make it perfectly satisfying, how about giving people satisfaction by going straight to the heart of the problem and man-aging their feelings? Everyone agrees that people work best when they work with a will. What a shame for the company not to get the benefit of super-nal motivation and for workers to be less than perfectly happy just because the real world is a place of inevitable compromise and dissatisfaction.

Managing feelings is of course an ancient art. Military leaders have known the importance of morale ever since they first led soldiers into battle. And Elton Mayo's industrial psychology was about nothing if not about managing feelings. But in our "psychological" age, psychological manipulation has become increasingly recognizable and only slightly less off-putting than martial law. In the early 1980s, when the management movement began to burst its cocoon and become part of mainstream Americana, the heirs of the human relations movement needed a new, more innocuous model. They found it in "culture."

In the 1970s, the concept of "culture"—the idea that socially incul-cated values are a powerful determinant of behavior—spread from an-thropology into other academic disciplines and became influential among the chattering classes. In 1978, the radical historian Christopher Lasch published a best-selling jeremiad, titled *The Culture of Narcissism,* that blamed the "contemporary malaise" and selfish values of the me decade on the "bureaucratization of the spirit" that had taken place in the "modern economy." President Jimmy Carter helped publicize Lasch's book by citing it as his inspiration for going on national television, hurting his re-election chances in the process, to chastise Americans for their "malaise."

Malaise in the ranks is the enemy of every manager. If it can be caused by bad cultural values, it's obviously time for a new culture. Managers spontaneously embraced the idea of "corporate culture," which sprang into life fully formed as the latest business buzz phrase, its provenance attributable to no single individual. In 1980, *Business Week* ran a cover story on corporate cultures, featuring a dozen CEO's anecdotes of how ignoring or attending to company values had hurt or helped the bottom line.

The gurus raced to catch up. Tom Peters, one of only two management consultants mentioned in the *Business Week* story, joined Robert Waterman in writing *In Search of Excellence* (1982). In traditional guru fashion, they described top-down "strong cultures" as instruments of bottom-up liberation. Successful companies had "loose-tight" qualities, with the result that "[i]n the very same institutions in which culture is so dominant, the highest levels of true autonomy occur. The culture regulates rigorously the few variables that do count . . . . But within those qualitative values (and in almost *all* other dimensions), people are encouraged to stick out, to innovate."

Other gurus such as Peter Senge, who did not explicitly deal with "culture," pushed some of the same buttons. Senge's *The Fifth Discipline* (1990), which popularized the idea of the "learning organization," drew a lot of credibility from the impressive sophistication with which the book applied models of self-defeating systems dynamics to managers and organizations. But Senge advocated integrating "systems thinking" with other, much more traditional disciplines such as "mental models" and "shared visions" that held the same appeal to managers as "culture" and "values." They promised "control without controlling."

The gurus saw culture as both a management tool and an instrument of human liberation. Whereas many anthropologists held that culture is a "kind of resource" that is used in the social "arena," management gurus tended to think that culture was all there was to social organization. Social scientists saw behavior as determined not just by internalized cultural values but by external "arrangements of status, power, and identity." Social scientists commonly acknowledge the objective reality of external power as opposed to internalized cultural values. But leading gurus used the culture concept to argue that freedom, aided by a new sense of organic wholeness, would abolish top-down power while simultaneously creating a more effective corporate order. Senge was only one of many who believed that "shared visions" would allow organizations to "be both more locally controlled *and* more well coordinated than their hierarchical predecessors."

This promise of coordination without coercion explains the twenty-year survival—a near record—of "culture" and "values" as management buzzwords and a vital part of the intellectual arsenal not just of gurus but of many ordinary managers. "Learning organizations" have all but disappeared into the hazy abstractions of systems analysis, "reengineering" is applied furtively under cover of John Doe aliases, and old jokes like Tom Peters's "liberation management" don't get a smile. But "culture" and "values" thrive in hearty good health because they give managers with democratic consciences a convincing way to speak about organizational coherence without acknowledging top-down power.

"Culture" helps both managers and employees deny the unpleasant fact of prescribed behavior. "Culture" suggests that people are acting not according to authority but out of commitment to internalized values, which is the essence of freedom. And when newly prescribed behavior meets resistance, "culture" is a polite way to explain the organization's inertia and to cover up whatever power struggles are going on.

Gurus and managers apply the culture concept to something very real in organizational life. But often they are misapplying it, using "culture" to describe what used to more accurately be called morale and procedures, not the deeply held values and mores to which anthropologists refer. The rubric "culture" seems applicable because morale and procedures, like values and mores, involve feeling and knowledge. But the feelings involved in morale are far less deeply rooted than those that operate in culture and values. And knowledge of procedures is far less a matter of tacitly understood mores than explicit understanding of "that's the way we do it here."

Employees are often emotionally involved and sometimes highly committed to a company, especially if their real, deeply held personal values are well aligned with the company's procedures and objectives. But for other employees, manipulative "corporate cultures" will not succeed in changing values.

That "corporate culture" does not usually refer to deeply held values and mores is made clear by the ease and rapidity with which managers claim to change it. Morale and procedures, however, are genuinely subject to rapid change because they have less to do with personal commitments and values than with a sense of being treated effectively and fairly. Anyone who has experienced injustice in the workplace knows how quickly an inept or unethical manager can depress morale.

Does it matter that morale and procedures are mistakenly called "culture?" Yes, it does. Misapplication of the culture concept can lead managers to try to manipulate values rather than to attack problems head on. Savvy employees understand the game and ingratiate themselves by propping up phony corporate cultures. Morale is probably often hurt rather than helped by the indirection and ineffectiveness that the culture concept promotes.

The effect on earnest employees can be even worse. They may buy into the new "culture" as if it were deeply held. If the organization has to abandon its new "values" as quickly as it adopted them, the shock will be worst among the believers. If they are hurt in the process, they may be turned into organizational cynics.

"Culture change" probably ought to be dropped as a management tool. Although it can be effective, its effectiveness too often depends on smoke and mirrors. Employees must either not see or pretend not to see that they are being manipulated by top-down power. If they do not see it, they are likely in for demoralizing disillusionment down the road. If they do see it, they will either cooperate hypocritically or else resist what they see as hypocritical management, damaging morale either way.

Managing morale is a less appealing job than managing "culture" because there is a lot less apparent room for indirection and manipulation. Morale is much more clearly a matter of justice and effectiveness. Managers who treat employees as fairly as they can without letting human relations techniques distract them from business goals have mastered two of the three principles for managing morale.

The third principle for managing morale is to avoid disingenuous denials of top-down power or, worse, self-righteous claims that power is earned by moral authority. That brings me back to the paradox I presented in the Introduction, namely, that the creation of as much justice as is possible in corporate life depends on honest recognition of its inherent injustice and compromises. Managing for morale requires recognition that employees trade freedom for work under top-down power because it pays better than working alone. Most employees know the score and are capable of high morale in imperfect and unjust situations as long as they believe managers are honestly doing the best they can. But managers who do not know that they are in possession of unjust top-down power are less likely to have enough moral humility to create the limited amount of justice that is all it takes for high morale.

Leadership

For more than half a century—going back at least to Chester Barnard—the belief that managers lead less by power than by moral authority has grown ever more popular. The claim of moral superiority, not always explicit, has helped support the recent cult of CEO celebrities. In the wake of Enron and other scandals, the mass media will probably stop celebrating CEOs for at least the near term. But there is a whole industry of business leadership gurus and consultants likely to use Enron as justification to keep on touting the idea that good management is a matter of moral authority.

The idea of the manager as a moral leader meshes well with the conventional wisdom about the new realities of business. Command-and-control bossism is outdated in a fiercely competitive global economy. Not top-down managers but leaders inspire bottom-up energy and fast, flexible teamwork that wins the race to market. Some of that may be true, but managers' top-down power to justly or unjustly reward and punish performance has not disappeared.

Leadership as a business school discipline is a crowded field. No wonder. It offers intriguing opportunities for the practitioner to dabble in the fascinations of psychology and have a gratifying impact on people of prominence while earning lucrative consulting fees. In this crowded domain there are senior statesmen such as Warren Bennis, but no one stands out with éclat from the multitudinous crowd of journeymen leadership gurus.

Maybe the leadership gurus are all too much of a piece in their well-balanced psyches. The most successful gurus have a common characteristic—personal charm—that puts them among the most attractive people on business school faculties. But the field's satisfying personal rewards also create its main occupational hazard, a sort of preening in the guru's own righteous humanism that pops up in the ideas of even the most scrupulous and that can create a moral insensitivity to the realities and dangers of power.

Because leadership is thought to be a matter of personality, the gurus focus mainly on psychological growth. The therapeutic orientation that Mayo applied so assiduously to workers is now devoted with far more intensity to managers. Leaders are change agents prepared not just to take "control of a political structure" but to transform it, just as they have already done with their own personality through some lonely "psychodrama" that has qualified them to lead others toward their revolutionary vision.

The leader, in short, is one of those "twice-born" souls whom William James celebrated a century ago in his *Varieties of Religious Experience* (1905), which is why leadership courses and workshops have a flavor of religious revivalism. Taking Erik Erikson's psychobiography *Gandhi's Truth* (1969) as their master text, the leadership gurus give their teachings a subtle spiritual appeal by making religious conversion their tacit model of the psychodynamics that create secular business leaders. Few of us, of course, actually wish to be spiritually reforged in the kind of psychological fire that created Gandhi, which is why saints are not found on every street corner. But the business leader needs at least to "begin the arduous process of becoming himself."

No one could object to the ideal personal characteristics and behavior that managers are supposed to develop as they undergo their spiritual metamorphoses into leaders—faithfulness to oneself, earning of trust by trusting others, willingness not just to take risks but to learn from inevitable mistakes. To judge by the leadership literature, the problem of management tyranny is restricted to pathological personalities who engage in "narcissistic leadership." The psychologically healthy leader exemplifies and therefore inspires in others openness, empathy, optimism, faith, and vision.

What gets left out or at least shortchanged in the leadership literature is power. The leadership gurus will sometimes use the word "power," but as with "culture," they misuse it or at least underuse it. Power, Warren Bennis and Bert Nanus have said, is "the basic energy needed to initiate and sustain action." So vague a definition allows power to be thought of mainly as the ability to influence, inspire, and empower others. Such abilities are only a limited aspect of power, though they fit very nicely with the benevolent, idealistic aspects of leadership as taught in the business schools. But other basic aspects of power, such as control of the social and institutional apparatus that enables the powerful to punish and reward others in order to coerce and entice behavior, are omitted. Or if these unpleasant aspects of power are included, they are described as a "misuse" of power. According to Bennis and Nanus, "Historically leaders have controlled rather than organized, administered repression rather than expression, and held their followers in arrestment rather than in evolution."

Control, repression, and arrest are ugly things, but they are not a "misuse" of power. They are its unavoidable essence. The point, for example, of the rule of law in democratic societies is not to abolish such things as control, repression, and arrest but to use them justly to deter and punish criminal behavior while guarding against tyrannically unjust application of such power to good citizens. It is the relative lack of legal restraint and large potential for injustice to the worthy within the thankfully limited world of the corporation that makes managerial power painful to accept in a democratic society.

The negative aspects of power may be hard to accept, but leadership gurus need to get real. To suppose that it is not sometimes the job of corporate leaders to use power to control, repress, and arrest the actions of their subordinates is wishful thinking in the extreme and a hindrance to achieving effective leadership. No one can prescribe the right balance in any particular situation, but successful leaders mix the gentle virtues with force. Gandhi's nonviolence gave him a moral advantage but scarcely relieved him of the necessity of using strikes, boycotts, and other forms of coercive power.

Only by omitting the reality of management power as arbitrary and coercive are leadership gurus able to describe corporate ideals in terms of "democracy," a "system of values" characterized by "communication," "consensus," "influence," "expression," and a "human" bias. That those are often good and useful qualities for corporations to possess will be disputed by few. But precisely because they are fostered from the top down by management rather than being the law of a sovereign people, they do not and cannot make the corporation democratic.

The enormously difficult challenge of the corporate leader is to encourage "communication," despite the existence of the manager's arbitrary top-down power to curtail it. Unlike a democratic government, management has the power to end discussions so that we can quit talking, get to work, and make money. The trick, of course, is to know when and how to end the conversation, which is one of the true marks of leadership. A good way to make a bad start as a manager is not to face up to the fact of one's power and to suppose that "communication" in corporations is the same sort of moral absolute that free speech is in democracies.

One could argue, of course, that the gurus' predilection for "democracy" is just a metaphor, and not to be mistaken for the reality of corporate life and its top-down power. When Warren Bennis calls for "leadership, not management," he is not claiming that we do not need managers but just emphasizing that the best managers are leaders. But what else can we understand Michael Hammer to be saying than that we no longer have either "managers" or "workers" because "neither of these terms has much meaning anymore?" When Peter Senge says that learning will become "an inescapable way of life for managers and workers (even if we bother maintaining that distinction)," the only reasonable gloss on his parenthetical phrase is that learning organizations will make managerial power passé.

Gurus will be gurus, but surely no living, breathing manager actually believes that there will ever be corporations without managerial power! Unfortunately, naked emperors really do sometimes mistake a fashionable whimsy for a handsome suit of clothes. Recently, a CEO proudly announced that workers at a company plant had voted to decertify their union, an action showing that the company's "philosophy of radically decentralized decision making puts them in control and effectively eliminates 'management.' Without a management to confront and with no one designated as 'labor,' these people did not see a substantial role for their union."

Decertification of the union may or may not show that something good is happening for those workers, but we may be confident that "management," even in quotation marks, is not being eliminated. And it would be a bet worth more than even money that that CEO believes he leads less with power than with moral authority.

Ethics

Although the gurus usually underestimate power, they are undoubtedly right that moral authority is an important aspect of leadership. But moral authority does not imply moral superiority. Morally inferior people can possess great moral authority. Hitler's followers, for example, believed profoundly in his ethical superiority.

The first thing to recognize about moral authority is that it is often immoral and toxic to those who possess it. It encourages self-satisfaction that is an ethical trap, promoting the self-righteousness that corrupts character and rationalizes injustice. Moral authority only increases power's tendency to believe, as Jefferson said, "that it has a great soul and vast views, beyond the comprehension of the weak; and that it is doing God's service while it is violating all his laws."

What a contrast with the naive moral philosophy of management as it has been espoused by gurus, business schools, and corporate leaders.

When the Enron scandal broke, the business press featured a naïve business-school professor claiming to have hard data proving that ethics pays. Some of the thieves at Enron and WorldCom may spend some time behind bars. But others, we may safely predict, will get off scot-free for looting their companies of tens and even hundreds of millions of dollars. Try telling them that they did badly, either ethically or financially!

Profit is an admirable thing, but not as a motive for ethics. We admire ethical conduct not when it's easy and profitable but when it hurts. The work of improving corporate morality and reducing the number of future Enrons is not just a matter of better accounting standards but of abandoning the gurus' illusions about managing through moral authority.

Managers often have and sometimes deserve moral authority. But they earn it by getting the job done and making money while treating others as fairly and honestly as they can, not by preaching and exhorting. The surest way to destroy moral authority is to try to use it as an instrumental tool, which is what some Enron managers did.

Contemporary gurus like Gary Hamel, who a few years ago enthusiastically embraced Enron as an example of "business concept innovation," could be made the butt of many jokes. That would not be fair. Hamel and his ilk were as duped as investors into believing Enron was immensely profitable.

But Hamel and even gurus who never breathed the name of Enron bear some responsibility, not for the company's financial corruption, but for creating and supporting the managerial fantasies that provided its moral cover. Hamel used Enron as a principal example of his idea—or rather the gurus' tired old idea—that companies "are going to have to become less like autocracies and more like democracies."

Hamel saw Jeffrey Skilling, the architect of Enron's strategy of "business concept innovation," as a generous-spirited manager who created an ambience of trust and empowerment. Skilling brought heavy hitters to Enron and encouraged them to swing for the fences, Hamel approvingly reported, by richly rewarding home runs while not punishing strikeouts: "At Enron, failure . . . doesn't necessarily sink a career."

The more recent picture of Enron as a citadel of top-down terror to rival the Death Star and of Skilling as the company's Darth Vader may be no more accurate. If the new image of Skilling as the prince of darkness goes unquestioned, gurus like Hamel could say they got the facts of this particular story wrong, but not the basis of management in bottom-up power and top-down morality.

What if Hamel came closer to getting the story right in the first place? What if there was something, maybe a lot, to his original finding that Enron was a high-spirited community of freedom and creativity because of Skilling's leadership? Only subsequently have Enron employees come forward to say that Skilling terrorized them. At the time, some of his colleagues and subordinates, especially those whom he made into multimillionaires, probably thought him a pretty decent fellow.

Maybe the idea of management by moral authority helped cause or at least support corruption at Enron. At some point, of course, Enron managers crossed a line beyond which it is hard to believe they had much room for self-deception as to their wrongdoing. That is why some teachers of business ethics say that Enron is useless as a case for sensitizing managers' consciences; Enron was just conscienceless thievery. But that is too narrow a notion of business ethics, which is not just a matter of keeping one's hands off other people's money but of maintaining a managerial worldview that does not corrupt the conscience. The idea of the manager as a moral leader is well adapted for corrupting the conscience.

Skilling himself may have believed he was a moral leader humanizing business. Coming to Enron in 1990 with a Tom Peters-like background of consulting at McKinsey and little experience in actually managing, he used the "loose-tight" language of *In Search of Excellence* to describe his idea of promoting bottom-up innovation while applying pressure from the top to make the numbers. The system of evaluation by coworkers that he put in place at Enron—now criticized for fostering fear but touted at the time as rewarding teamwork—resembles the traditional Harvard Business School emphasis on the small group as the organic, communal business unit that best liberates human potential.

Maybe it was only when Skilling's orthodox business-school faith in freeing people from control failed to work its promised alchemy of turning moral authority into gold that he ended up fiddling with the books. His erratic behavior in his last few weeks at Enron suggests less the desperation of a cornered crook than a neurotic crisis in the face of a collapsing dream castle.

Ken Lay, Skilling's predecessor as Enron CEO, took moral leadership no less seriously. After the Enron story broke, television news programs ran file footage of Lay sermonizing like a teaching elder on the "core of values" in the heart of every "leader." The TV coverage aimed to suggest that Lay was a pious hypocrite. But the subordinates who have come forward so far have reported that Lay, unlike Skilling, was a hands-off manager who lacked the accounting know-how to arrange Enron's complex deals. Lay probably truly, not hypocritically, believed he could run the company by going around telling others what a good person he was.

It will be a long time before we know the whole Enron story, but the gurus' notion of management by moral authority should not be let off the hook until we do. The role of false moral prophecy in corrupting Enron would make a great study if the principals could ever be persuaded to submit to in-depth examination or, most unlikely, would honestly examine themselves.

Regardless, the idea of top-down moral leadership ought to be abandoned as both an undemocratic conceit and a threat to business ethics. The gurus' notion of using moral authority as a management tool is misguided at best. Whether or not it played a direct role in the psychology of Enron's leaders, it is a recipe for their kind of false pride and spiritual corruption.

In the age-old debate among philosophers as to whether the purpose of ethical education is to improve the will or inform the understanding, the latter position makes the most sense in the corporate world. Most managers are already people of reasonably good will, but they need better understanding of the moral snares among which they work. Real business ethics begins with honest understanding of the unjust and undemocratic nature of managerial power and the temptations it creates for self-righteousness and self-deception. Only managers with that kind of understanding and humility have a shot at creating a corporate life that is reasonably just and ethical.

Genuine moral concern finds most of its expression in action and recognizes that moralistic talk is not only cheap but dangerous. It would be a sign of progress in business ethics if our corporate leaders spoke less about morals and more about what they are doing to promote real growth in the bottom line.

—◦—

The business world and all the rest of us, too, should demand more from management gurus. Walt Whitman said that there are no great poems without great audiences, and we may count on the gurus to give us advice no better than we demand.

Many able managers already know how imbalanced the gurus' teachings are on work, culture, leadership, and ethics. They know that:

1. It is counterproductive to oversell spiritual rewards and to pretend that a lot of work is not still an unpleasant necessity done mainly for money.
2. Morale or "culture" cannot be manipulated but arises from fair and effective management of people and real business problems.
3. Leadership is not just the inspiration of bottom-up participation but is also the imposition of control and direction through top-down power.
4. Managers' power endangers their souls, yet it is riskier still, both practically and ethically, to try to manage only with moral authority.

Not that the gurus' teachings are all bad or useless even to the best managers. There is still plenty of useful wisdom in thinking along the lines of Peter Drucker's half-century old idea of managing by objectives. Focusing on whatever pleasant or unpleasant work needs doing instead of pretending that all work is spiritually rewarding is the starting place for respecting employees' dignity and improving morale.

Mary Parker Follett's notion of the company as a potential person formed by employees' integration of their thoughts and desires into a harmonious whole is an unachievable ideal but is still far more practical as a guide for managers than manipulating "culture." Two people working together do sometimes have the satisfaction of creating a new self, different from that with which either of them began. But their catalyst can only be the need to solve a real problem. Able managers do not manipulate values but help employees do their jobs, which is the only source of any useful new spirit.

As Follett saw, not all opposing desires can be integrated. Even if it were possible, life is too short to do it. That makes the boss's top-down power an unavoidable necessity. Sometimes managers can minimize the use of power by working with employees to discover "the law of the situation" and taking their orders from it. That is how, as Follett said, leaders can follow and followers lead. But unfortunately, different people often read situations differently, which means that sometimes managers, not situations, have to give orders.

Because managers sometimes have to use their power arbitrarily, they cannot claim moral authority. Power and ethics, as Jefferson said, do not mix. Managers may earn some moral authority by acting as fairly and effectively as they can. But to try to use that moral authority as a managerial tool is to forfeit it. In management as elsewhere, honesty is its own reward—often its *only* reward—which is what makes integrity both difficult and admirable. Abandoning the self-righteous, moralistic pretense that has become fashionable for managers in recent decades may be a little hard on some managers' egos. But it would be the surest, though hardly perfect, safeguard against the moral arrogance that power can promote.

Many able managers already know these things. But it is not good enough for them to use that knowledge just to run their own companies. They have a responsibility to speak the truth about management and especially to make clear that the corporation, useful as it is, is not a good model for the rest of a democratic society. The best possible act of corporate "social responsibility" would be to acknowledge the conflict, and therefore help maintain the balance, between the top-down management power that has made us rich and the bottom-up political values that keep us free.

Not just managers but all citizens need to think hard and critically about the gurus' ideas. This book has been about the gurus' inadequate response to the conflict between corporate life and democracy, but another could and should be written about the increasing influence of management ideas on our political values and institutions. The gurus' idea of democratizing corporations and legitimizing management is a pipe dream, but it is all too possible to run a country like a company.

NOTES

Introduction

p. xiv. "chief executive of . . . " Alan M. Dershowitz, "Baseball's Speech Police," *New York Times,* February 2, 2000.

p. xv. "fellow citizens . . . " Thomas Jefferson, *Notes on the State of Virginia* (New York: Norton, 1972), 164–165.

p. xvi. "the real insight . . . " Joan Magretta and Ann Stone, *What Management Is: How It Works and Why It's Everyone's Business* (New York: Free Press, 2002), 195.

p. xvi. "[t]he best performers . . . " ibid.

p. xvii. "[h]istorically, organizations have . . . " ibid., 202.

p. xxvi. "Back when work . . . " ibid., 196.

p. xxxi. "everyone's business . . . " ibid., 1.

p. xxxi. "ask management to . . . " ibid., 220.

Chapter 1, Handling People in Early America

p. 5. "to beware lest . . . " Plato, *Epistles,* trans. Glenn R. Murrow (Indianapolis, IN: Bobbs-Merrill, 1962), 253.

p. 5. "despotic power benefits . . . " ibid., 229.

p. 6. "better to concentrate . . . " Machiavelli, *The Prince,* ed. Quentin Skinner and Russell Price (Cambridge: Cambridge University Press, 1988), 54.

p. 6. "often forced to . . . " ibid., 62.

p. 7. "The Jeffersonians believed . . . " Pauline Maier, *American Scripture: Making the Declaration of Independence* (New York: Knopf, 1997), 191.

p. 7. "that it has . . . " John Chester Miller, *The Wolf by the Ears: Thomas Jefferson and Slavery* (New York: Free Press, 1977), 42.

p. 7. "an obligation to . . . " Gordon Wood, *The Radicalism of the American Revolution* (New York: Knopf, 1992), 56; cf. Lance Banning, *The Jeffersonian Persuasion: Evolution of a Party Ideology* (Ithaca: Cornell University Press, 1978), 51.

p. 7. "on the casualties . . . " Thomas Jefferson, *Notes on the State of Virginia* (New York: Norton, 1972), 164–165.

p. 8. "Those who labour . . . " ibid.

p. 8. "drudgery . . . to those . . . " Jefferson, *Writings,* ed. Paul Leicester Ford (New York: G. P. Putnam's Sons, 1892–1899), vol. 8, 174.

p. 8. "Decision, activity, secrecy . . . " Lynton K. Caldwell, *The Administrative Theories of Hamilton and Jefferson: Their Contribution to Thought in Public Administration* (Chicago: University of Chicago Press, 1944), 25.

p. 8. "a vast mass . . . " ibid., 95.

p. 8. "greatest genius, hurried . . . " ibid., 97.

p. 8. "a tissue of . . . " Jonathan Daniels, *Ordeal of Ambition: Jefferson, Hamilton, Burr* (New York: Doubleday, 1970), 118.

p. 9. "How is it . . . " Samuel Johnson, "Taxation No Tyranny," available: www.samueljohnson.com/index.html.

p. 9. "Slavery caused rather . . . " Edmund S. Morgan, *American Slavery American Freedom: The Ordeal of Colonial Virginia* (New York: W. W. Norton, 1975), passim.

p. 9. "a much harsher . . . " Gordon Wood, *The Radicalism of the American Revolution* (New York: Alfred A. Knopf, 1992), 53.

p. 10. "Our children . . . " Jefferson, *Notes on the State of Virginia*, 162–163.

p. 11. "duty to know . . . " James O. Breeden, ed., *Advice Among Masters: The Ideal in Slave Management in the Old South* (Westport, CT: Greenwood Press, 1980), 8.

p. 11. "kill up and . . . " ibid., 40.

p. 11. "If the master . . . " ibid., 41.

p. 11. "His back very . . . " quoted in Charles Dickens, *American Notes* (Gloucester, MA: Peter Smith, 1968), 265–266.

p. 11. "Anger begets anger . . . " Breeden, *Advice Among Masters*, 45.

p. 11. "Negroes are by . . . " ibid., 22.

p. 11. "The only way . . . " ibid., 87.

p. 11. "most general defect . . . " ibid., 34.

p. 12. "[t]he most important . . . " ibid.

p. 12. "[E]ven in inflicting . . . " ibid., 86.

p. 12. "reduce the man . . . " ibid.

p. 13. "The 1850 U.S. . . . " Alfred D. Chandler, Jr., *The Visible Hand: The Managerial Revolution in American Business* (Cambridge: Harvard University Press, 1977), 65.

p. 13. "the curse of . . . " William Kauffman Scarborough, *The Overseer: Plantation Management in the Old South* (Baton Rouge: Louisiana State University Press, 1966), 16.

p. 13. "I think I . . . " ibid., 46.

p. 13. "I don't get . . . " ibid., 104.

p. 13. "when a manager . . . " ibid., 127.

p. 14. "all seem to . . . " ibid., 125.

p. 14. "Colonel Cottonbags" ibid., 122.

p. 14. "a favorable crop . . . " ibid., 104.

p. 14. "should always pull . . . " ibid., 102.

p. 14. "not encourage tale . . . " ibid., 120.

p. 14. "pride of character" William L. Van Deburg, *The Slave Drivers: Black Agricultural Labor Supervisors in the Antebellum South* (Westport, CT: Greenwood Press, 1979), 51.

p. 15. "curb his sanguinary . . . " Terry Alford, *Prince Among Slaves* (New York: Oxford University Press, 1977), 74.

p. 15. "They had to . . . " Eugene Genovese, *Roll, Jordan, Roll: The World the Slaves Made* (New York: Pantheon, 1972), 378–379.

p. 17. "arrangements for the . . . " Nathan Appleton, "The Introduction of the Power Loom, and Origin of Lowell," in Alfred D. Chandler and Richard S. Tedlow, eds., *The Coming of Managerial Capitalism: A Casebook in the History of American Economic Institutions* (Homewood, IL: Irwin, 1985), 161.

p. 17. "city way of . . . " Benita Eisler, ed., *The Lowell Offering: Writings by New England Mill Women (1840–45)* (New York: Harper, 1977), 43.

p. 17. "freedom and equality," ibid., 53.

p. 17. "independent of everyone!" ibid., 19.

p. 18. "very pretty women . . . " Harriett Robinson, *Loom and Spindle: Or, Life Among the Early Mill Girls* (New York: T. Y. Crowell, 1898), 82.

p. 18. "one young face . . . " Robert F. Dalzell, Jr., *Enterprising Elite: The Boston Associates and the World They Made* (New York: Norton, 1987), 45–46.

p. 18. "going home to . . . " Eisler, *Lowell Offering*, 28.

p. 19. "Because each overseer . . . " Thomas Dublin, *Women at Work: The Transformation of Women and Work in Lowell, Massachusetts, 1826–1860* (New York: Columbia University Press, 1979), 22.

p. 19. "engineering at a . . . " Nathan Appleton, *The Introduction of the Power Loom and Origin of Lowell* (N.p.: B. H. Penhallow, 1858), 34.

p. 19. "great potentate . . . " Robinson, *Loom and Spindle*, 8.

p. 20. "But there were . . . " ibid., 9.

p. 20. "They lamented, for . . . " Eisler, *Lowell Offering*, 15.

p. 21. "over-bearing tyrants" ibid., 55.

p. 21. "Puckersville" Robinson, *Loom and Spindle*, 14.

p. 21. "At least the . . . " Teresa Anne Murphy, *Ten Hours' Labor: Religion, Reform, and Gender in Early New England* (Ithaca: Cornell University Press, 1992), 11.

p. 21. "To strike a . . . " Eisler, *Lowell Offering*, 58.

p. 21. "The overseers' fault . . . " ibid.

p. 21. "ruffle the temper" and "tyrannical" James Montgomery, *The Carding and Spinning Master's Assistant*, ed. Alfred D. Chandler (Glasgow, 1832; reprint, New York: Arno Press, 1979), 219–220.

p. 22. "Invoking the spirit . . . " Dublin, *Women at Work*, 93.

p. 22. "on the rights . . . " ibid., 91.

p. 22. "amizonian [sic] display" ibid., 92.

p. 22. "the lordly avarice . . . " ibid., 98.

p. 22. "apparently harsh and . . . " ibid., 112.

p. 23. "As late as . . . " Merritt Roe Smith, *Harpers Ferry Armory and the New Technology: The Challenge of Change* (Ithaca: Cornell University Press, 1977), 283.

p. 24. "The foremen, according . . . " Chandler, *Visible Hand*, 74.

p. 24. "Situated dangerously close . . . " Smith, *Harpers Ferry Armory*, 30–31.

p. 24. "Forbidding gambling and . . . " ibid., 255.

p. 25. "to some extent . . . " ibid., 271.

p. 25. "especially when the . . . " ibid., 272.

p. 25. "hammer out their . . . " ibid.

p. 26. "court martial" Harold C. Livesay, *Andrew Carnegie and the Rise of Big Business* (New York: Longman, 2000), 40.

p. 26. "The enforcement of . . . " Alfred D. Chandler, Jr., Thomas K. McCraw, and Richard S. Tedlow, eds., *Management Past and Present: A Casebook on the History of American Business* (Cincinnati: South-Western College Publishing, 1995), 12.

p. 26. "While greeting passengers . . . " Edward Hungerford, *The Story of the Baltimore & Ohio Railroad, 1827–1927* (New York: G. P. Putnam's Sons, 1928), 279 (italics in original).

p. 27. "No man who . . . " ibid., 273.

p. 27. "Each officer . . . " Chandler, McCraw, and Tedlow, *Management Past and Present*, 13.

p. 27. "whip them or . . . " Wesley S. Griswold, *A Work of Giants: Building the First Transcontinental Railroad* (New York: McGraw-Hill, 1962), 197.

p. 27. "He had a mild . . . " Lynne Rhodes Mayer and Kenneth E. Vose, *Makin' Tracks: The Story of the Transcontinental Railroad in the Pictures and Words of the Men Who Were There* (New York: Praeger, 1975), 41.

p. 28. "The Central Pacific president . . . " ibid., 31.

p. 30. "lick any man . . . " Frank Gilbreth, *Scientific Management Course . . . 1912* (Easton, PA: Hive Publishing Co., 1980), 9.

p. 30. "The grafting system . . . " Thomas H. Patten, Jr., *The Foreman: Forgotten Man of Management* (N.p.: American Management Association, 1968), 17–18.

p. 30. "Some foremen had . . . " ibid., 18.

Chapter 2, The Demon: Frederick W. Taylor

p. 33. "So the story went . . . " Robert Kanigel, *The One Best Way: Frederick Winslow Taylor and the Enigma of Efficiency* (New York: Viking, 1997), 67.

p. 33. "All his life . . . " Charles D. Wrege, *Frederick W. Taylor, The Father of Scientific Management: Myth and Reality* (Homewood, IL: Irwin, 1991), passim.

p. 35. "I . . . broke my eyes . . . " Kanigel, *One Best Way*, 91.

p. 36. "Now, Fred, you know . . . " Frederick W. Taylor, *The Principles of Scientific Management* (New York: Harper, 1911), 49.

p. 37. "The machinists fought . . . " ibid., 50.

p. 37. "He got 'friendly' warnings . . . " Frank Barkley Copley, *Frederick W. Taylor: Father of Scientific Management* (New York: Harper, 1923), vol. 1, 167.

p. 37. "continuous struggle with . . . " Taylor, *Principles*, 52.

p. 37. "More honestly, Taylor . . . " ibid., 50.

p. 38. "Men will not . . . " Kanigel, *One Best Way*, 212.

p. 40. "where your conscience . . . " ibid., 77.

p. 40. "So he slept . . . " Sudhir Kakar, *Frederick Taylor: A Study in Personality and Innovation* (Cambridge: MIT Press, 1970), 19.

p. 41. "beyond the pale" Kanigel, *One Best Way*, 409.

p. 41. "He evened the score . . . " Frederick W. Taylor, "The Making of a Putting Green," *Country Life in America* (February 1915): 41–42.

p. 41. "Unlike the machines . . . " Daniel Nelson, *Frederick W. Taylor and the Rise of Scientific Management* (Madison: University of Wisconsin Press, 1980), 36–37; see also H. L. Gantt, "Frederick Winslow Taylor," Taylor Papers, Stevens Institute of Technology.

p. 42. "He kept a fierce watch . . . " Kanigel, *One Best Way*, 227.

p. 42. "crawled in through . . . " Copley, *Frederick W. Taylor*, vol. 1, 145.

p. 42. "Apparently, he attended . . . " Kanigel, *One Best Way*, 181–182.

p. 43. *"military type of* . . . " Taylor, *Shop Management* in *Scientific Management: Compiling Shop Management, the Principles of Scientific Management, and Testimony Before the Special House Committee by Frederick W. Taylor*, foreword by Harlow S. Person (New York: Harper, 1947), 98 (italics in original).

p. 43. "and if such . . . " ibid.

p. 43. "overhead charges on . . . " No author, probably Taylor, "The Foreman's Place in Scientific Management," in Clarence Bertrand Thompson, ed., *Scientific Management: A Collection of the More Significant Articles Decribing the Taylor System of Management* (Cambridge: Harvard University Press, 1922), 397.

p. 43. "spoilage and breakage . . . " John G. Aldrich, "Ten Years of Scientific Management," *Management Engineering* (February 1923): 88.

p. 45. "when the best results . . . " No author, probably Taylor, "The Foreman's Place in Scientific Management," 397 (italics in original).

p. 45. "where to start . . . " Taylor, *Shop Management*, 103.

p. 45. "Using a Barth slide rule . . . " Carl G. Barth, "Slide Rules for the Machine Shop as a Part of the Taylor System of Management," in Thompson, *Scientific Management*, 403.

p. 46. "These new men . . . " Taylor, *Shop Management*, 105.

p. 46. "To further speed . . . " Robert Thurston Kent, "The Tool Room Under Scientific Management," in Thompson, *Scientific Management*, 434–435.

p. 47. "the man with the slide-rule . . . " Taylor, *Principles*, 103.

p. 48. "I have you . . . " Kanigel, *One Best Way*, 226–227.

p. 48. "earned higher wages" Nelson, *Frederick W. Taylor*, 151.

p. 50. "Then Taylor cut . . . " ibid., 75.

p. 51. "Lacking 'perfect men' . . . " "Taylor's Notes for a Talk on Management . . . to the Leading officials of the Bethlehem Steel Co. in the Fall of 1899," Taylor Papers.

p. 51. "of the opposition . . . " Taylor, "Report No. 10—Progress Made in No. 2 Machine Shop and Further Improvements Needed," May 29, 1899, Taylor Papers.

p. 51. "without the help . . . " ibid.

p. 52. "Crowds gathered at . . . " Kanigel, *One Best Way*, 343.

p. 52. "Production, he claimed . . . " Taylor, *Principles*, 71.

p. 53. "the law of heavy . . . " ibid., 57.

p. 53. "Schmidt, are you . . . " ibid., 44–45.

p. 53. "rather rough talk" ibid., 45.

p. 53. "appropriate and not unkind" ibid.

p. 53. "so stupid and . . . " ibid., 59.

p. 53. "when he was told . . . " ibid., 47.

p. 54. "all of the pig . . . " ibid.

p. 54. "But a report . . . " Report by James Gillespie and H. C. Wolle, Table 1, Taylor Papers.

p. 54. "large powerful Hungarians" Report by James Gillespie and H. C. Wolle, p. 1, Taylor Papers.

p. 54. "The plant's assistant . . . " Kanigel, *One Best Way*, 320.

p. 54. "At least forty . . . " Report by James Gillespie and H. C. Wolle, p. 8 and Table 4, Taylor Papers.

p. 54. "the old idea . . . " Taylor, *Principles*, 63.

p. 55. "By the spring . . . " Kanigel, *One Best Way*, 353.

p. 55. "A few years before . . . " Nelson, *Frederick W. Taylor*, 79.

p. 55. "[C]onfine your entire time . . . " Kanigel, *One Best Way*, 348.

p. 55. "I respectfully request . . . " ibid., 355.

p. 55. "I beg to advise . . . " ibid.

p. 56. "Could you expand . . . " Margaret Ellen Hawley, *The Life of Frank B. Gilbreth and His Contribution to the Science of Management* (master's thesis, University of California at Berkeley, 1929), 63–64.

p. 56. "The processes and . . . " Alfred P. Haake, "From Scientific Management to Personal Relations," in John R. Commons, ed., *Industrial Government* (New York: MacMillan, 1921), 26–27.

p. 57. "better than average . . . " ibid., 27.

p. 57. "Taylor saw propaganda . . . " Gay to Taylor, September 13, 1908, Taylor Papers.

p. 57. "Besides making scientific . . . " Jeffrey L. Cruikshank, *A Delicate Experiment: The Harvard Business School, 1908–1945* (Boston: Harvard Business School Press, 1987), 58.

p. 58. "was the only system . . . " Copley, *Frederick W. Taylor*, vol. 2, 353.

p. 58. "Taylor subjected Brandeis . . . " ibid., 372.

p. 58. "The ICC denied . . . " Kanigel, *One Best Way*, 436.

p. 59. "gospel of hope," *New York Times*, November 22, 1910.

p. 59. "idea that the mission . . . " Ida M. Tarbell, "Taylor and His System," *Saturday Review of Literature* (October 25, 1914): 225.

p. 59. "rare high type . . . " Ray Stannard Baker, "Scientist in Business Management," *American Magazine* (February 24, 1911): 3.

p. 59. "those doing the practical . . . " Copley, *Frederick W. Taylor*, vol. 2, 381.

p. 59. "professors and literary . . . " ibid.

p. 60. "third great party . . . " *American Magazine* (February 24, 1911): 3.

p. 60. "the literary classes" Taylor, *Testimony Before the Special House Committee* in *Scientific Management*, foreword by Harlow S. Person, 10.

p. 60. "proper and legitimate . . . " Taylor, "A Piece-Rate System," *Transactions of the American Society of Mechanical Engineers* 16: 861.

p. 60. "necessity for the labor . . . " ibid.

p. 60. "Unions, Taylor said . . . " Taylor, *Shop Management*, 187.

p. 60. "reduces the laboring man . . . " Hugh G.J. Aitken, *Taylorism at Watertown Arsenal: Scientific Management in Action, 1908–1915* (Cambridge: Harvard University Press, 1960), 173.

p. 60. "during election time . . . " ibid., 138.

p. 62. "the ordinary pig-iron handler . . . " *Hearings Before a Special Committee of the House of Representatives to Investigate the Taylor and Other Systems of Shop Management* (Washington, DC: Government Printing Office, 1912), vol. 2, 1938.

p. 62. "Under our laws . . . " ibid., vol. 1, 213.

p. 62. "With flushed face . . . " Copley, *Frederick W. Taylor*, vol. 2, 348.

p. 63. "I have found it necessary . . . " ibid., 291.

Chapter 3, The Engineers: The Gilbreths and Gantt

p. 65. "motion study" K. H. Condit, "Motions and the Variable Factors That Affect Them," *American Machinist* (April 16, 1925): 609–610.

p. 65. "happiness minutes" Frank and Lillian Gilbreth, *Fatigue Study: The Elimination of Humanity's Greatest Unnecessary Waste* (New York: Sturgis and Walton, 1916), 159.

p. 66. "He would seal . . . " Edna Yost, *Frank and Lillian Gilbreth: Partners for Life* (New Brunswick, NJ: Rutgers University Press, 1949), 70, 12.

p. 66. "Instead of demanding . . . " William R. Spriegel and Clark E. Myers, eds., *The Writings of the Gilbreths* (Homewood, IL: Irwin, 1953), 46.

p. 67. "Analyzing all human . . . " K. H. Condit, "Analyzing the 'How' of a Job," *American Machinist* (April 23, 1925): 649.

p. 67. "sixty feet long . . . " Yost, *Frank and Lillian Gilbreth*, 142.

p. 68. "Here on this spot . . . " ibid., 155.

p. 68. Published in 1914 . . . " L. M. Gilbreth, *The Psychology of Management: The Function of the Mind in Determining, Teaching, and Installing Methods of Least Waste* (1914; reprint, New York: Macmillan, 1921), passim, but especially chap. 5.

p. 68. "entertained in the club . . . " Margaret Ellen Hawley, *The Life of Frank B. Gilbreth and His Contributions to the Science of Management* (master's thesis, University of California at Berkeley, 1929), 43.

p. 69. "pick up both . . . " Spriegel and Myers, *Writings of the Gilbreths*, 41.

p. 70. "raise the pay . . . " Yost, *Frank and Lillian Gilbreth*, 160.

p. 70. "He dramatically scooped . . . " Robert Kanigel, *The One Best Way: Frederick Winslow Taylor and the Enigma of Efficiency* (New York: Viking, 1997), 434.

p. 70. "Never . . . have I seen . . . " Hawley, *Life of Frank B. Gilbreth*, 104.

p. 70. "Yet Taylor, who . . . " Edwin T. Layton, Jr., *The Revolt of the Engineers: Social Responsibility and the Engineering Profession* (Cleveland: Press of Case Western Reserve University, 1971), 173.

p. 71. "Gilbreth saw that . . . " Gilbreth to John G. Aldrich, September 8, 1913, Gilbreth Papers, Purdue University.

p. 71. "An employee later . . . " Hawley, *Life of Frank B. Gilbreth*, 71.

p. 71. "He built tall stools . . . " Gilbreth to John G. Aldrich, September 8, 1913, Gilbreth Papers.

p. 71. "Taylor praised Gilbreth's . . . " Hawley, *Life of Frank B. Gilbreth*, 75.

p. 71. "Prominent psychology professors . . . " Yost, *Frank and Lillian Gilbreth*, 259.

p. 71. "Frank's innovative use . . . " Yost, *Frank and Lillian Gilbreth*, 110.

p. 72. "Showed micromotion film to . . . " Yost, *Frank and Lillian Gilbreth*, 225.

p. 72. "act of war" Daniel Nelson, *Managers and Workers: Origins of the Twentieth-Century Factory System in the United States, 1880–1920* (Madison: University of Wisconsin Press, 1995), 68.

p. 72. "In France, the . . . " Martial and Josette Andre to the author, May 5, 1997.

p. 72. "In England, a . . . " Keith Whitston, "The Reception of Scientific Management by British Engineers, 1890–1914," *Business History Review* (summer 1997): 207–229. For an alternative view, see Lyndall Urwick and E.F.L. Brech, *The Making of Scientific Management* (London: Management Publications Trust, 1945), 102.

p. 72. "The Americans found . . . " H. L. Gantt, *Industrial Leadership* (New Haven: Yale University Press, 1916), 14.

p. 73. "Comforting himself that . . . " Lillian M. Gilbreth, *As I Remember: An Autobiography* (Norcross, GA: Engineering and Management Press, 1998), 136.

p. 73. "Surely a German . . . " ibid., 130.

p. 73. "the enormous waste . . . " Irene M. Witte, "Frank Gilbreth—A Philosopher," in *The Frank Gilbreth Centennial* (New York: American Society of Mechanical Engineers, 1969), 104.

p. 73. "crippled soldier" Hawley, *Life of Frank B. Gilbreth*, 80.

p. 73. "done by a one-armed . . . " Frank and Lillian Gilbreth, *Motion Study for the Handicapped* (London: Routledge, 1920), 64.

p. 73. "hate pictures showing . . . " Hawley, *Life of Frank B. Gilbreth*, 92.

p. 73. "Back in the consulting game . . . " Hawley, *Life of Frank B. Gilbreth*, 83–86.

p. 74. "In 1924 he lured . . . " Harry Arthur Hoff, "'Pimco': An Interpretation," *Journal of Personnel Research* (December 1924): 282–288.

p. 74. "No. 8 hammer . . . " H. L. Gantt to Russell Davenport, March 19, 1900, Taylor Papers, Stevens Institute of Technology.

p. 75. "economical methods" L. P. Alford, *Henry Laurence Gantt: Leader in Industry* (New York: American Society of Mechanical Engineers, 1934), 78.

p. 76. "As with Frank Gilbreth . . . " Layton, *Revolt of the Engineers*, 173.

p. 76. "Joining Taylor in . . . " Gantt to Taylor, June 8, 1898, and September 22, 1998, Taylor Papers.

p. 76. "Rather than wait months . . . " H. L. Gantt, *Work, Wages, and Profits,* 2nd ed. (New York: Engineering Magazine Co., 1919), 107.

p. 76. "inspired the confidence . . . " Alford, *Gantt*, 89.

p. 76. "out into the shop . . . " ibid., 89–90.

p. 77. "utilize his brains . . . " ibid., 89.

p. 77. "who most needed . . . friend and helper . . . " Gantt, *Work, Wages, and Profits,* 109.

p. 77. "Unskilled workmen . . . " ibid., 120.

p. 77. "When Gantt sent . . . " Alford, *Gantt*, 131.

p. 77. "if we expect to" Nelson, *Managers and Workers*, 66.

p. 78. "Gantt's biographer tells . . . " Alford, *Gantt*, 135–136.

p. 78. "Here's a man who . . . " ibid., 136.

p. 78. "Too many businessmen . . . " Gantt, *Industrial Leadership* (New Haven: Yale, 1916), 112 (italics in original).

p. 78. "financiers, whose aim . . . " Gantt, *Organizing for Work* (New York: Harcourt, Brace, 1919), 32.

p. 79. "the manufacturer would . . . " ibid., 31–32.

p. 80. "Many manufacturers have . . . " ibid., 31.

p. 80. "This is primarily . . . " ibid., 38.

p. 81. "chronic derangement . . . " Thorstein Veblen, *The Theory of Business Enterprise* (1904: reprint, New York: Augustus M. Kelley, 1965), 38–39.

p. 81. "the technological expert . . . " Thorstein Veblen, *Imperial Germany and the Industrial Revolution* (1915; reprint, New Brunswick, NJ: Transaction Publishers, 1990), 195–196.

p. 81. "OUTLAW which must . . . " Alford, *Gantt*, 188.

p. 81. "large corporations are . . . " Gantt, *Work, Wages, and Profits*, 46.

p. 81. "some democratic evangelist . . . " Herbert Croly, *The Promise of American Life* (New York: Macmillan, 1909), 453–454.

p. 81. "economic discovery that . . . " Charles Ferguson, "Men of 1916," *Forum* (February 1916): 168.

p. 81. "Ferguson, a clergyman . . . " Samuel Haber, *Efficiency and Uplift: Scientific Management in the Progressive Era, 1890–1920* (Chicago: University of Chicago Press, 1964), 45.

p. 82. "wait for the crowd . . . " Ferguson, "Men of 1916," 178–179.

p. 82. "incompetency in high . . . " Alford, *Gantt*, 191.

p. 82. "industrial control is . . . " ibid., 266 (italics in original).

p. 83. "palaver about the war . . . " Ferguson, "Men of 1916," 172.

p. 83. "It arose out . . . " Alford, *Gantt*, 266.

p. 83. "call upon us . . . " ibid., 274.

p. 83. "Gantt and Ferguson advised . . . " ibid., 273.

p. 83. "debating-society theory . . . " ibid., 259–260.

p. 84. "not according to . . . " ibid., 196.

p. 84. "[T]he idea of politics . . . " ibid., 271.

p. 84. "After Congress declared . . . " Jordan A. Schwarz, *The Speculator: Bernard M. Baruch in Washington, 1917–1965* (Chapel Hill: University of North Carolina Press, 1981), 102.

p. 84. "Gantt believed they . . . " Gantt, *Organizing for Work*, 107.

p. 84. "not as a steel man . . . " Bernard M. Baruch, *Baruch: The Public Years* (New York: Holt, Rinehart, and Winston, 1960), 65.

p. 84. "a patrimonial band . . . " Robert D. Cuff, "We Band of Brothers—Woodrow Wilson's War Managers," *Canadian Review of American Studies* (fall 1974): 137.

p. 85. "of the 'business' type . . . " Gantt, *Organizing for Work*, 9.

p. 85. "Convinced that record-keeping . . . " ibid., 19.

p. 85. "Working at first . . . " Alford, *Gantt*, 195.

p. 85. "I am alone . . . " ibid., 197.

p. 85. "continually advised . . . " Gantt, *Organizing for Work*, 38–39.

p. 86. "was performing the work . . . " ibid., 79.

p. 86. *"lack of progress* . . . " ibid. (italics in original).

p. 86. "these charts assembled . . . " ibid., 80 (italics in original).

p. 87. "By September 1918 . . . " Bernard Bailyn et al., *The Great Republic: A History of the American People* (Lexington, MA: D. C. Heath, 1992), 299.

p. 87. "our industrial system . . . " Gantt, *Organizing for Work*, 20.

p. 87. "Among the 'higher . . . '" ibid., 9.

p. 87. "simply did not . . . " ibid., 20.

p. 87. "were much better satisfied . . . " ibid., 81.

p. 87. "risk any such attempt . . . " ibid., 7.

p. 88. "which should not be . . . " ibid., 72.

p. 88. "Soviet commissars would . . . " Alford, *Gantt*, 215.

p. 88. "Gantt finally gave up . . . " Gantt, *Organizing for Work*, 102.

p. 88. "to those who know . . . " ibid., 104.

p. 88. "reflected in an improved . . . " ibid., 91.

p. 88. "that industrial democracy . . . " ibid., 104.

p. 89. "business and industry . . . " ibid., 66.

p. 89. "Its faculty would . . . " Joseph Dorfman, *Thorstein Veblen and His America* (1934; reprint, New York: Augustus M. Kelley, 1966), 453.

p. 90. "By then, she . . . " Laurel Graham, *Managing on Her Own: Dr. Lillian Gilbreth and Women's Work in the Interwar Era* (Norcross, GA: Engineering and Management Press, 1998), 139.

p. 91. "Food Will Win the War . . . " Richard Norton Smith, *Uncommon Man: The Triumph of Herbert Hoover* (New York: Simon and Schuster, 1984), 89–90.

p. 91. "turning out the lighthouses . . . " ibid., 98.

p. 91. "whether people can . . . " ibid., 88.

p. 91. "The encouragement of solidarity . . . " Herbert Hoover, *American Individualism* (Garden City, NY: Doubleday, Page, 1922), 41.

p. 92. "the exaggerated idea . . . " David Burner, *Herbert Hoover: A Public Life* (New York: Knopf, 1979), 211.

p. 92. "In return she . . . " Lillian Gilbreth to Herbert Hoover, March 12, 1929, Gilbreth Folder, Presidential Papers, Secretary's File, Hoover Papers, Hoover Presidential Library.

p. 92. "[w]hat you say . . . " Laurence Richey to Lillian Gilbreth, March 15, 1929, ibid.

p. 93. "When he was commerce secretary . . . " William Barber, *From New Era to New Deal: Herbert Hoover, the Economists, and American Economic Policy, 1921–1933* (Cambridge: Cambridge University Press, 1985), 119–121.

p. 93. "Fearing to promote . . . " E. P. Hayes, *Activities of the President's Emergency Committee for Employment* (Concord, NH: Rumford Press, 1936), 132, 121.

p. 93. "one of the group . . . " ibid., 122.

p. 94. "Under Gilbreth's lead . . . " ibid.

p. 94. "Gilbreth's efforts, however . . . " Graham, *Managing on Her Own*, 226–228.

p. 94. "Some companies . . . " Lillian Gilbreth to S. J. Crumbine, January 4, 1933, Gilbreth File, American Child Health Association Papers, Hoover Presidential Library.

p. 94. "In 1931 when Hoover . . . " Herbert Hoover to Lillian Gilbreth, February 21, 1931, President's Personal File, Hoover Papers.

p. 95. "Feminist historians . . . " *Jesus as Mother: Studies in the Spirituality of the High Middle Ages* (Los Angeles: University of California Press, 1982), 154–158.

Chapter 4, The Optimist: Mary Parker Follett

p. 101. "gaunt Boston spinster" Lyndall Urwick, "Persons and Ideas," Follett Papers, Henley College of Management, Henley-on-Thames, England.

p. 101. "two minutes flat" ibid.

p. 101. "[c]leverness with no conceit . . . " Avrum Isaac Cohen, *Mary Parker Follett: Spokesman for Democracy, Philospher for Social Group Work, 1918–1933* (Ph.D. diss., Tulane University School of Social Work, 1971), 15.

p. 101. "one of the makers . . . " ibid., 12.

p. 102. "the most exciting . . . " Eduard C. Lindeman, "Mary Parker Follett," *Survey Graphic* (February 1934): 86.

p. 102. "Experience may be . . . " F. M. Stawell, "Mary Parker Follett," *Newnham College Register*, Follett Papers.

p. 103. "public affairs . . . " "Daniel Baxter," *Quincy Patriot Ledger* (January 3, 1885): 2.

p. 103. "His army enlistment . . . " Parker Collection, Quincy Public Library.

p. 103. "Charles's one success . . . " Follett File, Quincy Historical Society.

p. 104. "Proud of Mary's intelligence . . . " Katharine Furse, "M.P.F.," Follett Papers.

p. 104. "Perhaps he taught her . . . " Harriet Mixter's memory recorded in notes provided to the author by Pauline Graham.

p. 104. "But Mary—judging . . . " Unsigned typescript, "Elizabeth Balch," Follett Papers.

p. 104. "Even before her father's . . . " Furse, "M.P.F."

p. 104. "tall, pallid, peevish . . . " Unsigned typescript, "Elizabeth Balch."

p. 105. "Mother and son . . . " Stephen Follett to Katharine Furse, March 11, 1950, Follett Papers.

p. 105. "I knew a boy . . . " Mary Parker Follett, *Dynamic Administration: The Collected Papers of Mary Parker Follett* (New York: Harper and Brothers, 1942), 270.

p. 105. "she went to college . . . " Stephen Follett to Katharine Furse, March 11, 1950.

p. 106. "Royce, Harvard's leading . . . " Anna Thompson File, Radcliffe College Archives.

p. 106. "answered him straight . . . " Follett, *Dynamic Administration*, 15.

p. 107. "with affection and admiration . . . " Furse, "M.P.F."

p. 107. "Briggs had run a school . . . " Elliot Milton Fox, *The Dynamics of Constructive Change in the Thought of Mary Parker Follett*" (Ph.D. diss., Columbia University, 1970), 32.

p. 107. "would simply tell Isobel . . . " Unsigned typescript, "Elizabeth Balch."

p. 107. "Miss Briggs . . . supplied . . . " Stephen Follett to Katharine Furse, March 11, 1950, Follett Papers.

p. 108. "The outer evidence . . . " Harriet Mixter to Katharine Furse, September 3, 1934, Follett Papers.

p. 108. "always very . . . self-conscious . . . " Lyndall Urwick to Stephen Follett, February 27, 1950, Follett Papers.

p. 108. "another acquaintance noted . . . " Stawell, "Mary Parker Follett," 40.

p. 109. "[S]uperhuman unities . . . " William James, *A Pluralistic Universe* (Cambridge: Harvard University Press, 1977), 134.

p. 109. "a complex of experiences . . . " Mary Parker Follett, *The New State: Group Organization the Solution of Popular Government* (New York: Longmans, Green, 1918), 20.

p. 109. "in-and-through . . . " ibid., 8.

p. 109. "It would be absurd . . . " Mary Parker Follett, *The Speaker of the House of Representatives* (New York: Longmans, Green, 1896), 314.

p. 110. "private understanding" ibid., 330.

p. 110. "Woodrow Wilson, as . . . " Woodrow Wilson, "Committee or Cabinet Government," *Overland Monthly* (January 1884): 95.

p. 110. "facts as they are . . . " Theodore Roosevelt, *American Historical Review* (December 1896): 176.

p. 110. "to think and talk . . . " Unsigned typescript, "Elizabeth Balch."

p. 111. "married women are . . . " Fox, *Dynamics of Constructive Change*, 48.

p. 111. "Eventually the city . . . " Susan J. Ginn to Patrick T. Campbell, December 21, 1933, Follett Papers; cf. Dorothy Worrell, *The Women's Municipal League of Boston: A History of Thirty-Five Years of Civic Endeavor* (n.p.: Women's Municipal League Committee, 1943), passim.

p. 111. "the group, because . . . " Fox, *Dynamics of Constructive Change*, 46.

p. 111. "we have become . . . " Follett, *New State*, 25.

p. 112. "I asked a man . . . " ibid., 29.

p. 112. "Surgery to remove . . . " Richard C. Cabot to Katharine Furse, December 21, 1933, Follett Papers.

p. 112. "hard words" Stawell, "Mary Parker Follett," 40.

p. 113. "Ordinary living . . . " Unsigned typescript, "Elizabeth Balch."

p. 113. "creative statesmanship" Walter Lippmann, *A Preface to Politics* (New York: n.p., 1913), 213.

p. 113. "Instead of Lippmann's . . . " Follett, *New State*, 335.

p. 113. "The ballot box!" ibid., 5.

p. 114. "collective thought . . . " ibid., 22–23.

p. 114. "'War,' she said . . . " ibid., 357–358.

p. 114. "Therefore, she used . . . " ibid., 7.

p. 114. "so co-ordinated . . . " Follett, *Dynamic Administration*, 71; cf. 192.

p. 115. "Her utopian exhortations . . . " Follett, *New State*, 319.

p. 115. "[W]e should have . . . " Mary Parker Follett, *Creative Experience* (New York: Longmans, Green, 1924), 3.

p. 116. "see industry as . . . " Follett, *Dynamic Administration*, 26.

p. 116. "In her prewar . . . " See, for example, the correlation drawn between high wages and low selling costs in the *Second Annual Report of the Minimum Wage Commission of Massachusetts* (Boston: n.p., 1915), 100.

p. 116. "it was useless . . . " Furse, "M.P.F."

4–20 (huh?) "for some other . . . " "Six-Million-Dollar Firm Is Given to Employees," *Boston Post,* April 9, 1915; cf. Charlotte Heath, "History of the Dennison Manufacturing Company," *Journal of Economic and Business History* (August 1929): 182–183.

p. 117. "He had supported . . . " Follett to Dennison, March 1, 1917, Dennison Papers, Baker Library, Harvard Business School; cf. Susan Ginn, June 7, 1917, to Dennison, Dennison Papers.

p. 118. "In 1935, when . . . " James T. Dennison, *Henry S. Dennison, 1877–1952: New England Industrialist Who Served America* (New York: Newcomen Society, 1955), 34.

p. 118. "He sent employees . . . " Edna Yost, *Frank and Lillian Gilbreth: Partners for Life* (New Brunswick, NJ: Rutgers University Press, 1949), 320–321.

p. 118. "Influenced by Follett . . . " Henry Dennison, *Organization Engineering* (New York: McGraw-Hill, 1931), 192–193.

p. 118. "The solution came . . . " Follett, *Creative Experience*, 157–158.

p. 119. "every possible bit . . . " Follett, *Dynamic Administration*, 228.

p. 119. "The 'uncovering' which . . . " ibid., 38–39.

p. 119. "$8.00 or $9.00 . . . " ibid., 32.

p. 119. "ethical pre-judgment . . . " ibid., 30.

p. 119. "only integration . . . " ibid., 35.

p. 120. "If she erred . . . " ibid., 36.

p. 120. "I'm the boss . . . " ibid., 281.

p. 121. "The world . . . " ibid., 94.

p. 121. "Businessmen liked . . . " ibid., 269; cf. Lyndall Urwick, "The Problem of Organisation: A Study of the Work of Mary Parker Follett," *Bulletin of the Taylor Society* (July 1935): 166, and Henry Metcalf and Lyndall Urwick, introduction to Follett, *Dynamic Administration,* 22.

p. 122. "should be leader . . . " Follett, *Dynamic Administration*, 268.

p. 122. "[w]hoever connects me . . . " ibid., 294.

p. 122. "How did Kant . . . " ibid., 293.

p. 123. "As a social reformer . . . " ibid., 284.

p. 123. "ascendancy traits" ibid., 271.

p. 123. "Don't exploit your . . . " ibid., 273 (italics in original).

p. 123. "The industrial leader" ibid., 293 (italics in original).

p. 124. "She offered a homely . . . " ibid., 62 (italics in original).

p. 124. "Our job is . . . " ibid., 59.

p. 124. "partnership of following . . . " ibid., 290.

p. 124. "When she said . . . " Mary Parker Follett, "The Illusion of Final Responsibility," *Proceedings* (Oxford: Rowntree Lecture Conference, 1926); cf. Mary Parker Follett, "The Meaning of Responsibility in Business Management," in *Dynamic Administration*, 146–166.

p. 124. "The creative circularity . . . " Follett, *Dynamic Administration*, 54.

p. 125. "My cook . . . " ibid., 59.

p. 125. "we shall never . . . " Follett, *Creative Experience*, 206.

p. 125. "One of the tragedies . . . " Follett, *Dynamic Administration*, 290.

p. 125. "all talk of . . . " Follett, *Creative Experience*, 171.

p. 126. "sovereignties must be . . . " Follett, *Dynamic Administration*, 112.

p. 126. "fallacy . . . that the manufacturer . . . " ibid.

p. 126. "follow as one . . . " ibid., 290.

p. 126. "Dame Katharine later . . . " Furse, "M.P.F."

p. 127. "often suffered physically" ibid.

p. 127. "theorizing or dogmatizing . . . " Follett, *Dynamic Administration*, 18.

p. 127. "Her brother . . . " George Follett to Katharine Furse, January 25, 1934, Follett Papers.

p. 127. "all right" Stawell, "Mary Parker Follett."

p. 127. "The obituary . . . " *Quincy Patriot Ledger,* December 21, 1933.

Chapter 5, The Therapist: Elton Mayo

p. 130. "The solitary who . . . " Richard C.S. Trahair, *The Humanist Temper: The Life and Work of Elton Mayo* (New Brunswick, NJ: Transaction Books, 1984), 99.

p. 130. "Mayo broke his . . . " ibid., 45.

p. 131. "The marriage contained . . . " Elton Mayo to Dorothea Mayo, September 19, 1922, Mayo Family Archive, South Australia State Library, Adelaide.

p. 132. "real scientific mind . . . " Trahair, *Humanist Temper*, 84.

p. 133. "defensive, static, levelling . . . " Robert Hughes, *The Fatal Shore: A History of the Transportation of Convicts to Australia, 1787–1868* (London: Collins Harvill, 1987), 596.

p. 134. "The immigrant workers . . . " Verity Burgmann, *Revolutionary Industrial Unionism: The Industrial Workers of the World in Australia* (Cambridge: Cambridge University Press, 1995), passim.

p. 134. "do much to promote . . . " Trahair, *Humanist Temper*, 59.

p. 134. "When he took . . . " Elton Mayo to Dorothea Mayo, March 21, 1916, Mayo Family Archive.

p. 135. "Explaining the election . . . " Trahair, *Humanist Temper*, 96.

p. 135. "Published in 1919 . . . Elton Mayo, *Democracy and Freedom: An Essay in Social Logic* (Melbourne: Macmillan, 1919), 28–30.

p. 135. "Society, like an . . . " Trahair, *Humanist Temper*, 164.

p. 135. "But even in . . . " Mayo, *Democracy and Freedom*, 72.

p. 135. "intelligent collaboration" ibid., 60.

p. 135. "Mayo favored corporate . . . " ibid., 54–55.

p. 136. "assault on London" Trahair, *Humanist Temper*, 139.

p. 136. "Filling his days . . . " Elton Mayo to Dorothea Mayo, October 7, 1922, Mayo Family Archive.

p. 137. "He further impressed . . . " The prime minister's letter is in the Mayo Papers, Box 1, Folder 75, Baker Library, Harvard Business School.

p. 137. "Much later, after . . . " F. J. Roethlisberger, *The Elusive Phenomena: An Autobiographical Account of My Work in the Field of Organizational Behavior at the Harvard Business School* (Cambridge: Harvard Business School, 1977), 29.

p. 138. "perhaps we'll send . . . " Trahair, *Humanist Temper*, 148.

p. 138. "It's a great . . . " ibid., 149.

p. 138. "With his 'rambunctious' . . . " Barry D. Karl, *Charles E. Merriam and the Study of Politics* (Chicago: University of Chicago Press, 1974), 134.

p. 139. "We are 'placed' . . . " Trahair, *Humanist Temper*, 166.

p. 139. "Fortunately, the factory's . . . " Mayo to Joseph Willits, May 14, 1923, Mayo Papers, Box 1, Folder 75.

p. 139. "Moving on to . . . " Elton Mayo, "Revery and Industrial Fatigue," *Journal of Personnel Research* (December 1924): 279.

p. 139. "Turnover in the . . . " Mayo, "Day-Dreaming and Output in a Spinning Mill," *Occupational Psychology* 2 (5): 209.

p. 139. "Better still, output . . . " Mayo, "Revery and Industrial Fatigue," 277–278.

p. 139. "the fatigue and . . . " Mayo, "Day-Dreaming and Output," 209.

p. 139. "production . . . offers an . . . " Mayo, "Revery and Industrial Fatigue," 275–276.

p. 140. "To Charles Merriam . . . " Mayo to Merriam, July 21, 1925, Laura Spelman Rockefeller Foundation Archives, Folder 572, Rockefeller Archives Center, North Tarrytown, NY.

p. 140. "Mayo told Merriam . . . " Mayo to Merriam, July 21, 1925, Laura Spelman Rockefeller Foundation Archives, Folder 572.

p. 140. "Ruml, with his . . . " Ruml to Mayo, March 15, 1924, Laura Spelman Rockefeller Foundation Archives, Folder 572.

p. 140. "Mayo found it . . . " Elton Mayo, "The Business Problems Group," Mayo Papers, Box 5, Folder 13.

p. 142. "Mayo aided his . . . " Trahair, *Humanist Temper*, 350.

p. 142. "He recast his . . . " Unsigned typescript, "Elton Mayo," Laura Spelman Rockefeller Foundation Archives, Folder 572.

p. 143. "The next year . . . " Trahair, *Humanist Temper*, 202.

p. 143. "By 1940 the . . . " "Grant from the Foundation: $360,000 to Harvard University," Rockefeller Foundation Archives, 1937, Folder 4076, Box 342, Series 200, Record Group 1.1, Rockefeller Archive Center, North Tarrytown, NY. This document lists the total as $1,260,000, but a number of smaller grants followed. Richard Gillespie, *Manufacturing Knowledge: A History of the Hawthorne Experiments* (Cambridge: Cambridge University Press, 1991), puts the total, including John D. Rockefeller Jr.'s early personal gifts, at $1,520,000, p. 243.

p. 143. "The influence that . . . " Roethlisberger, *The Elusive Phenomena*, 29.

p. 144. "Over coffee and . . . " Mayo to Dorothea Mayo, March 2, 1935, Mayo Family Archive.

p. 144. "Protecting the flank . . . " Steven M. Horvath and Elizabeth C. Horvath, *The Harvard Fatigue Laboratory: Its History and Contributions* (Englewood Cliffs, NJ: Prentice-Hall, 1973), passim.

p. 145. "manner in conversation" George Homans, *Coming to My Senses: The Autobiography of a Sociologist* (New Brunswick, NJ: Transaction Books, 1984), 91.

p. 145. "Pareto held that . . . " Vilfredo Pareto, *The Mind and Society*, ed. Arthur Livingston (New York: Harcourt, Brace and Co., 1935), 1569–1570. Cf. Lawrence J. Henderson, *Pareto's General Sociology: A Physiologist's Interpretation* (Cambridge: Harvard University Press, 1935), 21.

p. 145. "either we must . . . " Wallace Brett Donham, *Business Adrift* (New York: McGraw-Hill, 1931), xxix.

p. 145. "as a kind . . . " Homans, *Coming to My Senses*, 147.

p. 146. "He argued that . . . " Elton Mayo, "The Choice of a Story," Mayo Papers, Box 5, Folder 16.

p. 147. "at a comfortable . . . " Gillespie, *Manufacturing Knowledge*, 21.

p. 147. "Yet Pennock immediately . . . " ibid., 76.

p. 147. "Further easing the . . . " ibid., 59.

p. 148. "Inevitably came the . . . " ibid., 61–62.

p. 148. "She asked for . . . " Daily History Record, June 25, 1927, Hawthorne Studies Collection, Baker Library, Harvard Business School.

p. 148. "Bogatowicz also got . . . " Gillespie, *Manufacturing Knowledge*, 59–64.

p. 148. "due to the . . . " ibid., 68.

p. 148. "a man come . . . " ibid.

p. 149. "As his first . . . " ibid., 73.

p. 149. "When he returned . . . " ibid., 76.

p. 150. "any theory that . . . " Elton Mayo, *Human Problems of an Industrial Civilization* (New York: Macmillan, 1933), 73.

p. 150. "the blind spot . . . " Elton Mayo, "The Blind Spot in Scientific Management," Mayo Papers, Box 5, Folder 9.

p. 150. "[T]he supervisor is . . . " Elton Mayo, "Changes in Industry: The Broad Significance of the Western Electric Investigations," *Research Studies in Employee Effectiveness and Industrial Relations: Papers Presented at the Annual Autumn Conference of the Personnel Research Federation at New York, Nov. 15, 1929* (n.p.: Western Electric Co., n.d.), 24.

p. 150. "Until Doctor Mayo . . . " Gillespie, *Manufacturing Knowledge*, 136.

p. 151. "[A]n attitude of . . . " ibid., 150.

p. 151. "continuous interviewing" ibid., 151.

p. 151. "Speaking to an . . . " Trahair, *Humanist Temper*, 234.

p. 151. "get the employee . . . " Gillespie, *Manufacturing Knowledge*, 149.

p. 151. "absence this year . . . " ibid., 169.

p. 152. *"The Function of . . . "* ibid., 164.

p. 152. "Dickson came around . . . " F. J. Roethlisberger and William J. Dickson, *Management and the Worker* (Cambridge: Harvard University Press, 1939), 548; cf. Mayo, *Human Problems*, 120.

p. 152. "He claimed it . . . " Mayo, *Human Problems*, 70.

p. 153. "an account of . . . " Gillespie, *Manufacturing Knowledge*, 180.

p. 154. "With his objectivity . . . " Mayo, *Human Problems*, 71–74.

p. 154. "To create such . . . " ibid., 166–167.

p. 154. "administrative *elite*" ibid., 178 (italics in original).

p. 154. "When the Hawthorne . . . " Roethlisberger, *Elusive Phenomena*, 52.

p. 155. "a new type . . . " Roethlisberger, *Management and the Worker*, 561.

p. 155. "Not realizing that . . . " ibid., 553.

p. 155. "pay has been . . . " Roethlisberger, *Manufacturing Knowledge*, 83.

p. 155. "an important factor . . . " Roethlisberger, *Management and the Worker*, 133.

p. 156. "On the basis . . . " ibid., 577.

p. 156. "Roethlisberger and Dickson . . . " ibid., 266–269.

p. 156. "fear of contracting . . . " ibid., 268.

p. 156. "had a bit . . . " Abraham Zaleznik, "Foreword: The Promise of Elton Mayo," in Trahair, *Humanist Temper*, 10.

p. 157. "Mayo replied with . . . " Mayo to Donald David, August 1, 1942, Mayo Papers, Box 1, Folder 5.

p. 157. "In 1939, she . . . " Gael Elton Mayo, *The Mad Mosaic: A Life Story* (New York: Quartet, 1983), passim.

p. 157. "Mayo spent his . . . " Elton Mayo, *The Social Problems of an Industrial Civilization* (Cambridge: Harvard University Graduate School of Business Administration, 1945), xii–xv.

p. 157. "If our social . . . " ibid., 123.

p. 158. "Negotiations for a . . . " Trahair, *Humanist Temper*, 344.

p. 159. "the way people . . . " Roethlisberger, *Elusive Phenomena*, 279.

Chapter 6, The Leader: Chester Barnard

p. 161. "worry, malnutrition, and . . . " Chester Barnard, *Organization and Management: Selected Papers* (Cambridge: Harvard University Press, 1948), 64.

p. 162. "revolutionary conditions" ibid., 62.

p. 163. "threatened . . . the relief . . . " ibid., 69.

p. 163. "that the least . . . " ibid., 65.

p. 163. "lost their heads . . . "New Violence Is Reported as Court Frees ERA Group," *Trenton State Gazette,* April 25, 1935.

p. 163. "Meanwhile, to forestall . . . " "Sympathy and Prudence," *Trenton Evening Times,* April 30, 1935.

p. 163. "The company had . . . " "Fifty Years of Service," *Communication* (no. 3, 1977), 13, in AT&T Archives, Warren, NJ, reference no. 38 10 03 15.

p. 163. "Because prices fell . . . " William G. Scott, *Chester I. Barnard and the Guardians of the Managerial State* (Lawrence: University Press of Kansas, 1992), 68.

p. 164. "Barnard patiently listened . . . " Barnard, *Organization and Management*, 71.

p. 164. "After two hours . . . " ibid., 73–74.

p. 164. "No, said Barnard . . . " ibid., 74–75.

p. 164. "we better leave . . . " ibid., 75.

p. 165. "What a triumph . . . " ibid., 75–77.

p. 165. "Barnard easily outshone . . . " L. J. Henderson, *L. J. Henderson on the Social System* (Chicago: University of Chicago Press, 1970), 41.

p. 165. "Henderson called the . . . " Henderson to Barnard, May 10, 1938, Barnard Papers, Box 2, Folder 59, Baker Library, Harvard Business School.

p. 166. "hostile or bellicose" Barnard, *Organization and Management*, 64.

p. 166. "Aside from mentioning . . . " ibid., 61.

p. 166. "The strike deprived . . . " "Barnard Will Hold Conference with Arbitration Committee of Mercer ERA Strikers on Tuesday," *Trenton State Gazette*, April 25, 1935.

p. 166. "Devaluing economics in . . . " Barnard, *Organization and Management*, 71–72.

p. 166. "amount allowed for . . . " "Thousand Marching Strikers Surround ERA Headquarters," *Trenton Evening Times*, April 23, 1935.

p. 166. "a very large . . . " "Confusion Hides Status of Strike," *Trenton Evening Times*, May 1, 1935.

p. 166. "And newspaper accounts . . . " "ERA Strike at End," *Trenton Evening Times*, April 30, 1935.

p. 167. "semi-aristocratic demeanor" Scott, *Chester I. Barnard*, 84.

p. 000. "I looked upon" Chester Barnard, *Philosophy for Managers: Selected Papers*, ed. William B. Wolfe and Haruki Iino (Ithaca: New York State School of Industrial and Labor Relations, Cornell University, 1986), 10.

p. 168. "nickel plater" Town Directories, Malden Public Library, Malden, MA.

p. 168. "[H]e taught me . . . " Chester Barnard, *The Functions of the Executive* (Cambridge: Harvard University Press, 1938), dedication page.

p. 168. "But elsewhere he . . . " William B. Wolf, *The Basic Barnard: An Introduction to Chester I. Barnard and His Theories of Organization and Management* (Ithaca: New York State School of Industrial and Labor Relations, Cornell University, 1974), 46.

p. 168. "Owing to his . . . " Barnard student File, Mount Hermon School, Northfield, MA.

p. 168. "In adulthood Barnard . . . " Warren Weaver, "Chester Irving Barnard," *Yearbook* (Philadelphia: American Philosophical Society, 1961), 109.

p. 169. "Suffering from 'nervous' . . . " William B. Wolf, *Conversations with Chester I. Barnard* (Ithaca: New York State School of Industrial and Labor Relations, Cornell University, 1973), 54.

p. 169. "In his Christian . . . " Barnard, *Functions of the Executive*, 256.

p. 169. "He left Harvard . . . " Barnard File, Harvard University Archives.

p. 170. "Thus, when America . . . " Robert D. Cuff, *The War Industries Board: Business-Government Relations During World War I* (Baltimore: Johns Hopkins University Press, 1973), 20.

p. 170. "Baruch preferred to . . . " ibid., 49.

p. 170. "Testifying to Congress . . . " ibid., 84.

p. 172. "Chagrined at protests . . . " Barnard, *Organization and Management*, 81.

p. 172. "Prosperity 'which is' . . . " Chester Barnard, *Philosophy for Managers* (Tokyo: Bunshindo, 1986), 81.

p. 172. "Although Barnard insisted . . . " Barnard to John Maurice Clark, February 15, 1956, Barnard Papers, Box 2, Folder 31.

p. 172. "In a mid–1930s . . . " Barnard, *Organization and Management*, 6–7, 16.

p. 172. "Profit, he said . . . " Wolf, *Conversations with Chester I. Barnard*, 28.

p. 172. "Asked by students . . . " Barnard, *Functions of the Executive*, 239.

p. 172. "A cautious manager . . . " Scott, *Chester I. Barnard*, 70–87.

p. 173. "Switchboard operators soon . . . " Wolf, *Conversations with Chester I. Barnard*, 26.

p. 174. "Now he had . . . " Barnard, *Philosophy for Managers*, 11–12.

p. 174. "Not 'in the' . . . " Barnard, *Functions of the Executive*, 295.

p. 174. "most vital of . . . " Barnard, *Philosophy for Managers*, 11–12.

p. 175. "Legions of leadership . . . " Barbara Kellerman, "Required Reading," *Harvard Business Review* (December 2001): 21.

p. 175. "Barnard's book announced . . . " Barnard, *Functions of the Executive*, 170–171; cf. Barnard, *Philosophy for Managers*, 152; Barnard to Bertrand de Jouvenel, May 22 and June 12, 1956, Barnard Papers, Box 2, Folder 32; Barnard to Mary Cushing Niles, September 5, 1958, Barnard Papers, Box 2, Folder 40; and Barnard's review of *Bureaucracy in a Democracy* by Charles S. Hyneman, *American Political Science Review* (December 1950): 1001.

p. 175. "Authority, he concluded . . . " Barnard, *Functions of the Executive*, 150.

p. 175. "An order is . . . " ibid., 170.

p. 175. "Low-level employees . . . " ibid., 170–171.

p. 176. "Even murderous tyranny . . . " ibid., 183–184.

p. 176. "Barnard spoke aloud . . . " ibid., 167.

p. 176. "Barnard admitted that . . . " ibid., 280–283.

p. 177. "By exemplary courage . . . " ibid., 282–284.

p. 177. "Like other top-down . . . " Scott, *Chester I. Barnard*, 84.

p. 178. "Preparing for the . . . " Barnard to Henderson, March 21, 1939, Barnard Papers, Box 2, Folder 55.

p. 178. "But in authoritarian . . . " Barnard, *Organization and Management*, 31.

p. 178. "The rise of management . . . " ibid., 44–45.

p. 178. "Does the democratic . . . " ibid., 29.

p. 178. "artificial questions of . . . " Barnard, *Functions of the Executive*, 167n.

p. 179. "In the summer . . . " Barnard to Henderson, August 7, 1940, Barnard Papers, Box 2, Folder 52.

p. 179. "He recruited Barnard . . . " Barnard to Rockefeller, January 17, 1950, Barnard Papers, Box 2, Folder 41.

p. 180. "Most famously of . . . " Barnard, *The Deeper Significance of the USO* (n.p., n.d.), 5. The pamphlet is in the historical files of the USO headquarters, Washington, DC.

p. 181. "Northern and Southern . . . " Barnard to Mark A. McCloskey, February 10, 1953, Barnard Papers, Box 2, Folder 38.

p. 181. "At least partly . . . " Barnard to Rockefeller, January 17, 1950, Barnard Papers, Box 2, Folder 41.

p. 181. "a big fight . . . " Scott, *Chester I. Barnard*, 84.

p. 181. "At the USO, . . . " Barnard, *Organization and Management*, vi–vii.

p. 181. "He advised USO . . . " Chester Barnard, *What It Takes to Do a Good USO Job* (n.p., n.d., n.pp.) (italics in original). The pamphlet is in the historical files at USO headquarters, Washington, DC.

p. 182. "To ensure that . . . " ibid.

p. 182. "two years only . . . " Barnard, *Deeper Significance of the USO*, 7.

p. 182. "By war's end . . . " Chester Barnard, *USO In Perspective: A Statement of the Historical Background of USO* (n.p., n.d.). The pamphlet is in the historical files at USO headquarters, Washington, DC.

p. 182. "Barnard answered that . . . " Barnard, *Deeper Significance of the USO*, 5–6.

p. 182. "Personal aversions based . . . " Barnard, *Functions of the Executive*, 147.

p. 183. "ordinarily associated with . . . " Scott, *Chester I. Barnard*, 76–77.

p. 183. "Yet Barnard developed . . . " Barnard, *Deeper Significance of the USO*, 8–11.

p. 184. "something new in . . . " ibid.

p. 184. "In race relations . . . " ibid.

p. 184. "USO clubhouses operated . . . " Julia M.H. Carson, *Home Away from Home: The Story of the USO* (New York: Harper and Bros., 1946), 181–199.

p. 184. "Barnard believed that . . . " Barnard, *Deeper Significance of the USO*, 8–11.

p. 185. "This is the . . . " David E. Lilienthal, *The Journals of David E. Lilienthal: The Atomic Energy Years, 1945–50* (New York: Harper and Row, 1964), 533.

p. 185. "In the anti-Communist . . . " "The New Attack on Lilienthal," *New Republic* (June 6, 1949): 5.

p. 185. "totalitarian government" Chester Barnard, "Arms Race v. Control," *Scientific American* (November 1949): 13.

p. 187. "Driving through the . . . " Barnard, "Atomic Energy Case," p. 8, Barnard Papers, Box 2, Folder 69.

p. 187. "Closeted together for . . . " Barnard et al., *A Report on the International Control of Atomic Energy* (Washington, DC: Government Printing Office, 1946), 6, 18.

p. 188. "After weeks of wheel-spinning . . . " Barnard, "Atomic Energy Case," p. 19, Barnard Papers, Box 2, Folder 69.

p. 188. "Atomic energy then . . . " Barnard, *Report on the International Control of Atomic Energy*, 18.

p. 188. "Reflecting Barnard's influence . . . " Lilienthal, *Journals of David E. Lilienthal*, 24.

p. 188. "By abandoning 'control' . . . " Barnard, *Report on the International Control of Atomic Energy*, 3.

p. 189. "Bush and Conant . . . " Richard G. Hewlett and Oscar E. Anderson, Jr., *A History of the United States Atomic Energy Commission, Volume I, The New World, 1939/1946* (University Park: Pennsylvania State University Press, 1962), 545.

p. 189. "Barnard and the . . . " Barnard, *Report on the International Control of Atomic Energy*, 4–8.

p. 189. "Later, in telling . . . " Barnard, "Atomic Energy Case"; cf. Dean Acheson, *Present at the Creation: My Years in the State Department* (New York: Norton, 1969), 153.

p. 189. "*Time* magazine . . . " "Atomic Age," *Time* (April 8, 1946): 27.

p. 189. "But Dorothy Thompson . . . " Hewlett and Anderson, *History of the United States Atomic Energy Commission, Volume I*, 558.

p. 189. "Meeting with a . . . " Barnard to Walter Lippmann, February 10, 1950, Barnard Papers, Box 2, Folder 36.

p. 189. "Barnard and the . . . " Jordan A. Schwarz, *The Speculator: Bernard M. Baruch in Washington, 1917–1965* (Chapel Hill: University of North Carolina Press, 1981), 287.

p. 190. "At a Blair . . . " Chester Barnard, "Atomic Energy Control," *Dartmouth Alumni Magazine* (February 1948), 35; cf. Barnard to Lilienthal, April 19, 1948, Barnard Papers, Box 2, Folder 36.

p. 190. "how well we . . . " Lilienthal, *Journals of David E. Lilienthal*, 454.

p. 190. "McGeorge Bundy, looking . . . " McGeorge Bundy, *Danger and Survival: Choices About the Bomb in the First Fifty Years* (New York: Random House, 1988), 189.

p. 191. "After Acheson became . . . " Barnard, *Philosophy for Managers*, 155.

p. 191. "And he held . . . " Barnard to Charles P. Curtis, September 26, 1955, Barnard Papers, Box 2, Folder 30.

Chapter 7, The Statistician: W. Edwards Deming

p. 199. "In just three years . . . " Deming Papers, Box 1, Folder 13, Library of Congress.

p. 200. "At fourteen, he . . . " Cecilia S. Kilian, *The World of W. Edwards Deming* (Knoxville, TN: SPC Press, 1992), 169.

p. 200. "chipping, filing, hacking . . . " ibid., 172.

p. 200. "While teaching, he . . . " Deming's civil service application, Deming Papers, Box 1, Folder 1.

p. 200. "Some people go . . . " Kilian, *World of W. Edwards Deming*, 174.

p. 201. "idea of equipotential . . . " W. Edwards Deming, *A Possible Explanation of Packing* (Ph.D. diss., Yale University, 1927), 39, 1.

p. 201. "There is no . . . " Kilian, *World of W. Edwards Deming*, 99.

p. 201. "If variable experience . . . " ibid., 99, 91.

p. 201. "into a man . . . " ibid., 175.

p. 202. "One of Deming's . . . " ibid., 173.

p. 202. "tried to understand . . . " ibid., 175.

p. 203. "breakdown of the . . . " Walter A. Shewhart, *Economic Control of Quality of Manufactured Product* (New York: D. Van Nostrand, 1931), 4.

p. 203. "the concept of . . . " Walter A. Shewhart, *Statistical Method from the Viewpoint of Quality Control*, ed. W. Edwards Deming (Washington, DC, Graduate School, Department of Agriculture, 1939), 4.

p. 203. "never ruffled, never . . . " Kilian, *World of W. Edwards Deming*, 92.

p. 203. "before it began . . . " ibid., 90.

p. 203. "operational . . . criteria of . . . " ibid.

p. 204. "accept as axiomatic . . . " Shewhart, *Economic Control of Quality*, 6.

p. 204. "lack of success . . . " Shewhart, *Statistical Method*, 5.

p. 205. "derived from past . . . " Shewhart, *Economic Control of Quality*, 15.

p. 206. "Now that the . . . " ibid., 21.

p. 206. "It is too . . . " ibid., 15.

p. 206. "Unaided by statistical . . . " Kilian, *World of W. Edwards Deming*, 80.

p. 207. "the world lives . . . " ibid., 89.

p. 207. "Deming got his . . . " Deming Papers, Box 1, Folder 1.

p. 208. "Roosevelt in the . . . " John C. Culver and John Hyde, *American Dreamer: The Life and Times of Henry A. Wallace* (New York: Norton, 2000), 227.

p. 208. "He reported to . . . " Deming to Leigh Page, October 23, 1930, Deming Papers, Box 107, Folder 9.

p. 208. "Dodge pithily summarized . . . " Kilian, *World of W. Edwards Deming*, 70.

p. 208. "He continued his . . . " Deming Papers, Box 1, Folder 13.

p. 208. "The visit to . . . " Egon Pearson, *The Application of Statistical Methods to Industrial Standardisation and Quality Control* (London: British Standards Association, 1935).

p. 209. "Back in the United States . . . " W. Edwards Deming and R. T. Birge, *On the Statistical Theory of Errors* (Washington, DC: Graduate School of the Department of Agriculture, 1938).

p. 209. "No, said Shewhart . . . " Kilian, *World of W. Edwards Deming*, 176.

p. 210. "An energetic spirit of . . . " W. Edwards Deming, *Out of the Crisis* (Cambridge: MIT Press, 1986), 206–207.

p. 210. "His methods for . . . " Deming Papers, Box 1, Folders 1 and 2; Deming, "Some Particulars Regarding the Shewhart Method of the Statistical Study of Causes," in Deming Papers, Box 108, Folder 3; and Deming, *Out of the Crisis*, 206.

p. 211. "In December 1940 . . . " Deming Papers, Box 1, Folder 2.

p. 211. "Manufacturers bought more . . . " Deming Papers, Box 1, Folder 2; Box 7, Folder 7.

p. 211. "Focusing on control . . . " Seminar participants to J. C. Capt, undated, Deming Papers, Box 108, Folder 3.

p. 212. "While at Stanford . . . " Deming, "Some Particulars Regarding the Shewhart Method."

p. 212. "Just as armories . . . " C. G. Darwin, "Statistical Control of Production," Deming Papers, Box 27, Folder 6.

p. 212. "But Ford, General Motors . . . " Deming Papers, Box 108, Folder 4.

p. 213. "SQC also seemed . . . " C. G. Darwin, "Statistical Control of Production."

p. 214. "The State Department . . . " Deming Papers, Box 1, Folder 3; Box 23, Folder 5.

p. 214. "keep aloft long . . . " William M. Tsutsui, *Manufacturing Ideology: Scientific Management in Twentieth-Century Japan* (Princeton: Princeton University Press, 1998), 194.

p. 215. "Protzman and Sarasohn" Kenneth Hopper, "Creating Japan's New Industrial Management: The Americans as Teachers," *Human Resource Management* (summer 1982): 15.

p. 215. "The CCS course . . . " Hopper, "Creating Japan's New Industrial Management," 28. Source books used by Protzman and Sarasohn to create the seminar came out of the Taylorist tradition, including *Principles of Industrial Management* (New York: Ronald Press, 1947) by Gantt's biographer, L. P. Alford; see Hopper, "Creating Japan's New Industrial Management," note on p. 20; and p. 30.

p. 215. "But the Japanese found . . . " Hopper, "Creating Japan's New Industrial Management," 30.

p. 215. "Yet even some . . . " ibid., 24, 28.

p. 216. "But they disapproved . . . " ibid., 16–17.

p. 217. "We are in . . . " Deming, *Elementary Principles of the Statistical Control of Quality: A Series of Lectures* (Tokyo: Nippon Kagaku Gijutsu Remmei, 1952), 1; cf. Peter J. Kolesar, "What Deming Told the Japanese in 1950," *Quality Management Journal* (fall 1994): 9–24.

p. 217. "Later in Japan . . . " See the balanced account by Izumi Nonaka, "The Recent History of Managing for Quality in Japan," in J. M. Juran, ed., *A History of Managing for Quality: The Evolution, Trends, and Future Directions of Managing for Quality* (Milwaukee: American Society for Quality, 1995), 519–520; cf. S. Miura, "Quality Control and Dr. Deming," Deming Papers, Box 111, Folder 4.

p. 217. "a necessary part . . . " Robert E. Cole, *Managing Quality Fads: How American Business Learned to Play the Quality Game* (New York: Oxford University Press, 1999), 74.

p. 218. "Recent studies—by . . . " Andrew Gordon, *The Wages of Affluence: Labor and Management in Postwar Japan* (Cambridge: Harvard University Press, 1998); Tsutsui, *Manufacturing Ideology*; Michael A. Cusumano, *The Japanese Automobile Industry: Technology and Management at Nissan and Toyota* (Cambridge: Harvard University Press, 1985).

p. 219. "In 1951, on . . . " Deming Papers, Box 111, Folder 5.

p. 220. "The 'servile spirit' . . . " Kilian, *World of W. Edwards Deming*, 27.

p. 220. "Explaining SQC in . . . " ibid., 77.

p. 220. "In Japan later . . . " Deming Papers, Box 111, Folder 4.

p. 221. "the theory of . . . " Kilian, *World of W. Edwards Deming*, 9.

p. 221. "Earlier, in his . . . " ibid., 9–10.

p. 221. "the spotlight on . . . " ibid., 46.

p. 221. "Deming offered a . . . " ibid., 76, 45.

p. 222. "A few years . . . " ibid., 188.

p. 222. "active of their . . . " *Cases from Japan's Manufacturing and Service Sectors with Special Contribution by Prof. Kaoru Ishikawa* (Tokyo: Asian Productivity Organization, 1984), 5.

p. 223. "a better product . . . " Kilian, *World of W. Edwards Deming*, 69 (italics in original).

p. 224. "larger role in . . . " Clare Crawford-Mason, Summary of "If Japan Can . . . Why Can't We?" in Kilian, *World of W. Edwards Deming*, 16.

p. 224. "sold 30,000 copies . . . " Deming to Andrew Deming, August 31, 1980, Deming Papers, Box 1, Folder 9; Cole, *Managing Quality Fads*, 56.

p. 224. "Donald Petersen, president . . . " Paul Ingrassia and Joseph B. White, *Comeback: The Fall and Rise of the American Auto Industry* (New York: Simon and Schuster, 1994), 140.

p. 224. "a burr under . . . " Cole, *Managing Quality Fads*, 74.

p. 224. "would need years . . . " Deming to Petersen, June 28, 1982, Deming Papers, Box 16, Folder 3.

p. 224. "Ford surpassed GM . . . " Ingrassia, *Comeback*, 136.

p. 225. "Petersen authored the . . . " Donald E. Petersen and John Hillkirk, *A Better Idea: Redefining the Way Americans Work* (Boston: Houghton Mifflin, 1991), 248, 7.

p. 225. "a merciless tyrant . . . " Ingrassia, *Comeback*, 221.

p. 225. "many elements of . . . " "Petersen Restructures Ford's Future," *Automotive Industries* (February 1982): 53.

p. 225. "But many lower-level . . . " Cole, *Managing Quality Fads*, 94.

p. 225. "Ouichi offered the . . . " William G. Ouichi, *Theory Z: How American Business Can Meet the Japanese Challenge* (Reading, MA: Addison-Wesley, 1981), 68–69, 129.

p. 226. "Deming deplored the . . . " Deming, *Out of the Crisis*, 137.

p. 226. "originally meant a . . . " A. V. Feigenbaum, *Total Quality Control* (New York: McGraw-Hill, 1991; first printing 1951), 6.

p. 226. "came to stand . . . " Deming, *Out of the Crisis*, 141.

p. 226. "damned American management . . . " Deming, *Out of the Crisis*, 85, 129.

p. 227. "In 1989, an . . . " Jerry Bowles and Joshua Hammond, *Beyond Quality: How Fifty Winning Companies Use Continuous Improvement* (New York: G. P. Putnam's Sons, 1991), 148–149; Cole, *Managing Quality Fads: How American Business Learned to Play the Quality Game*, 68–69.

p. 227. "its core emphasis . . . " Cole, *Managing Quality Fads*, 148.

p. 227. "Acting the part . . . " Mary Walton, *The Deming Management Method* (New York: Dodd, Mead, 1986), 40–54.

p. 227. "[T]he ranking of . . . " Deming, *The New Economics for Industry, Government, Education* (Cambridge: MIT Press, 1993), 173.

p. 228. "Dispensing with grades . . . " ibid., 149–150.

Chapter 8, The Moralist: Peter Drucker

p. 233. "To hobble his . . . " C. A. Macartney, *The Habsburg Empire* (New York: Macmillan, 1969), 410.

p. 233. "There is no . . . " Andrea Gabor, *The Capitalist Philosophers: The Geniuses of Modern Business—Their Lives, Times, and Ideas* (New York: Times Business, 2000), 300.

p. 234. "Vienna remained a . . . " Peter F. Drucker, *Adventures of a Bystander* (New York: Harper and Row, 1978), 84.

p. 235. "A nation that . . . " Peter F. Drucker, *The Future of Industrial Man: A Conservative Approach* (New York: John Day, 1942), 71 (italics in original).

p. 235. "Marxism was no . . . " Peter F. Drucker, *The End of Economic Man: A Study of the New Totalitarianism* (New York: John Day, 1939), 26, 33.

p. 235. "Christianity, at least . . . " ibid., 66–67.

p. 235. "He heard Hitler . . . " ibid., 124.

p. 235. "Drucker also saw . . . " ibid., 15.

p. 236. "Once in power . . . " Drucker, *Adventures of a Bystander*, 165.

p. 236. "This incident stuck . . . " Drucker, *End of Economic Man*, 36–37.

p. 236. "*Die Judenfrage in* . . . " Austrian National Archives, call number C54,052.

p. 237. "Drucker would soon . . . " Drucker, *Future of Industrial Man*, 84, 97.

p. 238. "The earlier influences . . . " Drucker, *End of Economic Man*, 42.

p. 238. "In *The End* . . . ibid., chap. 6.

p. 238. "The American founders . . . " Drucker, *Future of Industrial Man*, 243.

p. 239. "Propertied Americans did . . . " ibid., 244.

p. 239. "But there was . . . " ibid., 80.

p. 239. "more power over . . . " ibid., 79.

p. 240. "denial of the . . . " Drucker, *Concept of the Corporation* (New Brunswick, NJ: Transaction Books, 1993; orig. pub. 1946), 9.

p. 240. "[T]here has never . . . " Drucker, *Future of Industrial Man*, 99.

p. 240. "The difference, Drucker . . . " ibid., 294–295.

p. 240. "In his book . . . " ibid., 291–295.

p. 242. "a cog in . . . " Drucker, *Adventures of a Bystander*, 257.

p. 242. "The chairman of . . . " ibid., 258.

p. 244. "The resident intellectual . . . " Drucker, *Future of Industrial Man*, 158.

p. 244. "Although Brown had . . . " Drucker, *Adventures of a Bystander*, 263, 258.

p. 245. "subterranean race war" Alfred McClung Lee and Norman Daymond Humphrey, *Race Riot* (New York: Dryden Press, 1943), 106.

p. 245. "Top GM managers . . . " Frank Cormier and William J. Eaton, *Reuther* (Englewood Cliffs, NJ: Prentice-Hall, 1970), 94.

p. 246. "Sloan worked as . . . " Drucker, *Adventures of a Bystander*, 285, 280.

p. 246. "More volatile than . . . " Drucker to author, November 13, 2000.

p. 247. "What an absurd . . . " Drucker, *Adventures of a Bystander*, 282.

p. 248. "Drucker noted that . . . " Drucker, *Concept of the Corporation*, 64–65.

p. 248. "Yet he disliked . . . " Drucker, *Adventures of a Bystander*, 288.

p. 248. "recently been disputed . . . " Daniel Seligman, introduction to John McDonald, *A Ghost's Memoir* (Cambridge: MIT Press, 2002), xiv–xv.

p. 248. "But Drucker somewhat . . . " Drucker, *Adventures of a Bystander*, 292.

p. 248. "Drucker believed not . . . " Drucker, *Concept of the Corporation*, 11.

p. 248. "According to Drucker . . . " ibid., 10–11.

p. 249. "Drucker claimed that . . . " ibid., 11.

p. 249. "socially constitutive sphere" Drucker, *Future of Industrial Man*, 158.

p. 249. "Drucker saw the . . . " Ducker, *Concept of the Corporatio*, 123, 115.

p. 249. "One of decentralization's . . . " ibid., 127, 123.

p. 249. "Wherever Sloan stood . . . " ibid., 122, 129.

p. 250. "Drucker also wrote . . . " ibid., 130–136.

p. 250. "Sloan must therefore . . . " ibid., 198–199.

p. 250. "[t]he primary object . . . " Alfred P. Sloan, *My Years with General Motors* (Garden City, NY: Anchor Books, 1963), 70.

p. 250. "In *My Years* . . . " ibid., 237.

p. 250. "become again predominately . . . " Drucker, *Concept of the Corporation*, 100.

p. 250. "Sloan also dismissed . . . " Sloan, *My Years with General Motors*, 59.

p. 251. "However, McNamara, with . . . " Gabor, *The Capitalist Philosophers*, 139.

p. 252. "In *Concept of* . . . " Drucker, *Concept of the Corporation*, 155–156.

p. 252. "thumbed his nose . . . " Richard C.S. Trahair, *The Humanist Temper: The Life and Work of Elton Mayo* (New Brunswick, NJ: Transaction Books, 1984), 337.

p. 253. "Drucker, however, believed . . . " Peter F. Drucker, *The Practice of Management* (New York: Harper and Bros., 1954), 124–125.

p. 253. "To liberate employees . . . " Drucker, *Practice of Management*, 119.

p. 253. "Hence, Drucker voiced . . . " ibid., 281.

p. 253. "Nor did Drucker . . . " ibid., 391–392.

p. 254. "Over time, Drucker . . . " ibid., 310–311.

p. 254. "Recently, Drucker . . . " Peter F. Drucker, "The Next Society: A Survey of the Near Future," *Economist* (November 3, 2001), 17–18.

p. 255. "Drucker supplied Welch . . . " Jack Welch, *Jack: Straight from the Gut* (New York: Warner Business Books, 2001), 108.

p. 255. "Drucker's other contribution . . . " ibid., 314.

p. 256. "conscious transfer of . . . " ibid., 398.

p. 256. "He had thought . . . " Peter F. Drucker, *The Unseen Revolution: How Pension Fund Socialism Came to America* (New York: Harper and Row, 1976), 4.

p. 256. "But the pension . . . " Peter F. Drucker, *The New Realities in Government and Politics/in Economics and Business/in Society and World View* (New York: Harper and Row, 1989), 228 (italics in original).

p. 257. "Reluctantly, he admitted . . . " *Drucker on Asia: A Dialogue Between Peter Drucker and Isao Nakauchi* (Newton, MA: Butterworth-Heinemann, 1997), 149.

p. 257. "Now he hoped . . . " Drucker, *New Realities in Government and Politics*, 176.

p. 257. "a sense of . . . " Peter F. Drucker, *Managing the Non-Profit Organization: Practices and Principles* (New York: HarperCollins, 1990), xviii.

p. 257. "What could come . . . " Drucker, *New Realities in Government and Politics*, 226.

p. 257. "*changed human being* . . . " Drucker, *Managing the Non-Profit Organization*, xiv (italics in original).

p. 258. "Better yet, a . . . " ibid., 15, 17.

p. 258. "According to Drucker . . . " Drucker, *New Realities in Government and Politics*, 204.

p. 258. "Drucker thought, probably . . . " Drucker, "Next Society," 10.

p. 258. "Drucker evidently believed . . . " ibid., 8, 14, 16–17.

p. 259. "Yet Drucker believes . . . " Drucker, *Managing the Non-Profit Organization*, xiv.

p. 260. "Yet as soon . . . " Drucker, *Managing the Non-Profit Organization*, 117, 3, 145–146.

Conclusion

p. 264. "Profit is fine . . . " "Tom Peters's True Confessions," *FastCompany* (December 2001), available: www.fastcompany.com/online/53/peters.html.

p. 264. "They overreach for . . . " Jedidiah Purdy, *For Common Things: Irony, Trust, and Commitment in America Today* (New York: Knopf, 1999), 30.

p. 265. "Life at work . . . " "Tom Peters's True Confessions."

p. 266. "Marketing surveys report . . . " Daniel Yankelovich, *New Rules: Searching for Self-Fulfillment in a World Turned Upside Down* (New York: Random House, 1981).

p. 266. "Information technology is . . . " Peter M. Senge, *The Fifth Discipline: The Art and Practice of the Learning Organization* (New York: Doubleday, 1990), 172.

p. 266. "Michael Hammer, one . . . " Michael Hammer, *The Agenda: What Every Business Must Do to Dominate the Decade* (New York: Crown, 2001), xiv.

p. 266. "Unfortunately, the reengineers claimed . . . " Michael Hammer and James Champy, *Reengineering the Corporation: A Manifesto for Business Revolution* (New York: Harper Business, 1993), 69–70.

p. 267. "And because process-centered . . . " Michael Hammer, *Beyond Reengineering: How the Process-Centered Organization Is Changing Our Work and Our Lives* (New York: HarperCollins, 1996), 59–60.

p. 268. "Like the pitchmen . . . " ibid., 60–61.

p. 269. "In the 1970s . . . " Christopher Lasch, *The Culture of Narcisissm: American Life in an Age of Diminishing Expectations* (New York: W. W. Norton, 1978), 90.

p. 270. "*Business Week* ran . . . " "Corporate Culture: The Hard-to-Change Values That Spell Success or Failure," *Business Week* (October 27, 1980), 148–160.

p. 270. "The gurus raced . . . " Thomas J. Peters and Robert H. Waterman, Jr., *In Search of Excellence: Lessons from America's Best-Run Companies* (New York: Harper and Row, 1982), 105 (italics in original); cf. Terrence E. Deal and Allan A. Kennedy, *Corporate Cultures: The Rites and Rituals of Corporate Life* (Reading, MA: Addison-Wesley, 1982), 3–19.

p. 270. "But Senge advocated . . . " Senge, *The Fifth Discipline*, 287.

p. 271. "arrangements of status . . . " The anthropologist Sidney Mintz, quoted in Herbert G. Gutman, "Work, Culture, and Society in Industrializing America, 1815–1919," *American Historical Review* (June 1973): 542.

p. 271. "Senge was only . . . " Senge, *The Fifth Discipline*, 289 (italics in original). Senge sometimes brought power in through the back door. He called, for example, for preserving systemwide interests against selfish local managers by establishing "signals, perhaps coupled to rewards and costs, that alert local actors that a 'commons' is in danger" (298).

p. 274. "Because leadership is . . . " Abraham Zaleznik, "Managers and Leaders: Are They Different?" *Harvard Business Review* (May–June 1977): 70.

p. 274. "The leader, in short . . . " Warren Bennis, *On Becoming a Leader* (Reading, MA: Addison-Wesley, 1989), 49.

p. 275. "begin the arduous . . . " ibid., 32.

p. 275. "Power, Warren Bennis . . . " Warren Bennis and Burt Nanus, *Leaders: The Strategies for Taking Charge* (New York: Harper and Row, 1985), 17.

p. 275. "According to Bennis . . . " ibid., 16.

p. 276. "Only by omitting . . . " Warren Bennis and Philip Slater, "Is Democracy Inevitable?" in Warren Bennis, *An Invented Life: Reflections on Leadership and Change* (Reading, MA: Addison-Wesley, 1993), 42, originally published in the *Harvard Business Review*.

p. 276. "leadership, not management" ibid., 88.

p. 276. "But what else . . . " Hammer, *Beyond Reengineering*, 61.

p. 276. "When Peter Senge says . . . " Peter Senge, "Building Learning Organizations," *Journal for Quality and Participation* 15 (2): 32.

p. 277. "Recently, a CEO . . . " Annual Report 2000, the AES Corporation, p. 7.

p. 277. "Moral authority only . . . " John Chester Miller, *The Wolf by the Ears: Thomas Jefferson and Slavery* (New York: Free Press, 1977), 42.

p. 278. "Hamel used Enron . . . " Gary Hamel, *Leading the Revolution* (Boston: Harvard Business School Press, 2000), 153.

p. 278. "Hamel saw Jeffrey . . . " ibid., 216.

p. 278. "At Enron, failure . . . " ibid., 218.

p. 279. "Coming to Enron . . . " April Witt and Peter Behr, "The Fall of Enron" (July 29, 2002), available: www.washingtonpost.com/wp-dyn/articles/A14229–2002July 28.htm.

INDEX